PARENTING
A PRESCHOOLER

KNACK

PARENTING A PRESCHOOLER

A Complete Guide to Preparing Your Child for the Classroom—Ages 3 to 5

Robin McClure and Vince Iannelli, MD

Photographs by Susana Bates

KNACK
MAKE IT EASY

Guilford, Connecticut
An imprint of Globe Pequot Press

Copyright © 2010 by Morris Book Publishing, LLC

Editorial Director: Cynthia Hughes
Editor: Lara Asher
Project Editor: Tracee Williams
Cover Design: Paul Beatrice, Bret Kerr
Interior Design: Paul Beatrice
Layout: Maggie Peterson
Cover Photos by: Susana Bates
Interior Photos by: Susana Bates

Library of Congress Cataloging-in-Publication Data
McClure, Robin.
  Knack parenting a preschooler : a complete guide to preparing your child for the classroom—ages 3 to 5 / Robin McClure and Vince Iannelli ; photographs by Susana Bates.
     p. cm.
  Includes index.
  ISBN 978-1-59921-875-5
  1. Preschool children. 2. Child rearing. 3. Early childhood education. I. Iannelli, Vincent. II. Bates, Susana. III. Title. IV. Title: Parenting a preschooler.
  HQ774.5.M3927 2010
  649'.68--dc22
                                          2010003882

The following manufacturers/names appearing in Knack Parenting a Preschooler are trademarks:
EpiPen®
FluMist®
Duplos®
Lincoln Logs™
Band-Aid®
Play-Doh®
Popsicle®
Disney®
Fisher-Price®

Printed in China

10 9 8 7 6 5 4 3 2 1

To my loving parents, who have supported every decision I've made and who have always been quick with hugs and slow with criticism. To my husband's parents and family, who eagerly await us with open arms whenever we visit and overlook the messes we leave behind. To the devoted child care professionals and educators who give generously of their hands and hearts to help raise my children. To my loving husband Rick, who always stands proudly by my side. And to my three perfectly imperfect children: Hunter, Erin, and Connor. I cannot imagine a greater gift than each of you!

~Robin

Acknowledgments

There is perhaps no "best" stage of childhood; each transition has its joys and challenges. At the same time, my heart fills with an overwhelming amount of joy and sentimentality when I look back on my three children's preschool-age years. Even now, I clearly recall their absolute belief in all things wonderful and right with the world, how everything was magic, and how every day was an opportunity for an amazing adventure into the world of pretend and imagination.

My oldest son Hunter lived most of his preschool years (and beyond) as a pirate, even to the point where he once snuck a permanent marker from my desk drawer and drew a beard and mustache on his face. He also once asked his doctor if he could have a peg leg instead of his own. My daughter briefly toyed with the notions of being a ballerina and cheerleader, but quickly settled on wanting to be someone who helps others—a doctor, teacher, or veterinarian—an unwavering desire that continues today. My youngest lives to race—he talks about how he will be the champion of all things that go, including planes, trains and automobiles. Such sweet times!

I would like to thank child care professionals everywhere—in part because it can often be such a thankless job. Kids are incredibly hard work, and while it would be so easy to let our guard down and relax, it doesn't fall into the responsibility that comes with caring for children. It's people like "Miss Nanny," a family child care professional from Hurst, Texas, who has talked of retiring for years but is always convinced by families to stay on for just "one more year." With her, I always knew that my children had a loving home away from home.

I'd also like to again thank my agent, Barb Doyen, and fellow Texan and pediatrician Vince Iannelli for his valued contributions to this book. A special thanks to the folks at Globe Pequot Press for providing me the opportunity to write another amazing KNACK book. Finally, I'm blessed to again work with the superior talent of photographer Susana Bates, whose portraits beautifully capture the spirit and essence of preschoolers—even those who never miss a beat of action!

Photographer Acknowledgments

I would like to thank author Robin McClure for requesting that I work on this book with her. Thank you to Michael Michel, Dorothy Wagner, and the staff at Christ the King Community Day Care/Preschool, Cecilia Barry and MaryLynn Dinu at ACDS, Rysa Scibilia and the staff at All Star Studios, and Kye Hyun Kim at Kim's Martial Arts Corp.

I would also like to thank the families who invited me into their homes to photograph their children as well as the parents who allowed me to photograph their children at the preschool, in karate class, and at dance class. Children from the Ducks, Turtles, Dolphins, Bears, Pandas, Sunflowers, and Chipmunks classrooms at Christ the King Community Day Care/Preschool were featured.

Finally I would like to thank Thoth, Theresa, Warren, Marge, and Louise for their input.

CONTENTS

INTRODUCTION

You've survived the exhausting and exhilarating first year of your baby's birth and have overcome the daily challenges that can occur with a toddler. Your youngster has transformed into an increasingly self-assured, in-control, and ever-curious and active child now known as a preschooler. Congratulations! You've entered a new phase of parenting!

Most likely you've bought this book in the quest to be a better parent for your preschool-age child (defined as being between the ages of three and five). Since your child has now mastered many of life's basic developmental skills, you're apt to be more interested in what you can do to aid in your child's social, physical, and emotional needs and to provide the best preparation possible for kindergarten and subsequent school years.

The preschool years are often viewed as the magical years of childhood. Your youngster is growing in independence, yet is driven by the need to please others. He is learning respect, is practicing self-control, and is gaining new skills almost daily. Many parents remark that their preschool-age children are a constant source of surprise and inspiration because of how often they demonstrate newfound abilities that only yesterday seemed impossible to master. Perseverance, curiosity, and a positive attitude are typical traits of a preschooler, as are occasional tantrums and public meltdowns, whining, and even boastful behaviors.

How can you help your preschooler successfully and safely explore his growing world?

Positive parenting

Engage your child in **interactive play** free from life's distractions and really pay attention to your preschooler's thoughts and actions. There is a big difference between truly engaging with a child and just passively watching.

Provide your child with **opportunities to explore** and discover his environment. Kids at this age are extraordinarily curious. Parents need to slow down at times and let their children touch, feel, and experience things at their own pace.

Don't speak down to your child, thinking it will help her to better understand you. **Use adult language** and normal tone and teach your child how to speak in complete sentences using words and phrases correctly. Baby talk is best kept for babies!

Read to your child daily. Pop-up and other types of interactive books are good, but you can also read the funnies from the newspaper or even the back of cereal boxes.

Establish a routine and provide consistency in your child's life. Preschoolers crave schedules that they can anticipate and follow. Establish consistent eating schedules, sleep routines (including naps), and daily activities.

Boost social skills

Preschoolers love **playing with other children,** and learn best about sharing, caring, and even compromise through interactions with their peers. Introduce your child to a wide variety of new faces.

Your child is able to **learn proper table manners,** to show respect, and to say "please" and "thank you" at appropriate times.

Your child will begin to more easily **adapt to new situations,** and begin to separate from loved ones—just a bit—and enjoy experiences apart from parents.

When out in public, preschoolers tend to be better behaved than when they were toddlers. Be sure to go over expectations and rules beforehand; do not give in to "the gimmes" and whining tactics. Your child is now old enough to understand that he doesn't always get what he wants and that **rules must be followed**—although he may not like it.

Promote a healthy lifestyle

Sedentary lifestyles are having a negative effect on children as well as adults, as more and more kids are becoming overweight at a younger age than ever before. **Limit time spent watching television** and playing video games, and instead encourage physical fun.

Parents who ride bikes and take daily walks with their preschoolers are themselves more apt to be physically fit, and the emphasis on health and activity will help **promote positive health** habits for kids.

Watch the junk food and **minimize the "drive-through" meal routine** as much as possible. If you and your family are so busy that there is no time for nutritional meals, perhaps it is time to slow down on the activities. Families who eat at least one meal together each day without distractions are more likely to have a stronger, happier relationship overall.

Since preschoolers may begin to compare themselves with others, avoid using words such as "fat" or "overweight" and simply encourage **healthy eating** and being **physically fit.** You don't want your child to enter school worried about body image or to have low self-esteem.

Maintain a focus on safety

A growing independence means that kids at this age may have a tendency to get into more dangerous situations. Preschoolers think that nothing bad will happen to them and that all people are their friends, so **safe practices** must be put into place.

Teach your preschooler about **fire safety,** what to do in an emergency, and how to respond if he gets lost or separated from you.

Parents must stay vigilant about **protecting their youngsters from moving vehicles.** Preschoolers often

consider themselves "too big" to hold your hand when in public (they aren't), and may unexpectedly dash off when in parking lots—sometimes with tragic results. It might help to say that you need them to guide you in parking lots and other areas of potential danger, and to hold onto you! You'll both be safer as a result!

Preschoolers often are fearless and **think no harm can come** their way. After all, on television kids can fly or breathe under water, so why shouldn't they be able to in real life as well? It's more important than ever to keep a close watch on your preschooler and help them to understand that not everything they see and read about is real!

Preparing for school

Before you know it, your precious preschooler will transition into a young school-age child. Rather than spending too much time focusing on and worrying about your child's academic future, the best thing parents can do for their kids at this stage is to **enjoy them as they are!**

There's plenty of time to learn how to read and write, and know math facts. This is not to say that these skills aren't important, it's just that providing your child with a **rich exposure to the world** around him is truly the best way to prepare your child for academic success.

Let your child experience life by exploring objects of interest the way she wants to learn and with you serving in the role of nurturer, guide, and promoter. Your preschooler will most likely reintroduce you to the fascinations of the world and will help you rediscover the sense of wonder you may have long forgotten from your own youth. Everything is an adventure, and you will be in for quite an **exciting journey** with your child if you allow yourself the freedom, creativity, imagination, and patience to let them take the lead.

Making the connection

Just as with formal school work, there is plenty of time for enrichment programs and classes as a child gets older. For now, make it a priority to **share laughs and forge a loving bond** while making sure that your child is healthy, happy, physically active, and developing appropriately.

Too often parents are overworked and kids are over-scheduled to the point where good ol' family fun gets left out of the schedule. Make it a priority to connect with your preschooler as a way to forge a long-term, **close relationship** and promote a happier, healthy childhood.

Preschoolers typically thrive on spending quality time with grandparents and other family members, and learning about their heritage. They may **cherish family time** with relatives and embrace traditions and customs that help them to learn about who they are and where they fit into the world. Preschoolers love routine and holiday rituals, adding to the fun and excitement of the changing seasons, weather, and special occasions.

BEYOND TODDLERHOOD

Transformations combined with trials and tribulations are part of raising well-adjusted preschoolers

A lot happens between the ages of three and five—when youngsters are officially referred to as preschoolers. Transforming from a toddler to a preschooler doesn't guarantee the end of tantrums and other toddler-like behavior any more than turning five means your child is ready to begin school.

However, preschoolers are truly butterflies in the making. Ever-incessant questions, a developing will tempered with a great need to please, and truly enjoying being part of the family all contribute to the wonderful—and sometimes wild—world of preschoolers.

Parents will typically find that their values and beliefs can

Parent Connection

- Your preschooler will love sharing information, and may even teach you a thing or two. You may be surprised at how many things your preschooler is learning that you'd forgotten you knew!

- Newfound confidence and newly emerging abilities will provide endless entertain-ment and hours of engaging conversations—although topics will typically be about things of particular interest to your child.

- Your child will enjoy being the leader and instigator of family fun, so whenever possible let her lead the way!

Focus on Fun

- Preschoolers are always seeking out the next big adventure. The good news is that they want their family to be part of the action.

- Structures and rituals become very important to preschoolers, and many do best in knowing ahead of time what is planned for the day. Surprises aren't always welcome.

- Simple games such as hide and seek, tag, and no-stress contests that encourage quickness and coordination are skills-builders.

more easily be taught and put into practice during the preschool-age years. Whether it is environmental consciousness, helping out with chores, tending to a younger sibling in age-appropriate ways, or even following rules that have been established, many tasks are indeed doable for most preschoolers. It's just that preschoolers may need extra nudging or reminding to do them successfully.

By learning what things motivate your preschooler and then giving them specific responsibilities that match up to those interests, parents can help foster independence.

GREEN LIGHT

Preschoolers are the perfect age to be taught to "go green" and learn how to take care of Mother Earth. By demonstrating recycling and other green efforts early, you can help your preschooler grow up green naturally. Show your child how to separate out recyclables, reuse products, and choose reusable instead of disposable containers. Even opting for washable cups or water bottles rather than purchasing single-use drinks is a start!

Emotional Control

- Preschoolers still mostly believe that everything in their world revolves around them, although parents will notice a broader viewpoint and increased empathy as youngsters near school-age.

- Preschoolers are also learning right from wrong, but may continuously test boundaries and become upset over being told no.

- Preschoolers are heavily influenced by what they see and experience. It is vital that parents actively screen what their child is exposed to in terms of media, language, and even parental interactions.

Maturing Interactions

- Preschoolers are learning listening skills, and may increasingly demonstrate the ability to avoid interrupting others—although it still takes constant reminders.

- Practice active listening with your youngster, and make sure you provide your full attention. If you tune out your preschooler, she will learn to do likewise with others.

- A sense of ethics is forming at this stage, and your preschooler may begin to experience more complex emotions such as pride, guilt, empathy, and regret.

DAY IN THE LIFE
Load up on energy and patience, as you'll need both

Spending the day with a preschooler can be a lot of fun with shared laughs and entertaining times together. It can also be nerve-wracking, stressful, and exhausting when you have to redirect behaviors and render discipline.

Your preschooler will likely be expanding her interests and becoming increasingly experimental in terms of attempting new activities, food, and friendships.

The thing that you'll most want when parenting a preschooler is energy, as three- to five-year-olds are constantly on the go. Learning comes through active physical and dramatic play. Even eating can become an experience in trial and error and experimentation.

While preschoolers are a whirlwind of action, parents need to keep close reins on their schedules and activities. Most kids

Energetic Activities

- Skills such as jumping, hopping, balancing, skipping, galloping, and running are developed at this stage.

- Preschoolers are coordinated enough to master skills like pedaling and steering a tricycle or similar riding toy.

- Preschoolers love obstacle courses and park equipment that involves sliding, swinging, and climbing.

- They can still get themselves into situations where they are afraid to come down or let go of equipment, so close adult supervision is still needed.

Eating Habits

- Much of a preschooler's day revolves around food and mealtimes, so set the stage now for healthy eating.

- Don't be surprised if your preschooler is still reluctant to try new and different foods, although willingness to experiment may increase as social eating opportu-

nities at preschool or at a friend's house become more common.

- Preschoolers should be able to eat successfully with a fork and spoon.

- Ask your pediatrician if your child needs a multi-vitamin, but most kids don't.

don't have a strong sense of taking on too much, needing to rest, slowing down to rehydrate, or simply relaxing. Tantrums and meltdowns at this stage are more apt to be caused by a lapse of routine than anything else.

Also, preschoolers may not fully comprehend their own physical limitations and may be confused by what they see on TV or in the movies. You'll need to closely supervise activities to avoid having a child think he can fly off a high object like a favorite action hero or that he's immune from injury or pain.

Emerging Social Life

- While family is still important to your child, the preschool years are a time for learning social skills and making new friends.

- Most preschoolers want to play with friends and can easily socialize with kids they have just met.

- Blending in and being similar to other children is often important to preschoolers.

- They can still become overwhelmed and shy in unfamiliar situations, but tend to adapt more quickly than they did as toddlers.

Dramatic Play

- Preschoolers often learn and thrive through dramatic play and pretend.

- Relating to imaginary figures, cartoons, and action heroes helps preschoolers better understand their world.

- They may become some-what obsessive about certain fantasy characters and may want to dress like them, act like them, and even live like them.

- Fantasy and dress-up is considered a normal phase of development, but not all children will participate in dramatic play.

EXPANDING WORLD
Preschoolers are ready to hit the ground running, although they still prefer home sweet home

Your child's world is constantly expanding, and places that were cozy and familiar before may now suddenly seem too confining. Preschoolers love to explore and learn through active play, experimentation, and satisfying their seemingly insatiable curiosity.

While toddlers often wrestle with being separated from home and loved ones, preschoolers typically have mastered those hesitancies and simply want to go, go, go! This age devours newfound knowledge, which they gather from interesting books, while out and about on errands, and during activities that older family members might find dull or just routine. Retrieving the newspaper or watering plants can be

Outdoor Adventures

- Satisfy a preschooler's sense of adventure through plenty of unstructured free play at your local park or nearby playground.

- Be sure to establish safety rules with your child ahead of time, and make sure you can see her at all times.

- Look for exposed nails, rotting wood, or unsafe structures before letting your child play.

- Preschoolers may spontaneously create new games and adventures with children they have just met.

Reading Readiness

- At this age, most children enjoy books that feature humanized animals and objects that talk and have emotions.

- Pop-up books or books with interactive features are frequent favorites.

- Expect your child to want a cherished book to be read to her over and over again. Repetition not only provides consistency and comfort but is a common method for early childhood learning.

- Be sure to turn the tables and regularly ask your preschooler to "read" to you as well.

educational and utterly fascinating to a preschooler. You'll constantly be urging your child to keep pace and quit dawdling. Because preschoolers really do take time to pick the daisies!

Parents can help children to more fully comprehend their ever-expanding world through active participation and meaningful exploration of day-to-day life. If you can slow down just a bit, you can ask your preschooler to help decide what to buy at the store and then have her help you find specific items. Preschoolers really want to please, so constantly look for ways to help them succeed!

GREEN ● LIGHT

There are ample opportunities for free fun and enrichment that will satisfy your preschooler's desire to learn. Ask about reading hours at your local library or bookstore, twilight walks at a nearby nature center, or even free fishing or outdoor fun days sponsored by the local park department. Local businesses may offer free tours showing how money or candy is made, for example, and grocery stores occasionally feature free cookie decorating.

On-the-Go

- Little outings can be big adventures. While out and about, look for opportunities and activities that encourage curiosity and promote learning, while maintaining close supervision.

- Many preschoolers will begin to expand their boundaries naturally at this stage, and to feel comfortable going places without a parent right by their side.

- Encourage your preschooler to take the lead and plan places to walk and visit, but limit most outings to 20 minutes or less so kids don't become restless and even disruptive.

Helping Hands

- Find ways to let your child help you with basic household chores and tasks.

- Provide your preschooler with a personal shopping list (with pictures) when running errands, and ask him to help you. Some grocery stores even stock child-size carts.

- Since younger preschoolers may still struggle with self-control, establish ground rules ahead of time when running errands and provide rewards for a job well done and good behavior.

- Job charts and stickers are good motivational tools.

5

CHILD CARE OPTIONS

Not all child care is equal; research programs and providers carefully

Choosing child care for preschoolers can sometimes be more complicated than choosing basic care for infants or toddlers. While safety, health, and nutrition continue to be integral reasons for choosing a particular child care program, many families also look for enrichment activities and early childhood learning opportunities. That's because preschoolers thrive in settings where they have an opportunity to explore, learn, and enhance their social skills.

Many child care providers offer special programs that are either built into the daily curriculum or are available on an optional basis, including on-site dance, language, and soccer classes, to name a few. And some even offer age-appropriate field trips. Often, add-on programs are tailored to help busy parents while providing kids with exposure to activities they

Family Care Providers

- Family care providers, commonly called in-home care, typically are individuals who offer child care services out of their home.

- State guidelines designate how many children can be cared for by a single individual and may vary depending on the age of the children being cared for.

- Qualifications may vary from degreed early educators to caring adults who simply "love kids."

- Ask about first-aid, CPR, and other safety training and whether the home has been safety inspected.

Daycare Programs

- Daycare programs may be independently owned or part of a chain of operations.

- Many programs offer convenient drop-off and pick-up options for off-site activities, tutoring programs, and even enrichment programs like swimming lessons.

- Daycare centers may divide children into same-age classrooms for social enrichment.

- Staff turnover is common, and workers may not have much, if any, early childhood education training.

might not otherwise have the opportunity to participate in.

While all types of child care can provide safe, nurturing and quality services, additional factors such as cost, convenience, and flexibility can determine the specific type of child care option you choose. Regardless of whether you opt for home care, a formal program, or a friend or relative, you want to make sure your child is happy and receives age-appropriate fun and learning opportunities. If possible, you'll also want your preschooler to be able to interact with similar-age peers.

Relatives Providing Child Care

- The most affordable option is to have a relative or close friend watch your child.

- Disadvantages include the possibility that your child may not receive quality learning and enrichment opportunities and may not regularly socialize with other children.

- Different parenting approaches can also lead to strained relations.

- Grandparents watching their grandkids may find that their energy levels can't keep up with preschool-age children.

Nannies and Au Pairs

- Child care providers who reside with the family or watch your kids in your home can provide the greatest flexibility and convenience for working parents, but the arrangement may be expensive.

- Nannies and au pairs are represented by an agency.

- A key difference is that au pairs are typically young and from another country, while nannies are usually from the U.S., are of various ages, and have more extensive training. Nannies may remain with parents until a child starts school, while au pairs work for a family for about one year on average.

EARLY CHILDHOOD EDUCATION
Educators consider the preschool years an important foundation for later success

While many preschoolers learn best through unstructured play, some parents want early academic skills to be taught to their children to help them get a head start for school.

A variety of early childhood programs are available to help preschoolers bridge the gap between early childhood and school readiness. The years before kindergarten are often considered among the most critical stages that influence learning and overall school success.

As part of the United States' educational initiatives, many preschool-age programs receive funding to help train teachers and provide young children with appropriate care and access to learning. A variety of federal and state grants are

Head Start

- Head Start is considered the most successful national school readiness program in America.

- It provides early education, health, nutrition, and parent involvement services, primarily to low-income children and their families.

- Head Start targets children ages three to five whose family qualifies based on a low income level in accordance with federal poverty guidelines.

- Preschoolers who are in foster care or from families receiving public assistance are eligible for Head Start.

Preschool Prep

- Many child care centers tout "preschool programs," but they may simply be general programs that serve preschool-age kids.

- Preschool preparatory programs have a specific curriculum targeted to academic goals for achieving early learning skills.

- Academics aren't the only area of focus: some programs specialize in the arts, sports, dual language, and extra-curricular areas.

- Prep programs typically have higher structure and enhanced expectations, and may be more expensive.

dedicated to children who are identified "at risk" due to educational, economic, or language disadvantages or special education needs.

A federal commitment to an early childhood initiative means that state governments are being asked to impose high standards across all publicly funded early learning settings, develop new programs to improve opportunities and outcomes, engage parents in their child's early learning, and develop and improve the early education workforce.

PPCD and ESL

- The Individuals with Disabilities Improvement Act (IDEA), entitles children with disabilities to a "free appropriate public education." For children ages three to five, the program is called the Preschool Program for Children with Disabilities, or PPCD.

- If you suspect your preschooler has disabilities, contact your school district for an evaluation. If your child qualifies, free preschool services will be offered.

- State-funded preschools may offer special programs for speakers of English as a second language.

Is Early Education Important?

- Studies show that kids who participate in early education programs may have an advantage in school for the first two or three years, but children who don't participate in early programs do typically catch up academically and socially.

- Long-term program benefits include greater parental involvement, fewer referrals to special education or remedial services, better social skills, and greater ability to focus.

PRESCHOOLER INSIGHTS
This age is often considered the most fun for parents and kids alike

By three to five years old, children have mostly mastered the fundamentals of coordination, speech, and basic needs. The ability to walk and run, communicate well enough to be understood, listen, and follow directions, and possess greater control of their body and mind means that preschoolers can spend more time in exploring their ever-broadening world and their place within it.

This isn't to say that they have the necessary maturity and wisdom to do what is considered right and to keep them out of harm's way. They don't. Parents still need to be hands-on and actively involved as preschoolers continue to test their physical limits, to explore, and to seek out new experiences. They often seem like whirlwinds of never-ending activity, sometimes only slowing down long enough to provide their

Preschooler: Age 3

- The challenging "terrible twos stage" will diminish or end, as your child gains better control and is better able to express her wants and needs through words.

- Three-year-olds begin to form strong likes and dislikes.

- They are often quite fun to be around and will speak their minds—often at inappropriate times!

- They are developing a sense of humor and may even be able to tell simple jokes!

Preschooler: Age 4

- Four-year-olds are typically considered social butterflies. They may start to make friends independently of you and to look forward to playdates more than ever before.

- They are able to describe how objects are used.

- Four-year-olds love dramatic play and pretend, and may struggle to understand the difference between make believe and reality.

- They will most likely enjoy physical activities that can range from basic body movement and motion to age-appropriate sports.

growing bodies with required food and rest before they are ready to hit the ground running once again.

For parents, preschoolers' emerging sense of responsibility, wanting to please, and learning right from wrong are a welcome break from the infant and toddler years. Or maybe it only seems easier because it is more fun!

Be prepared for your child to transform daily—sometimes even hourly—both in a physical sense (from a princess to a pirate, from a lizard to a ladybug) as well as emotionally. You'll experience moments of self-control followed by unexpected tantrums and meltdowns, although luckily these behaviors become less frequent with time.

What should you expect when you are parenting a preschooler? A lot of exploring boundaries, endless curiosity and enthusiasm, some ups and downs as they process all the new information they're learning, and exponential growth in their developing sense of self. With preparation and patience, combined with the ability to adapt to just about anything that you and your child can imagine, you'll both be off to a great start!

Preschooler: Age 5

- Five-year-olds may vividly describe specific actions and events and often remember fine details.

- They have increased coordination and demonstrate an enhanced ability to focus and follow increasingly complicated and multi-step directions.

- Five-year-olds show a sense of increased independence and responsibility, and may have an easier time separating from parents.

- Self-control is becoming more the norm and meltdowns and tantrums the exception.

Preschool-Age Multiples

- Multiples may begin to express more individuality as preschoolers than they did at the baby and toddler stages. This may affect friendships, food choices, and activities.

- Parent each child individually, and allow multiples to have their own separate friends, playdates, and interests.

- Avoid grouping multiples together, such as saying "the twins." Instead, refer to each by name.

- Find ways to encourage cooperative play among same-age siblings.

APPEARANCE

Leaner physique and loss of baby fat are sure signs your preschooler is growing up

Of course your preschooler is still your little cherub, but as each day passes, you'll see small but notable physical changes that serve as unmistakable proof that your baby is growing up.

Chubby cheeks, plump thighs, and extended bellies are giving way to a sleeker, slimmer look—in part due to all the energy and calories your child expends during each waking hour. But those big, bright, and ever-inquisitive eyes and mouth full of baby teeth let you know you still have a youngster in tow.

Parents may also notice changes in the shape of their child's feet and more proficient use of their hands as other signs of

Height and Weight

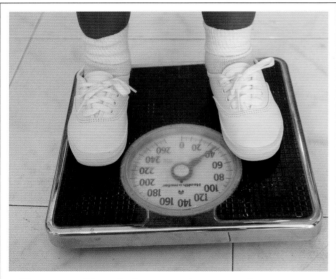

- Three-year-olds typically weigh between 25 and 40 pounds.

- Typical height is between 34 and 40 inches.

- Doctors generally use a growth chart to determine how well a child is growing, but parents can use them at home as well.

- Growth charts should be followed over time rather than just read at a single point in order to more accurately track overall growth patterns and percentages as compared with like-age peers.

Body Basics

- Three-year-olds will typically develop a taller, thinner, and more proportioned body appearance.

- So-called "baby fat" should be gone or significantly reduced at this stage. If your child appears to be heavier than most of his peers, you may need to revisit activity levels and calorie consumption.

- Three-year-olds need approximately 1,300 calories a day.

- Preschoolers like demonstrating their strength and enhanced coordination.

continued maturation and development of fine motor skills.

Three-year-olds may begin to take great pride in their appearance and strongly express their preference for certain hairstyles and accessories. Many boys find it hilarious to spike their hair or to personalize it with a particular cut, while some girls may adore headbands and fancy bows. Of course, some three-year-olds may not care one way or another about hair or grooming in general. Either way is completely normal, and individual preferences are another sign that your preschooler is learning about choices and developing a self-image.

ZOOM

Most children grow about 2 inches per year from age three to puberty. If your preschooler grows more or less, however, it doesn't mean there is a problem. No child grows at a perfectly steady rate through childhood. Genetics also play a key role. Some kids may start slow and hit a huge growth spurt later—a growth pattern known as "late bloomers."

Baby Teeth

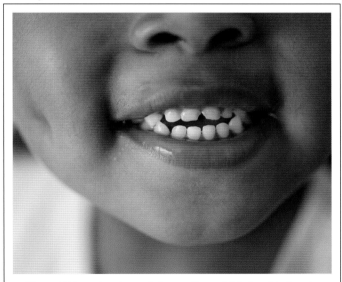

- Most children develop a full set of 20 baby teeth, also called milk teeth, by their third birthday.

- Tooth decay is a common problem for preschoolers. Some studies have shown that nearly 60 percent of three-year-olds have had at least one cavity.

- Your child should already be seeing a dentist. If not, schedule an appointment!

- Cavities in baby teeth should not be ignored. An untreated cavity can enlarge until the internal parts of the tooth are involved and lead to infection and tooth loss.

Hands and Feet

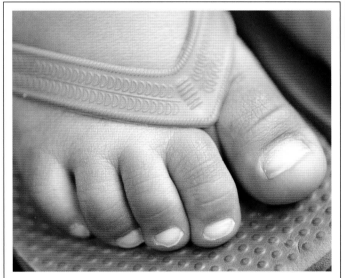

- Kids may want to touch and feel everything with their extremities as a form of tactile learning.

- Most preschoolers still have flat feet. The arch on the inside of the foot develops as the child grows.

- Observe your preschooler's normal walking gait, and note any toeing in or out, toe-walking, knock knees, or other gait abnormalities. If you see any, check with your doctor.

- Going barefoot exposes feet to dangers such as cuts, sprains, fractures, or even plantar warts.

WELL-CHILD VISIT

Annual checkups are opportunities to gain an overall assessment of your child's development

Annual checkups with your pediatrician provide an important opportunity to candidly discuss your child's physical, emotional, social, and intellectual changes and to ask about any potential concerns. Checkups are a nice way to provide extra assurance that your child is growing and developing on schedule!

Long gone are the times when you needed to bring your child to the doctor every few months; for preschoolers annual checkups are considered routine and should be continued into adulthood. The well visit will include basic measurements and checks followed by a quick examination of your child's body. Depending on the doctor's preference, your

What to Expect:

- Measurement of height and weight

- Blood pressure check

- An examination of typical growth and development as compared with peers

- Check of reflexes, motor skills, and spine

- Discussion of toilet training, social skills, and proper nutrition

- Review of sleep schedule

- Review of behavior and discipline

- Counseling of safety practices

Vision Screening

- Your child's eyes should be evaluated every year.

- Routine screenings can uncover many abnormalities, including misalignment of the eyes, reduced vision in a single eye, or nearsightedness or farsightedness.

- Testing may vary according to a child's willingness at this stage. It may include an observation of how kids fixate on and track objects and a thorough examination of eye alignment, eye movements, and reflexes.

child may be asked to disrobe to underwear only or wear a dressing gown for the examination.

As part of the exam, the pediatrician may listen to your child's heart, check breathing, and examine ears, eyes, and throat. Additional evaluations of your child's coordination, body tone, and motor skills may be conducted.

Your doctor will then ask you some questions about your child's overall development. There's no better time than right then to ask about any questions or concerns or to request professional advice. You are your child's advocate, after all!

ZOOM

Parents sometimes make the pediatrician the "bad guy" in order to make their child not mad at them. The strategy can create an extreme fear of going to the doctor. Instead, talk to your child about how the doctor will check things like weight, their ears and tummy, and how they are growing. You want your child to be reassured that a doctor helps keep them healthy and strong.

Concerns

- Think about questions ahead of time that you may want to ask your pediatrician, and write them down so you will be prepared.

- Many parents' questions are about what is considered "normal" for a three-year-old child, and often pediatricians can provide basic information that allays those concerns.

- If you've noted a physical characteristic or trait that seems out of the ordinary, address it with your child's doctor. Further evaluation may be warranted.

Immunizations

- As long as all immunizations are current, the 3-year-old well-child visit should not include any vaccinations. That's great news for both you and your preschooler!

- Your child should still receive an annual influenza shot. Flu shots or FluMist nasal flu vaccine sprays are typically administered throughout the fall and early winter, so depending on the timing, the flu vaccination may need to be scheduled separately from the well-child visit.

SELF

Youngsters are learning to control their emotions and finding their place within the world

At three years old, kids mostly understand that the world doesn't truly revolve around them and their needs—although they may not like it. They still struggle with self-control and keeping their emotions in check, but parents should see a marked improvement over the so-called "terrible twos" stage.

Preschoolers at this age may still be quite insistent about things they want, and are prone to occasional meltdowns and tantrums when circumstances don't go their way. But because they have an increased ability to communicate, they are now beginning to express their frustration more through words than through physical action. Whines and verbal demands now replace hitting and biting, and parents' ability

Being in Control

- Three-year-olds have developed a strong will about their wants and needs, and may not always maintain control of their emotions.

- Emerging independence should be encouraged, and parents should provide increasing opportunities for three-year-olds to have control over portions of their life.

- Letting kids choose between two or three parent-approved choices is one way to support their need for control.

All about Me

- Your child may love looking at baby pictures of herself and others, and asking detailed questions about what it was like to be little.

- Seeing themselves as babies and through various stages of development

helps three-year-olds better understand that they will become an adult one day.

- Seek opportunities to discuss what it might be like to be younger or older, and share some of your favorite memories at that age.

to talk with them using words they understand helps keep a better check on their emotions and desires than ever before.

Three-year-olds are also learning about their place in the world, and may find family history and photographs interesting to look at—to a point. Don't expect your preschooler to become interested in your family genealogy. He may, however, love hearing stories about how times were different when grandma or grandpa were little. Seeing dad's baby booties, for example, can help a child better understand that big people were once young children, too!

My World

- Your child's sense of "family" is developing.

- This is a good age to begin teaching customs or family traditions to your three-year-old. Explain why certain actions, clothing, or activities are important to your family, and how your child can take part in them.

- Show your child a globe and explain where family members previously emigrated from.

- Your child may enjoy participating in and learning about special religious observances in age-appropriate classes like Sunday school.

Curbing Tantrums

- While tantrums may be decreasing, kids may still have emotional blow-ups when they feel enormous frustration or feel out of control in their ever-growing world.

- To diffuse tantrums, try talking calmly with your child about her feelings and removing her from potentially volatile situations.

- Teach your child ways to express feelings and emotions in socially acceptable ways, such as remaining calm while using words rather than actions.

BEHAVIOR

Increased attention span and ability to follow simple directions provides for successful routines and structure

You can't help but notice how three-year-olds seem to be emotionally maturing right before your eyes. While far from being focused all the time, kids at this age have typically developed a three-minute attention span and are often captivated by observing routine activities and normal conversations. It is as if kids are "soaking up" newfound knowledge in all aspects of their ever-broadening world—why do you think their minds are often referred to as sponges?

Expect lots of questions from your inquisitive youngster— who, what, where, when, and why questions are often intermingled with "let me try it" or "I can do that" responses. Your child is anxious to please and will often go out of her way to

Improved Attention Span

- An increased attention span and understanding of language means your child will be more receptive to communications.

- Encourage eye contact with your child, not only because it is a way to determine whether she is paying

attention, but because it models the right way to talk with people.

- Whenever possible, instead of towering over your child, lower yourself to her level and talk in a friendly, conversational tone.

Repetition Promotes Learning

- Your child may enjoy repeating back words and sounds, so use that to your advantage by asking her to repeat back important things you say.

- Demonstrate a chore or task you'd like your child to do and explain how to do it; then let your child try.

- Choose age-appropriate tasks such as putting napkins at each table setting. Don't choose anything too difficult; start small and simple, and remember the praise!

"help"—even though much of the learning is experienced through not always successful trial-and-error methods.

Your child's ability to follow two-step directions combined with a strong desire to please and to do the right thing provides a prime opportunity for establishing order and routine. Allow your youngster to perform basic chores and provide simple age-appropriate services to others.

Be careful not to provide rewards for anything that should be done routinely or your child will learn to expect something for what should be a selfless act.

MAKE IT EASY

Many families utilize this period of learning receptivity to create age-appropriate job or behavior charts. Since kids this age can't read, a photo or similar visual reminder works best. Remember to keep the rules simple and focus only on a single task or two at a time to keep your three-year-old motivated. Possible chart categories might include not interrupting, saying "please," or feeding the family pet.

Establishing a Routine

- Most kids this age like routine and structure, and children will more likely stick with a task if it becomes part of normal expectations.

- Kids learn tasks well if they know to do something "right after breakfast" or after they are dressed for the day, for example.

- Find ways to help tykes be more successful at their first tasks, such as pre-measuring things or asking for only a small area to be swept.

Modeling Good Behaviors

- Parents are a child's best role model for behaviors, and you should know that preschoolers are watching your every move and reaction.

- Kids don't innately know right from wrong, so be sure to explain good behaviors every chance you get.

- Appeal to a child's emerging sense of judgment and frequently ask what she would consider the right thing to do.

INDEPENDENCE

Letting go is a first step in encouraging learning through trial-and-error, repetition, and practice

One of the most exciting and rewarding transitions from the toddler stage to early childhood is when your child begins doing things for himself instead of having you do everything for him!

At this stage, parents will be able to teach eager youngsters certain aspects of independence, although close supervision and constant monitoring are still a must. Kids won't just know how to do certain skills or activities; they need training and reinforcement, and may need constant reminders until they understand a new concept. With a little practice, your child won't think twice about doing something for himself!

Let your child learn a task through trial and error. Too often,

Self-Service Drinks

- Preschoolers may be able to pour a drink from a container to a cup, but expect some spills.

- Avoid one-gallon jugs and huge pitchers—they are heavy even for adults.

- Though advertised as being kid-friendly, juice bags with punch-in straws are often difficult for preschoolers to master. Frequently the wrong part of the bag ends up getting punctured!

- Individual paper cups are a perfect size for small hands.

Using Silverware

- Your child should now be able to sit at the table and eat properly using a fork and spoon.

- Using a knife correctly (and injury-free) should be reserved for later years.

- Preschoolers should be able to use a fork to stab cut-up meat and to spoon up most food items, although they may need constant reminders to not use their fingers as scoops.

- Complex food items like spaghetti will still take some practice!

well-meaning parents continue to perform tasks for their youngsters, who are fully capable of doing them themselves. While three-year-olds are extremely eager and enthusiastic, the "I can do it" spirit found in young preschoolers typically wanes with time. If you don't start encouraging independence now, your child may become perfectly content for you to do it all. The result is you have another problem on your hand: motivating uninspired and complacent kids!

YELLOW ● LIGHT

Overzealous moms and dads who swoop in to protect their children from every difficult situation have been given a name: helicopter parents. It's natural to want your child to be successful and frustration-free, but the truth is that not succeeding at something—at least initially—is how we learn! If parents hover and always save the day, then a child may struggle with independence, parental separation, and dealing with stressful situations. So, lighten up!

Food Preparation

- Preschoolers will want to spread their own jelly or butter on toast. Now's a good time to also show them how to clean up the mess they make, but don't expect perfection!

- Kids love using condiments such as mustard or ketchup on food items, but be careful of "oversqueezing" from the convenience bottles.

- Kids can learn to make their very own peanut butter and jelly or meat and cheese sandwiches!

Fostering Independence

- Provide your child with two- or three-choice options as often as possible.

- Don't question their final choices, especially if you've provided the options in the first place.

- Let your child know which choices are negotiable and which ones are not (anything relating to health, safety, or bedtime, for example), and then don't give in.

CELEBRATIONS

Holidays and special occasions can cause much excitement, but prolonged waiting can lead to frenzied behavior

Celebrating a special occasion with a three-year-old just begs of excitement and frenzied fun. Whether participating in holiday rituals in conjunction with popular events like Valentine's Day, Easter, 4th of July, Halloween, and Christmas or Hanukkah, or simply celebrating a new season or skill, kids this age relish any reason to celebrate!

Preschoolers often learn about holidays and their meaning from care providers, who might also offer age-appropriate crafts and activities related to the occasion. If your child stays at home full time, don't forget to expose him to holiday rituals through family and playgroup celebrations.

Birthday parties are also becoming a common practice

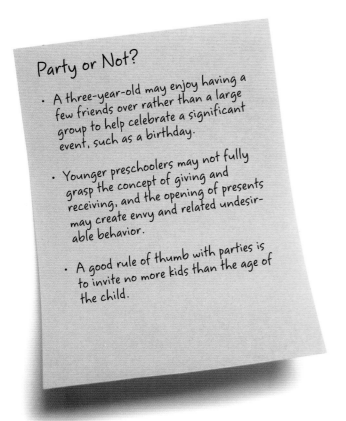

Party or Not?

- A three-year-old may enjoy having a few friends over rather than a large group to help celebrate a significant event, such as a birthday.

- Younger preschoolers may not fully grasp the concept of giving and receiving, and the opening of presents may create envy and related undesirable behavior.

- A good rule of thumb with parties is to invite no more kids than the age of the child.

Proper Party Behaviors

- If your child is invited to a party, talk about and practice proper behavior ahead of time.

- Most kids behave better when they know what to expect. Discuss with your child what will be happening at a party and even whether food will be served.

- Tell your child you will help her maintain self-control, but that she will be removed from the party if she starts behaving badly. Then, follow through. Other guests will thank you!

22

for many preschoolers and your child may begin receiving invitations to special parties and celebrations. Parties may either be in a child's home or at a kid-friendly venue. You'll need to prepare your child as to what to expect, how to act in someone else's home or in public, review basic manners and expectations (such as the birthday gifts are not for your child if he is going as a guest), and plan to stay with your child throughout the party.

The build-up of attending a party may sometimes become bigger than the event itself, resulting in meltdowns or out-of-control behavior. Anticipation is an emerging emotion for three-year-olds, so avoid telling kids about celebrations so early that they have to wait for an extended amount of time before the event actually occurs. Also, minimize exposure to commercialism or overhyping of key events. Retailers are starting their holiday marketing earlier and earlier, but the time lag between promotion and the actual date of an activity may be difficult for preschoolers to comprehend.

Party Poopers

- Too much sugar, missed naps, overly anxious kids, jealousy, and length of time spent on various activities just beg for meltdowns to occur.

- Make sure your child is well rested and has eaten before bringing to a party.

- Preschoolers may be so busy having fun that they forget to use the bathroom—make sure you bring a change of clothes for your child, just in case.

- Parents should keep parties small and simple, and no longer than 1½ hours . . . max!

Party Ideas

- Avoid mealtime parties for three-year-olds. There are too many picky eaters and adult assistance is often still needed for many foods.

- Keep activities short and simple; three-year-olds can have a blast just playing with bubbles or sidewalk chalk, and playing traditional party games like "Pin the Tail on the Donkey."

- Open presents privately when party guests are gone to avoid jealousy and hurt feelings.

23

POTTY HABITS

Toilet training is in full effect for preschoolers at this age, although accidents still happen

Maybe your child is already potty trained by the age of three. Or, perhaps, success may ebb and flow (so to speak) depending on your child's mood and circumstances. Many children at this age are able to stay dry throughout the day, but still require nighttime pull-ups because of frequent overnight accidents.

Regardless of whether your child is potty-trained, mostly trained, or still working on it, your preschooler is considered normal. As with all growth and development milestones, not all kids master potty-training at the same age. Yet, with few exceptions, all are able to stay dry and in control of their urination and bowel movement needs by the time they enter kindergarten. So, relax!

Ready or Not?

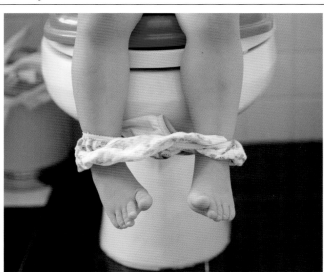

- By age three, your child should be showing signs of potty readiness if she isn't already trained.

- While some preschoolers may be perfectly content in diapers, the social pressure of seeing other kids going to the bathroom and wearing underwear or panties is often enough of a motivation to encourage kids to become potty trained.

- Team with your child's caregiver to make sure potty training methods are consistent between home and while in child care.

Transitional Success

- It's not unusual for kids to be more successful at potty training at either home or at child care, but not necessarily at both places initially.

- Accidents are most likely to occur in public, when a child is too excited or busy. Parents may need to set ground rules taking frequent bathroom breaks while out.

- Many three-year-olds still have accidents at naptimes, bedtime, and even when falling asleep in their car seat while on the road; plan accordingly.

Even if your child is toilet trained, there are still ample opportunities to have accidents. Sometimes three-year-olds are simply too busy at an activity to notice their body's cues that a visit to the bathroom is in order—often until it is too late. If your child becomes overly tired and takes a nap without visiting the bathroom first, then an accident may very well occur.

Most preschoolers are able to successfully stay dry—at least during waking hours—with regular potty breaks. Many daycares offer in-classroom bathrooms and add frequent bathroom breaks into the daily schedule.

Wiping and Frequency

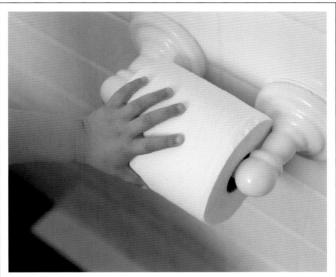

- Proper wiping still requires parental assistance, especially after bowel movements.

- Parents may struggle with a child who wants to do it "himself" or seeks privacy.

- Girls should still be supervised to make sure they know how to properly wipe from front to back.

- Some kid-friendly and flushable wet-wipe products can help young preschoolers to better clean themselves than by using just toilet paper.

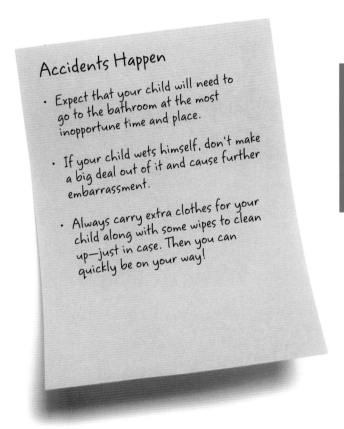

Accidents Happen

- Expect that your child will need to go to the bathroom at the most inopportune time and place.

- If your child wets himself, don't make a big deal out of it and cause further embarrassment.

- Always carry extra clothes for your child along with some wipes to clean up—just in case. Then you can quickly be on your way!

DRESSING

Kids use clothing for fantasy and pretend, and strong wills can contribute to power struggles

Preschoolers at this age have mostly mastered getting dressed—as long as the attire is basic. Forget about outfits with complex fasteners or ones that involve multiple layers if you want to promote independent dressing. Save those for special occasions, and keep it simple other times.

The very act of getting dressed or undressed may become a

big deal to a three-year-old. Your child may want to choose her own outfits, or transform into a superhero instead of wearing ordinary attire, and exert strong resistance to wearing something considered as boring as a plain T-shirt and shorts. Why do you think clothing retailers promote clothing with an array of glitter, built-in capes, action hero imprints, or sequins?

Taking Clothes On and Off

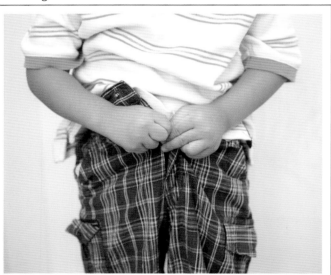

- Choose simple styles like T-shirts and pull-on shorts, skirts, or pants whenever possible, to make it easier for your child to dress and undress themselves.

- Kids at this age may be able to work buttons, zippers, and snaps, but may not

always be successful. Snaps around the waistline on clothing are often stiff and hard to snap into place.

- Bottoms should be able to be easily pulled down for those last-second bathroom emergencies.

Socks and Shoes

- Putting on socks can be difficult for a three-year-old.

- Shorter "no-show" styles are easier to put on than longer, crew-length styles.

- Make sure your child doesn't have bunching in the toe or heel area, or else

rubbing or discomfort can occur.

- Look for shoe styles that do not require lacing. Velcro or pull-on styles are popular with this age group.

- Taking off socks and shoes is never a problem!

Clothing wars are commonplace, and can be as frustrating for the child as they are for the parent. Parents really have to pick their battles in this area, and decide whether it really matters if their child wants to wear their favorite princess pajamas to the grocery store or a cape to the movies.

Finding solutions to help your child feel some control over clothing choices may mean overlooking mismatched clothes on occasion, and accepting that what you like and what your child prefers may not always be compatible. Remember that dressing independently is a major milestone!

ZOOM

The "flip flop factor" refers to children who arrive at child care dressed inappropriately for play and comfort. Wearing flimsy shoes for rugged outdoor activities, clothes that make bathroom breaks difficult (such as overalls), or wearing outfits that are either too warm or too cold for the weather are common complaints by staff. Make sure your child is dressed for comfort and fun.

Personal Style

- Most preschoolers love having special "flair" in their wardrobe, and what they love may change daily.

- Accessories such as hats, jewelry, scarves, kid-friendly watches, and forms of so-called "bling" (flashy) items are popular with this age group.

- Hairstyles may become important for both girls and boys alike. Boys may like to wear gelled looks for fun while many girls like certain hairstyles—sometimes complete with bows to match their outfit.

Dressing Battles

- Clothing wars are often the result of a child's love of fantasy and pretend, and how clothing puts him "into character."

- Rules about acceptable attire and why a jacket is needed or why a swimsuit can't be worn to daycare, for example, are battles that parents must always win.

- Help your child with decision-making by picking out outfits together the night before, with a "no change of mind" rule enforced.

AGE 3: CARE

HYGIENE
Teach healthy habits now to promote a lifelong routine of proper care

Since preschoolers are eager to learn and master skills that are as simple as putting toothpaste on their toothbrush or combing their hair, teaching general body hygiene is usually easy and sometimes even fun. While it's true a bit of dirt never hurt anyone, preschoolers may quickly look like they've rolled in it—maybe it's because their hands are into everything and they often end up with sticky things like glue or maple syrup on them. That's okay—that's what cleanup is for!

Parents should model good hygiene. Let your child see that you're brushing your teeth thoroughly twice each day, washing up before meals and after going to the restroom, and always making sure your hair is well groomed. As long

Brushing Teeth

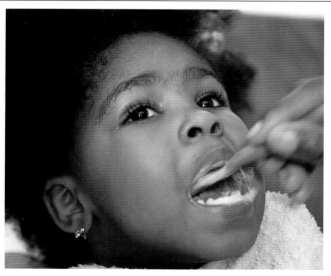

- Your child can brush her own teeth, though she won't be able to do a thorough job.

- Let her put a small amount of toothpaste on the toothbrush and have her brush her teeth while you brush yours.

- Make sure you have the right size toothbrush. Many parents pick brushes that are too big for children's small mouths.

- You will still need to brush your preschooler's teeth afterward. Make yourself the tooth inspector and keep things simple and stress-free.

Hair

- Morning "bed head" is a common look for preschoolers, and a mess of tangles can lead to howls and dressing struggles. Look for child-friendly detangle sprays to help minimize the ouchies.

- This age group may resist complicated hairstyles

- or extensive grooming, so parents should seek out options for providing simple and easy-to-maintain styles.

- Buy your preschooler a brush and comb and encourage her to groom her own hair as part of her daily routine.

28

as you matter-of-factly show preschoolers that these things are routine, expected, and are non-negotiable, they'll start to practice the same habits as well.

Resistance to hand washing and similar hygiene habits can sometimes occur when rules are inconsistent. If your child attends daycare, be sure to ask how these practices are handled. If your child is told to sing a certain song while washing hands to help track how long they are being scrubbed, for example, then by all means sing the same silly song with your tot when at home as well!

Hands and Nails

- Provide your child with a sturdy stepstool so she can wash and dry her hands (while supervised) at the bathroom sink.

- Show your child how to turn the faucet on and off and how to adjust the water temperature. Make sure you set rules around faucet use.

- Make sure the water heater is set at a safe 120 degrees Fahrenheit and consider using a faucet cover.

- Nails grow fast and can be quite sharp! Trim them regularly.

Body and Bath

- Preschoolers' faces are often as dirty as their hands! Show your child how to use a washcloth to clean her face and how to avoid getting soap in her eyes.

- Consider keeping a tub of towelettes next to your child's sink area for fast and convenient face cleaning.

- Your child can learn to soap her own body.

- Your child may prefer to take a shower over a bath.

- Always directly supervise your child when bathing.

SLEEPING

Sleep—lots of it—is still required to recharge young minds and bodies

Sleep routines should be well-established at this stage. After all, your three-year-old requires plenty of rest in order to rejuvenate for his always-on-the-go schedule when awake.

Many three-year-olds take daily naps, although the time spent either napping or relaxing may be shrinking. Consider naps an opportunity for your child to recharge his batteries;

hopefully, you'll be able to take advantage of that downtime as well! Parents should avoid too lengthy of a nap, however. An extended nap may mean kids will have difficulty falling asleep at their normal time and you might end up with a grumpy tot come morning.

If your child hasn't already been moved from his toddler

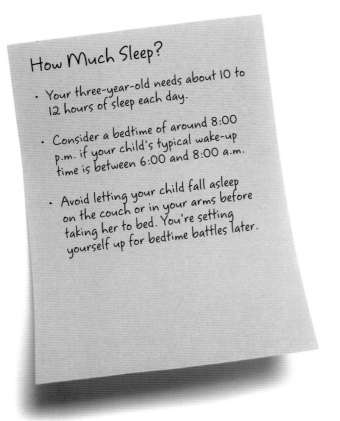

How Much Sleep?

- Your three-year-old needs about 10 to 12 hours of sleep each day.

- Consider a bedtime of around 8:00 p.m. if your child's typical wake-up time is between 6:00 and 8:00 a.m.

- Avoid letting your child fall asleep on the couch or in your arms before taking her to bed. You're setting yourself up for bedtime battles later.

Naps or Not?

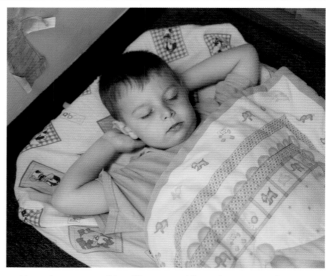

- Most three-year-olds still take naps. In fact, until they are five, most kids should take a nap.

- Preschoolers may seem ready to give up their nap, but it is usually because they want to keep playing, etc., not because they are truly ready to stop napping.

- Many daycares enforce an early afternoon nap or "quiet" time for preschoolers.

- Naps are typically shorter now than during the baby or toddler stages; an hour nap is considered average.

bed, this is the age where many preschoolers transition to a twin-size bed and away from a baby-themed room to one that is reflective of current interests.

While your toddler may have been easy to put to bed, don't be surprised if your three-year-old develops a fear of the night. An active imagination about monsters and similar scary objects combined with a keen awareness that adults are in another part of the house can disrupt sleep routines. A night light or a flashlight for a child to use if desired can help squelch fears of the dark.

Bedtime Rituals

- Establishing familiar and comforting bedtime rituals helps provide a gradual transition between the day's activities and sleep time.

- Getting ready for bed should be as low-key and relaxing as possible.

- Some preschoolers prolong bedtimes by stretching out the ritual as long as possible, so set a schedule and stick with it.

- Typical routines may include a relaxing bath, brushing teeth, picking a favorite stuffed animal, prayer, and reading a bedtime story.

········ YELLOW ● LIGHT ·········

Kids creeping out of bed in the middle of the night to wake up a parent is a common behavior that can affect the quality of sleep for all family members. Parents need to determine what is acceptable behavior, and then be consistent and firm about the rules. If you don't want your child coming to snuggle with you in bed in the middle of the night, then don't let him start the habit. It becomes harder to break with each exception.

Wetting the Bed

- Most three-year-olds occasionally wet the bed at night, and many don't stop until they are five or six years old.

- Exhaustion, not using the bathroom prior to falling asleep, genetics, or having too much to drink before bedtime are key contributors to bedwetting.

- Don't make a big deal out of wetting the bed.

- Some kids do not awaken when their body signals a need to urinate. Pull-ups and a waterproof mattress pad can help prevent stains or wet spots.

AGE 3: CARE

31

SAFETY

Parents must be vigilant about ensuring their child's safety around motor vehicles and water

Your three-year-old is developing better judgment and possesses a basic understanding of danger, but that doesn't mean you can let your guard down when it comes to safety. Kids this age are still easily distracted. And they may truly believe that no harm will come to them because loved ones will always protect them.

Dashing away in a parking lot or retrieving a lost item (like a bouncing ball) in the street and forgetting to look both ways can have devastating consequences, so adults must instill stringent rules about safety around cars.

Water safety becomes particularly important for your child to learn. Many children this age learn to swim—if they haven't

Water Awareness

- Curiosity about water contributes to accidental drownings of young children each year.

- Leaning over to look at water and then falling in is a common mishap. Kids can drown in as little as an inch of water.

- Never leave kids alone around water—even for the few seconds it takes to answer a phone. Drownings can occur swiftly and silently.

- If your child has a fear of water, taking lessons or playing in a wading pool or with water toys can encourage enjoyment.

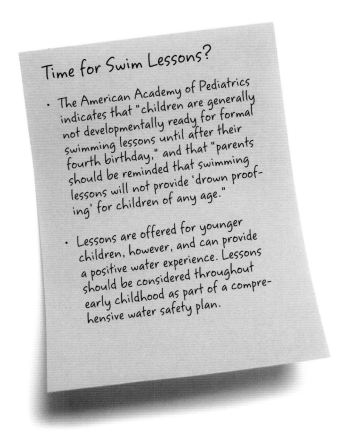

Time for Swim Lessons?

- The American Academy of Pediatrics indicates that "children are generally not developmentally ready for formal swimming lessons until after their fourth birthday," and that "parents should be reminded that swimming lessons will not provide 'drown proofing' for children of any age."

- Lessons are offered for younger children, however, and can provide a positive water experience. Lessons should be considered throughout early childhood as part of a comprehensive water safety plan.

already. Swim classes are increasingly offered for young children, beginning at the infant and toddler level. For the preschool group, safety is the primary skill taught. Your child can learn to float and to swim back to the edge of the pool and get out—a potentially lifesaving skill. Don't expect for your child to take one two-week course and be safe. Repetition and practice are important aspects of swimming success.

If you have a backyard pool or hot tub, then a comprehensive water safety plan is a must. A backyard fence is not enough; parents need to consider a separate pool fence with a childproof entrance, pool cover, lock for hot tubs, and locked backyard access from the home—in addition to swim lessons. Don't be afraid to ask about pool safety if your child is invited to play at a friend's home with a pool. And keep in mind that stringent water safety rules need to be established and communicated if staying with grandparents or other relatives as well.

Car Safety

- Enforce a no-exception "hold hands" rule when walking with your child in parking lots and public areas.

- Explain that motorists may not see them, and individuals must be responsible for themselves when walking amongst vehicles.

- Show how you can tell a car is backing up from their tail-lights.

- Teach your child about staying on the curb or sidewalk and other pedestrian rules. Teaching safety guidelines now and reinforcing them regularly will help your child later.

Independence Factor

- Preschoolers want to exert their independence and may start to resist being at your side when in public.

- Kids can become separated from parents in a matter of seconds. A momentary distraction, such as a cell phone call or chatting with an acquaintance, can cause a parent to lose focus and lead to a lost child.

- Parents should establish safety rules before every public outing.

- Develop a plan and discuss with your child what to do in the event that someone gets lost.

GEAR

It's out with the old, in with the new as toddlers become preschoolers

Items your child may have become quite familiar with—and even cherished—may not be suitable for a preschooler. Often, it's simply because the gear is either too small or is considered too babyish by your child. As your child develops greater cognitive and motor skills, learning needs and activities change as well. Achieving the milestone of preschool-age may ultimately mean out with the old and in with the new (or gently used) to keep up with your quickly growing child.

Safety and convenience gear may need to be updated or acquired. Parents should thoroughly check their child's car seat and ensure it still fits properly and is designed for your child's changing body shape and height. Booster seats for tables, child-friendly step stools, and potty chairs are other items that may be helpful for your child's emerging independence.

Car Seat Considerations

- Your child's car seat should be evaluated for fit and safety. Check straps and fittings while your child sits in the seat.

- Hand-me-down car seats may not meet current safety standards.

- Do not use a booster car seat. Three-year-olds are too young for these types of car seats.

- If a preschooler outgrows his car seat harness before age four, find one with an adjustable harness that has higher weight and height limits instead of a booster seat.

Boosters and Aids

- Booster seats can help your child to sit at the proper height at adult tables. Look for styles that can be fastened to a chair to minimize the risk of the seat sliding off with the child in it.

- Many restaurants and movie theaters provide booster seats for children to use. If possible, wipe them down first with an antibacterial wipe.

- Three-year-olds may need sturdy single-step stepstools for reaching the sink and some toilets.

While you may hate the notion of swapping out your child's nursery-style room, many preschoolers seek out themed bedrooms to reflect their current interests and favorite pretend-play fantasies. Beds may become bigger and the room design can now take a child through preschool and early elementary years.

You've undoubtedly noticed that your child's interest in toys is rapidly changing. Creative toys that allow assembly, experimentation, fantasy or pretend top the list, and toys don't need to be purchased to be educational or entertaining.

Movement and Exploration

- Your preschooler has the gross motor skills needed to successfully ride a tricycle or similar pedaled riding toy, but may still prefer easier scoot-riding toys.

- Three-year-olds can usually successfully operate slow-powered riding toys.

- Look for educational toys that promote free thinking and creativity.

- Don't force your child to assemble toys based on the manufacturer's example. He may have a better idea based on his imagination.

Room Updates

- Simple updates to your child's room can let your three-year-old feel like a "big kid" without spending a lot of money.

- Consider reusable wall stickers, painting the room a different color, or providing new accent pillows or bedding as inexpensive options.

- A twin-sized bed is a good option and still allows space in the bedroom for toys and unstructured play.

- Avoid overemphasis on a single theme; preschoolers quickly change their minds about favorite characters.

HOW PRESCHOOLERS LEARN

Forget structured learning; your child will learn best through engaging play and social interactions

The best part about delivering learning to preschoolers is that the formula for teaching is simple: Preschoolers learn best through engaging play and social interactions! While flash cards, so-called "brain time," and early math and reading skills do indeed help older preschoolers prepare for school, routine interactions are all that is needed for three-year-olds. In other

words, involve your child with your daily routine and responsibilities, taking time to explain objects and processes along the way, and your child will be learning at an incredibly fast rate.

While preschoolers may still crave familiarity, especially when it comes to books or routines they know and cherish, they may also love spontaneously making up activities and

KNACK PARENTING A PRESCHOOLER

Unscripted Stories

- Your child will draw from familiar stories and newly acquired skills to create made-up stories that show off tremendous imagination and creativity.

- Make up a story together with your child by taking turns creating characters and talking about the

adventures they take.

- Encourage your child to act out and "become" his character through facial expressions, movements, and tone of voice.

- Play a simple game of charades using well-known characters or activities.

Imitation and Observation

- Encourage your child to observe and then imitate you and add her own take on things.

- Promote silliness through talking in a mom or dad voice, or reverse role play.

- Read your child a beloved book with silly voices for all characters and then ask your child to do the same.

- Ask your child to see if he can think of what the family pet might be thinking or what his infant sibling might say if he could talk.

adventures. The fun part is your child may fluctuate between wanting the known versus the unknown.

Most three-year-olds will listen attentively to short stories and like familiar stories that are told again . . . and again . . . without any changes in words. They may relate to certain animal characters, especially those with human characteristics and responsibilities such as talking, going to school, or learning new skills. Once your child has learned the book's characters and essentially memorized the sequence of events, he'll be able to "read" it back to you with amazing accuracy!

ZOOM

Just how many times will your three-year-old want to put together and then take apart that same puzzle anyway? Doing something over and over again is a crucial sequence-building skill. Later, this knowledge becomes a learning building block for understanding concepts of grouping and sorting things that are similar, the same, or different, as well as determining consistency.

Music and Movement

- Most three-year-olds respond positively to upbeat music and child-friendly tunes.

- Favorite songs are often ones that involve silly motions and movements, such as the "Hokey-Pokey" or "The Wheels on the Bus."

- Dancing can be a great way to exercise and to work on coordination.

- Your child may love to hum and make silly sound effects, but be sure to explain when it is and isn't appropriate!

The Five Ws and an H

- Your child learns from asking questions—an endless stream of them. Sometimes the questioning is cute, but other times it can become downright annoying!

- Common questions are simply the five Ws: Who, What, Where, When, and Why, and then the H question: How?

- Encourage questions, but set a limit if your child is incessant.

- Maintain a positive attitude about questions, and avoid the "just because" answer.

TYPICAL SKILLS

Drawing shapes, identifying colors, and using math and logic are tasks to be mastered

As they transition from the toddler stage to early preschoolers, children's interests and abilities grow more complex. Preschoolers' attention spans are increasing quickly, in part due to their strong interests in observing how things are done. Fine motor skills are rapidly being tweaked and mastered, and a child who could barely hold a crayon one day seems to be coloring with great skill the next.

Many three-year-olds find shapes, colors, basic math, and problem-solving most fascinating at this stage, and may zealously study similarities and differences. Others may begin tracing shapes or even connecting base shape patterns to create objects from their imagination.

Shapes and Objects

- Your child can hold a pencil now, although she may not be using the correct form.

- She can usually draw a simple shape, such as a circle. Copying more complex shapes like a square or triangle is typically mastered at an older age.

- Three-year-olds can match an object to a picture of the object.

- They can talk about similarities and differences between objects, and use proper words to explain the answers correctly.

Math and Logic

- Three-year-olds can count up to three objects successfully, and sometimes more.

- They can use logic to solve problems, particularly ones that are simple and straightforward as well as real and immediate.

- Preschoolers at this stage do not typically understand hypothetical problems.

- Most three-year-olds can make a choice and then explain why they chose what they did—if they choose to tell you.

- Your child may like sorting things by shape and size.

Every child is unique, and the same holds true with interests and abilities. Just because your child couldn't care less about coloring or refuses to count objects, it doesn't mean anything is wrong. Your job as a parent is to find out what does interest your child, and to work on sparking areas that appeal to your preschooler. A preference for math and logic or creativity and abstracts may begin to surface, although it is much too early in a child's development to determine where your child's true passions may eventually lie.

ZOOM

Personality and patience can play a key role in what captures your child's attention. Some tots may sit quietly working hard at a skill, while others are a whirlwind around the table and may more likely be found rolling on the floor or making silly noises. Parents often find that the "timing" of when certain activities are scheduled has a great impact on a child's focus and interest in the subject.

Colors

Green — Frog

- Three-year-olds are interested in colors. They should know most common colors (such as red, blue, green, white, and black), and can usually identify them by name.

- Preschoolers may associate colors with certain activities or interests, which explains why they develop a sudden passion for specific colors.

- Encourage color recognition by asking basic questions, such as what color are leaves, your eyes, or the collar on the family pet.

Singing

- Your child can sing simple songs using proper words, and may like to repeat them until he gets the words right.

- Three-year-olds also like to make up silly songs, and may especially love singing into a microphone to hear their own voices.

- Your child may be able to carry a simple tune, and may like practicing to recorded music.

- Provide your child with some shakers or simple home-made noise makers to practice the beat.

GAMES & CHALLENGES
Encourage your preschooler to find his own path and reach a creative solution

Most three-year-olds absolutely love a good challenge. That's why so many preschool-age toys and games are created to encourage open-minded thinking and creative solutions. Having more than one way to build something rather than having a single right or wrong answer encourages youngsters to use their imagination. That's why products like

building blocks, interlocking plastic pieces like Duplos, and Lincoln Logs are so popular with the three-year-old set.

You don't have to buy these toys to provide your child with a challenge. Enterprising three-year-olds are master recyclers, and can transform boxes, empty cans, milk jugs, and just about any item from nature—everything from sticks and

Puzzles

- Three-year-olds love puzzles, and will spend significant time putting them together and taking them apart, only to put them together again.

- Most can put together a five-to-seven piece puzzle at this stage.

- Simple puzzles where kids choose a piece to fit into a pre-cut opening are typically too easy for your preschooler.

- Look for larger puzzle pieces that interlock and require kids to think about its shape and overall design.

Blocks and Stacking

- Blocks are a terrific child-size manipulative that provide hours of educational stacking fun. You don't have to go out and purchase blocks; anything stackable works just as well as long as it isn't too big or too heavy.

- Three-year-olds can typically stack five to seven objects successfully.

- Stacking and sorting by making two equal piles or counting each block as it is stacked onto another can help preschoolers to understand basic math concepts.

stones to pieces of wood or even shells—into a masterpiece.

Three-year-olds love creating their own set of rules to made-up games . . . just don't be surprised when those rules keep changing to give them the ol' preschooler advantage! That's why games without rules amongst three-year-olds typically end with someone's feelings hurt.

While young preschoolers revel in the challenge, and love to be declared the champion, they don't yet have the coping skills to handle losses well when things don't go their way.

Matching

- Simple card games like "Go Fish" (especially ones tailored to young preschoolers) are a fun way to teach matching and logic skills.

- Many preschoolers can play games where they match cards by turning up two at a time and then back down until they find a successful pair. Start with just four cards and then build up to prevent your preschooler from becoming frustrated.

- Help your child to learn object names, colors, and shapes by playing "I Spy" or games where she finds the answer from various options.

Problem Solving

- Most three-year-olds love a good challenge . . . as long as they ultimately win. That's why games requiring logic and trial-and-error are often fascinating for this stage.

- Ask your child what he would do in certain situations to help promote thinking skills. You might be surprised at the level of thought your youngster puts into a scenario.

DISCOVERY

Every outing is an opportunity for exploration and new experiences, especially when shared with peers

Consider yourself a tour guide for your child, as just about everything your preschooler experiences is another opportunity for discovery.

While your child can easily draw circles and lines, she may not have thought about how they can be connected to become a stick figure person, for example, or at least not until you show her. Then watch as her imagination soars and she starts showing stick figures holding things or engaging with one another (be sure to show how to draw happy, sad, angry, and surprised faces to show emotions).

Playgrounds offer endless fun and exploration. While toddlers may be hesitant to try some of the equipment,

Repeat and Go

- Your child may spend hours doing the same thing over and over again, and parents often make the mistake of redirecting a child's attention to something else.

- Repetition helps your child determine how doing things differently results in different outcomes.

- Avoid providing your child with too many activities at once. You may think you're providing enrichment opportunities, but you're actually interfering with him learning a skill thoroughly before moving on.

- Follow your child's lead when he's bored.

Let's Play Ball

- Your child runs and jumps easily, and playing with a ball is a way to practice motor skills while enjoying energetic play.

- Encourage your child to play with balls of various sizes and shapes.

- Explain how certain types of balls are used for various sports or games.

- Let your child feel the different hardness and texture of balls, such as comparing a foam ball to a baseball.

preschoolers may be more eager to learn to swing by themselves, try the monkey bars, and even take a turn down the covered slide that twists and turns.

Your child will be coordinated enough to play with a ball, and can toss it into the air and perhaps catch it, can throw it into a box or similar opening successfully, can kick it when rolled, and may even roll it up and down an incline.

While playing with your child and encouraging active discovery is important for development, look for opportunities for your child to have these adventures peers.

All Things Art

- Avoid asking your child what he is drawing or creating. He may not know, or care, and may simply just enjoy the art process itself.

- Play-Doh provides the opportunity to roll, stretch, shape, and smash a soft object. Preschoolers may like to squish the dough into shapes or just feel its texture. Show preschoolers how to blend two colors to make a new one.

- Finger painting lets children enjoy free expression art without any end goal.

Animal Activities

- Three-year-olds like to copy things you do, so have some fun teaching them animal-like behaviors and movement.

- Demonstrate how to hop like a frog, run like a rabbit, or sniff like a dog.

- Your child will like crawling on all fours, or doing the crab walk with tummy up.

- Slithering like a snake while flicking the tongue or making bunny ears out of arms can provide a laugh.

FAMILY FUN

It's all about the family; seek fun ways to promote togetherness and belonging

Family dynamics play a very important role in the development of a preschooler's sense of self, security, and place in the world. A positive family environment surrounded by loved ones helps a child flourish and feel safe enough to reach out and try new activities and skills.

Today's "families" are defined differently than in generations past, and no longer only refer to a household of mother, father, and a sibling or two. Many children today are raised in "blended" families while others are raised by a single parent. Regardless of how your household is made up, providing a sense of inclusion, nurturing, involvement, and good basic fun provide a preschooler with a strong family

Pretend and Fantasy

- Join your child's world of imagination and pretend. Help your preschooler brainstorm ways to create play settings in your own home.

- Actively participate in pretend adventures. Don't worry if your child prefers a fantasy world over real-

ity. It's a normal stage of development.

- Host a family campout in your living room, which can be as simple as hanging sheets over a couple of chairs, and tossing in a blanket, pillow, and flashlight.

Role Playing

- Why be just yourself when you can be anyone or anything you want to be? That's the thinking of many three-year-olds, so expect frequent role-playing transitions from pirate to princess to an airplane even.

- Three-year-olds love to role play, and may want to be

"mommy" or "daddy" by imitating things they see their parents or caregivers do.

- Avoid stereotyping roles or telling your child how a particular character should be played or dressed.

foundation for the present and future.

So what to do with your preschooler? Look for activities that promote shared experiences and encourage curiosity, pretending, leadership, and a sense of teamwork. Remember that simply making breakfast together or retrieving the morning newspaper provides a preschooler with a sense of responsibility and family contribution.

Parents need to step back from the role they assumed for the first three years of their child's life, in which they did everything for their tot and made all the decisions.

Creating Traditions

- Begin a few meaningful rituals you can begin now that can continue through childhood as a way to promote a sense of family and memories.

- Consider simple activities like movie nights (child's choice of movie) with popcorn and everyone snuggling in their PJs. What you pick isn't important; it's doing it together in a loving way.

- Preschoolers love most holiday traditions and learning how they can be a part of a variety of celebrations.

Fun in the Kitchen

- The kitchen is the perfect place to involve young children and stir up some food fun.

- Keep safety first and avoid having your preschooler around a hot stove or oven.

- Three-year-olds can help measure and pour, stir, and spread. Use this opportunity to talk about healthy eating choices, and you may be on your way to raising a kid who likes to cook and understands nutritional value as well!

IDEAS

Practically nothing is off limits when it comes to providing educational fun for your child

There's no shortage of ideas of what to do with your pre-schooler to keep him preoccupied and learning. That's because just about everything you can think of has the opportunity for fun. The simplest way to entertain your three-year-old is through inclusion—involving him in even the most routine of activities and household duties.

But sometimes you want to do more than chores, and the good news is that some of the most creative and educational activities use items or ingredients you already have at home.

Planning multistep activities can help build anticipation and lengthen the amount of time from start to finish. Keep in mind a preschooler's quickly wandering attention span,

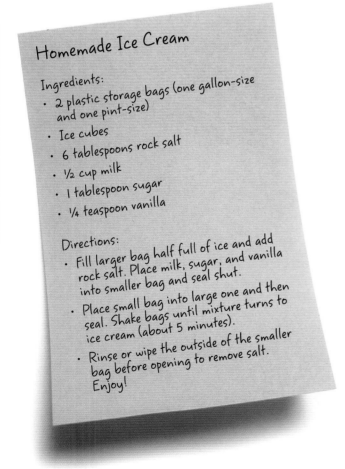

Homemade Ice Cream

Ingredients:
- 2 plastic storage bags (one gallon-size and one pint-size)
- Ice cubes
- 6 tablespoons rock salt
- ½ cup milk
- 1 tablespoon sugar
- ¼ teaspoon vanilla

Directions:
- Fill larger bag half full of ice and add rock salt. Place milk, sugar, and vanilla into smaller bag and seal shut.
- Place small bag into large one and then seal. Shake bags until mixture turns to ice cream (about 5 minutes).
- Rinse or wipe the outside of the smaller bag before opening to remove salt. Enjoy!

Hand-Eye Coordination

- Boost your three-year-old's hand-eye coordination skills by showing her how to thread pasta shapes onto shoe strings or yarn. Large plastic, child-friendly needles with blunt ends can also be used.

- Similar skills can be taught through stacking small

- objects into bigger ones.

- Have your child practice buttoning items (they don't need to be wearing the clothes with buttons to practice).

- Small jingle bells can be threaded onto pipe cleaners for holiday fun.

46

however. Activities work best when broken into smaller chunks. Consider tasks as centers: First you do this, then you accomplish that, then you put it all together and you have something amazing and new.

Using simple two- and three-step processes to achieve an end result helps a child to learn patience, enhances their span of focus, and teaches them that things don't always "just occur" without work and effort. These skills may take time, but are great for promoting learning readiness for preschool and ultimately kindergarten.

········· GREEN ● LIGHT ·············

Parents often make mistakes in trying to pre-plan outings rather than just letting their child take the lead. It can create frustration for both parent and child if you've paid for tickets to the zoo but your child really just wants to play with the water hose in the backyard. Consider starting an "idea jar" of activities with your child, and then pull one out when you're in search of some fun.

Puppet Play

- There are countless easy ways to make puppets. Socks, paper bags, paper plates, or even Popsicle sticks and foam paper can all make great puppet characters.

- Decorating the puppets is half the fun, so don't forget markers, glitter glue, or other kid-friendly supplies for unique designs.

- Puppet talk improves language skills by encouraging your child to get "into character" and think creatively about scenarios and words and descriptions.

Make-It-Yourself Playdough

Ingredients:
- 1 cup flour
- 1 tablespoon powdered alum (available in the spice section at many grocery stores)
- ½ cup salt
- 1 tablespoon oil
- 1 cup water
- 2 tablespoons vanilla
- Food coloring

Directions:
- Mix together all dry ingredients into a saucepan, and then add oil and water.
- Cook over medium heat, stirring until it reaches the consistency of mashed potatoes.
- Remove from heat and add vanilla. Divide into balls and knead in food coloring.

SOCIAL

Heightened interactions, emerging abilities to work things out with peers mark maturing social skills

A key social difference between toddlers and early preschoolers lies in how children relate to one another. While toddlers begin to interact with one another in a limited fashion, they still don't truly play "with" one another. That changes when your child becomes a preschooler. That's when the social butterflies begin to emerge and kids are quick to express that they want to play with their friends.

Small groups work best at this age, as too-large groups of children invite trouble. What's even more exciting about the emerging social skills of three-year-olds is that they may even begin to work things out (not always successfully) and engage in share situations—increasingly without adult

Eager to Please

- Your child is turning into a "people pleaser" and is learning new skills such as empathy, courtesy, and politeness.

- Explain what a compliment is, and encourage your child to give and receive compliments. At the same time, be sure to discuss how saying

certain things—even ones that are true—can sometimes hurt a person's feelings.

- Teach your child niceties like allowing guests to be first at something and opening doors for others. Praise generously!

Emerging Humor

- Your preschooler may begin to enjoy silly pranks—as long as they don't come at his expense.

- "Knock-knock" jokes and similar rhyming jokes and tongue twisters may have special appeal for preschoolers.

- General silliness, often demonstrated at picture-taking time and other occasions when the spotlight is on them, is to be expected.

- Your child will love laughing at your jokes—you've found the perfect audience!

intervention. That doesn't mean meltdowns or bad behaviors will never occur—that would be far too unrealistic—but you will find your child behaves well more often than not. That's definite progress!

You'll note increased cooperative play, as this age group becomes less selfish and more inclined to give and take in play situations. In other words, they'd rather have a friend to play with than keep a treasured toy all to themselves—at least most of the time.

Boys and girls play well together at this stage.

Little Helper

- You'll most likely never have such an enthusiastic helper as you do at this age. Your child will practically beg to assist you with about everything.

- Avoid being overly critical or refusing your child's help. Assign small tasks, and look the other way at not-so-perfect attempts. That's how young children learn.

- Be careful that your preschooler doesn't try something that is potentially dangerous. Make it clear which tasks are only for grown-ups and why.

Spontaneous Play

- Your three-year-old will begin to play spontaneously with other children, often joining in games and activities with kids she hasn't even formally met.

- Shy kids may play nearby while observing others and then quietly slip in on the action.

- Your child may not require your direction and attention as much as before, instead entertaining herself more.

- Look for toys and activities that allow your child the freedom and flexibility to play without structured rules.

PHYSICAL

Even with constant movement, some kids this age don't get enough physical activity

Learning is commonly expressed through physical action—lots of it! Kids combine their insatiable curiosity with endless energy, stacking up an array of physical achievements that demonstrate their burgeoning gross motor skills.

It's important that preschoolers have daily opportunities for extended unstructured physical play. This is why parks and kid-friendly obstacle courses hold so much appeal for youngsters, especially ones that include outdoor imagination stations with steering wheels, boat-shaped play apparatuses, and even command centers.

Your three-year-old will most likely thrive on being able to climb, hop, jump, leap, crawl, run, skip, and other age-

Hopping and More

- Your child can hop on one foot. Play games like hopscotch to encourage mastery of this skill.

- Three-year-olds can run easily. Have races to promote speed and physical activity.

- Have your child march to music, and lead a parade with friends or family.

- Your child can balance on one foot. Have timed contests to see how long your preschooler can balance on one foot, then the other. She may like to practice balancing on low (and safe) objects.

Walking

- Your child can walk in a straight line, toe to heel.

- Encourage different types of walking styles, such as walking backward, walking to the side by crossing one leg in front of the other, and walking in shapes (such as walking in a circle).

- Three-year-olds can go up and down stairs unassisted, usually placing one foot on each step (depending on the depth).

- Observe your child's walking to assure proper gait and sequence.

appropriate physical milestones for this age—although he may still be clumsy. With all the energy preschoolers exhibit, it's hard to believe that many children don't get enough activity.

If your child isn't physically active, and seems to prefer being more sedentary, it's your job to find ways to get him up and moving. Physical development and motor skills will be needed later on for school, in sports, and in other physical enrichment activities, so do your part to promote physical activity today.

Tiptoeing

- Many kids like to occasionally walk on their tiptoes. If your child walks on tiptoes all or most of the time, however, it is a sign that something could be wrong. Have your child evaluated by a doctor.

- Show your child the art of "sneaking" as a way to practice tiptoeing.

- Demonstrate pointed toe and flexed foot stances. Show how foot position can change how your child walks, from waddling like a duck to gliding like an eagle.

Jumping

- Your child can successfully make two-footed jumps over small barriers, not to exceed six inches high.

- Challenge your child to jump over a small branch or have him jump over cracks in the sidewalk.

- Demonstrate how to jump and leap while crouched down like a frog.

- Many three-year-olds can complete sequence steps such as "hop-hop-jump."

- Jumping jacks exercises that involve separate foot and hand motions are often still too complex to master.

INTELLECTUAL

Past, present, and future are concepts being learned as cognitive development continues to evolve

Not only does your three-year-old seem smarter, he is beginning to show examples of wisdom and logic that weren't noticeable even a few months earlier. The cognitive development of a young preschooler is ever-changing, and each child develops at his own unique pace. Factors such as genetics, environment, enrichment activities, and even nutrition

play a role in a child's intellectual development. The best thing parents and caregivers can do to promote cognitive development is to constantly expose their children to quality learning opportunities. It's that simple!

Three-year-olds think in the here and now, and are not truly aware of concepts that involve change over time. Confusion

Nature

- Three-year-olds like to relate their sense of place within the world and how things work together in nature. Making connections such as rain providing plants and trees with nutrients just like kids needing food to eat are especially interesting.

- Your child likes learning how wooden furniture and flooring once came from trees and that milk comes from cows, for example.

- By the end of the third year, your child should know about the four seasons and related activities and weather.

Family

- Three-year-olds relate better to the abilities and development of same age peers and younger children, but don't grasp the same concepts as kids who are older than them.

- Most preschoolers have a strong sense of family. Pretend activities such as

playing house, with role-playing and chores, reflect a growing understanding of family structure.

- Your child may enjoy drawing human figures and may begin to add additional details and body parts such as fingers by the end of the third year.

between fact and fantasy is common, as young preschoolers have a difficult time understanding the difference. To them, a person in costume truly is that character, which is why many kid-targeted restaurants and retailers utilize caricature-influenced marketing tactics to woo young people.

Your child may begin to understand yesterday, today, and tomorrow, but many youngsters may not grasp anything beyond "now" and "later." Most three-year-olds don't understand the concept of a calendar and don't comprehend what it means for something to be months, or even years, away.

ZOOM

Your child has mostly mastered concepts of physical and behavioral actions. For example, he knows that if the doorbell rings, someone is there, or if he presses a certain button, the light will turn on. Preschoolers also understand that if they hit someone, they will be disciplined, or if they cry, an adult will respond to them. They may still struggle with the idea of something being broken.

Self

- Your child understands the concepts of in, out, under, over, in front of, behind, on top of, and bottom. He may enjoy demonstrating this to you as well, actually hiding under the bed or standing behind the fountain and describing what he is doing.

- He may provide detailed descriptions about what he plans to do or what he has just done.

- Your preschooler may begin to compare himself with others, but may still be oblivious to most differences.

Memory and Memorization

- Your child may remember things he did the day before or a short time ago. That doesn't mean he understands when he did it, only that he recalls the activity itself.

- Three-year-olds are capable of memorizing details and facts, an early sign of learning readiness.

- Your child should be able to state her first and last name and age correctly.

CREATIVE

Avoid the push for perfection; encourage free-spirited thinking and unstructured processes

Creativity at this stage involves much more than just pretend and imagination. Your child's lack of preconceived notions or rules means that every task or process starts as a blank sheet of paper, and your child will fill it in the way she chooses to! That's creativity in its truest form.

Creativity is expressed by your child's extreme interest in putting things together, through a child's view of style or placement, and even through a simplistic love of colors, actions, or deeds.

While certain things do need to be done in a specific order or way to provide the desired result, three-year-olds cherish the ability to do things without an instruction book. Even the

Avoiding Perfectionism

- Avoid encouraging perfectionism. Just admire your child's creativity and talents—whatever they might be.

- Many parents make the mistake of running with whatever new interest their child might exhibit at a given time. That's usually a big mistake. Just because your child likes to walk around on her tiptoes doesn't mean she wants to take ballet lessons.

- Seek out process-oriented toys that have multiple uses rather than types that can only be assembled in one way.

Creative Processes

- Encourage creativity by finding activities that promote free-spirited thinking. For example, choose finger painting on a blank sheet of paper over a simple paint by number.

- Let your child think as abstractly and illogically as she likes when it comes to creative expression. Many parents push "expected" outcomes to the point where kids avoid trying because they are afraid of failure.

- Display your child's artwork so he will know you are proud of his efforts.

way your child chooses to eat a particular food or examine a flower is a marvel in creativity. Since kids at this age are mostly unaffected by the thoughts and actions of others, they feel a pure sense of freedom in trying out new, untested, and not-always-successful ways of reaching the end result.

Parents can help nurture a child's spirit and curiosity by following a child's lead and providing appropriate tools and assistance as needed, supporting the process along the way. Avoid over-directing or setting requirements; grass doesn't always have to be green, after all!

Downtime and Daydreaming

- Simple daydreaming without a purpose or end goal is a great way to boost creativity.

- Arrange for ample unstructured free time away from television and guided activities.

- Creativity blossoms when your child is responsible for entertaining himself. Kids don't need to rely on others to entertain them at every waking minute.

- When away from television, computers, and video games, kids may showcase enhanced creativity skills.

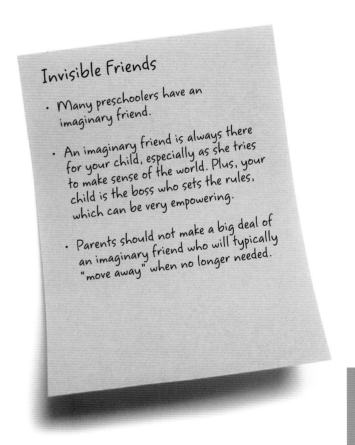

Invisible Friends

- Many preschoolers have an imaginary friend.

- An imaginary friend is always there for your child, especially as she tries to make sense of the world. Plus, your child is the boss who sets the rules, which can be very empowering.

- Parents should not make a big deal of an imaginary friend who will typically "move away" when no longer needed.

EMOTIONAL

Your child craves parental approval and attention from adults but is gaining emotional independence

It's not hard to figure out what your three-year-old is feeling. Social skills and language have advanced to the point where your child can tell you in great detail about his emotional state. Advancements in maturity and ability to better understand his own needs allows a young preschooler the ability to understand why he feels the way he does, and what can be done about it, resulting in fewer meltdowns from loss of control.

That's not to say that three-year-olds aren't emotional or needy. They are still subject to tantrums, whining, or crying when they are tired. The difference is that they are more easily soothed—and even able to comfort themselves—a skill that will continue to be enhanced in the coming years.

Shock and Awe

- Three-year-olds are typically in awe of just about everything. Expressive looks and gestures let you know exactly how fascinating little details or objects can be.

- Their range of emotions continues to expand, and they may need tender loving guidance to help them navigate new feelings.

- Encourage your preschooler to use words to express emotions, and to enhance communication overall.

- Find ways to surprise and delight your youngster with small marvels and watch their reactions.

Frustration, Anger, and Disappointment

- Your preschooler is capable of great anger and may need guidance in learning how to control it. Demonstrate appropriate ways to handle this very normal human emotion.

- Preschoolers become frustrated easily, and tasks that are too difficult or things that break can result in meltdowns. Remember your child wants to do things for himself, so don't over challenge him at this stage to avoid discouragement.

- Your child will most likely say when he is disappointed.

Preschoolers also have a broader range of emotions than what they experienced as toddlers. No longer are emotions limited to the basics: happy, sad, mad, scared, and surprised, among others. New emotions have emerged and begin to take shape: perplexed, embarrassed, awed, exhausted, frustrated, insecure, as well as many others.

Kids this age are excited about new skills, and want you to acknowledge their efforts. They readily follow suggestions and simple directions. They love to laugh and be silly but really like amusing you most of all!

················· YELLOW ● LIGHT ·················

Your three-year-old may have extremely tender feelings, which can be hurt by something as simple as a raised tone of voice or stern look. Early preschoolers are extremely sensitive about what others—especially adults—think and say about their actions. If they don't get the reaction they expect, preschoolers can become embarrassed or even experience humiliation, and will require extensive comforting.

Love and Insecurity

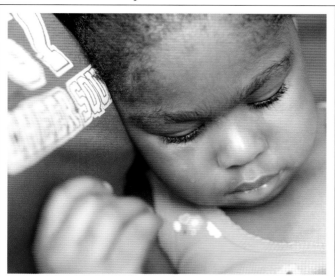

- Most preschoolers genuinely adore being snuggled, and will still seek out loved ones for reassurance and affection.

- Many preschoolers begin to favor one parent over another, and at this stage it is often the opposite-gender parent.

- Separation anxiety has mostly passed, but preschoolers may still feel insecure with new situations and in meeting new people.

- Your child may still crave a comfort item, such as a favorite toy or even a blanket.

Are Movies Too Scary?

- Taking your preschooler to a movie can be a fun family experience, but make sure the selection and your child's temperament and sensitivity are a good match.

- Because three-year-olds have difficulty separating fantasy from reality, even G-rated movies—including beloved Walt Disney classics—can over stimulate and frighten them.

- Another option is waiting for the DVD and fast-forwarding through scary parts.

57

AGE 3: MY WORLD

LANGUAGE
Communications improve as words are used over emotions

One of the most notable transitions between the toddler and preschooler years is the vast improvement of language skills. Not only does your child speak more, but he understands more as well, and he is learning the meaning behind words spoken. As a result, parent-child communications improve vastly and emotions calm down. Your three-year-old is beginning to "use his words" to express wants and needs instead of the emotional outbursts from before.

Many preschoolers speak well enough so that about 75 percent of speech is understandable. Your child may still stumble over words sometimes, but that is typically more of a normal word mastery process and is not indicative of a speech problem. You'll note that preschoolers may even practice certain words over and over until they become

Growing Vocabulary

- Three-year-olds have acquired 500 to 800 words, although they may still confuse meanings and word choices.

- Your child should be able to understand and use the right word for common objects.

- Pronouns (I, you, they, us, we, and they) are usually used correctly, such as "I need to go potty," instead of just "go potty."

- Your child may also begin to use plurals correctly, such as "Those horses are big," instead of just pointing and saying "horse."

Promoting Word Comprehension

- Promote word comprehension by having active conversations with your child, using short sentences and concise thoughts.

- Ask your child lots of questions and actively listen to her responses.

- Add descriptions in the

- form of extra adjectives to what your child says and then repeat it back. This gives your child additional word choices.

- Avoid overcorrecting grammar, and instead simply re-state the sentence using the proper word choices.

confident in saying it. After all, they have a great sense of pride in getting things right!

Your three-year-old is now able to talk in complete sentences using three-to-five words strung together. Instead of simply saying, "More milk," your child should be able to say something like "My milk is gone. I need more milk please." Note the use of "please" in that example, as your child is perfectly capable of learning proper manners and how to make a request rather than a demand at this age and stage!

ZOOM

Many preschoolers go through a stage when they stutter. Often, the stuttering goes away on its own as your child learns how to speak better and masters the coordination of muscles used for speech. In other cases, stuttering may continue into the school years, and speech therapy may be needed to help children overcome the speech difficulty.

Clarity and Phonemic Awareness

- Avoid guessing what your child is saying when unclear. Ask her to say her words differently.

- Encourage your child to talk with other adults and listen to determine how well others can understand what is being said. Parents are familiar with their children's language and speech patterns but the goal is for others to understand what your child says as well.

- Introduce phonemic awareness by showing letters and teaching the corresponding sounds.

Speech Delays

- Does your child have speech delays or is he simply a "later talker?"

- About 5 to 10 percent of kids have a developmental disability that causes a delay in speech.

- There are two main types of speech delays: expressive delays, the inability to generate speech; and receptive delays, the inability to understand the speech of others.

- Most delays improve with time but may require speech therapy. Ask your doctor if you have concerns.

APPEARANCE

Growth is steadier and body shape begins to reflect that of a school-age child

Four-year-olds don't look much different from three-year-olds, with one notable exception. A four-year-old's overall body shape may continue to slim down as your preschooler grows in height. Four-year-olds typically weigh between 27 and 46 pounds and are from 37 to 43½ inches in height. Separate growth and height charts for boys and girls are readily available online. Here is one example: http://pediatrics.about.com/cs/usefultools/l/bl_kids_centils.htm.s.

Growth rates from now on are typically slower and steadier. Pronounced growth spurts are not usually obvious; your child may actually begin to wear out clothing instead of simply outgrowing it so quickly!

Changing Looks

- Chubby cheeks and a cute-as-a-button nose may be replaced by features equally as adorable: thinner face, expressive eyes, and an impish grin.

- Preschoolers typically have extreme facial expressions. A quick look can show parents and caregivers how a child is feeling or even what she is up to.

- Hair may grow faster or slower, depending on growth cycles and genetics. Texture and wave patterns may change as hair follicles mature and a child ages.

On the Grow

- Average growth in height between ages three and four is 2½ to 3 inches, according to pediatric growth charts issued by the Center for Disease Control.

- Average weight gain during that same period is four to five pounds.

- Children typically advance a size or even two in clothing, although clothes may be too short but still fit properly around the waist and hips.

- Diet, illness, genetics, and even emotional well-being can affect a child's rate of growth.

A striking characteristic of most children at this stage is how they suddenly seem to have become a total package in terms of coordination, agility, and energy. While youngsters may still have bouts of clumsiness, the majority of kids flourish in their mastery of enhanced physical abilities and overall body mechanics.

Parents should pay particular attention to a child's physical abilities and overall physical appearance. While skills develop differently for each child, if you feel your four-year-old is lagging in key areas, ask your doctor for an evaluation.

ZOOM

How tightly or loosely is your child's body put together, and does it matter? Muscle tone is checked when a child is evaluated for gross motor development. If your child's body is too tight, then her movements may seem disconnected or even jerky. A child with tone that is considered too loose may lack strength and have sluggish movements.

Body Frame

- Physical growth occurs mostly in the legs and trunk areas of preschoolers' bodies.

- Four-year-old body shapes begin resembling that of a school-age child as they continue to lose so-called "baby" features.

- They have mostly lost their rounded belly shapes and have thinned out in their thighs.

- Clothing is typically sized for height and not weight. Many outfits include adjustable waistbands or elastic to allow for greater growth flexibility and diverse body shapes.

Hands and Feet

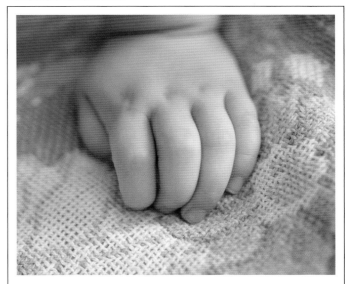

- Fingers may appear longer and slimmer.

- Feet that previously seemed extra wide as a baby or toddler now may seem to be more proportional.

- Average shoe size varies greatly, but typically ranges from size 9 to 13. Wide width shoes for children are readily available at many shoe stores.

- Feet grow quickly, but avoid buying shoes that are more than a half-size too big. Ill-fitting shoes can cause young kids to stumble and walk improperly.

WELL-CHILD VISIT

Doctor will review developmental milestones and overall wellness, and booster shots will be given

KNACK PARENTING A PRESCHOOLER

Yearly checkups are essential for keeping kids healthy and administering immunizations against many potentially life-threatening diseases and illnesses. Well-child visits also give parents an opportunity to discuss any behavioral or developmental concerns, health and safety issues, or just to seek guidance on what is considered normal child development.

A four-year-old checkup will be a busy one, and immunizations and boosters will most likely mean your child won't be leaving the doctor's office with a smile. But shots are typically done at the very end of a visit, and parents should take full opportunity at the start to ask questions and provide the doctor with details about your child's everyday life. It's your

What to Expect:

- Measurement of height and weight
- Blood pressure check
- An examination of growth and development
- Check of reflexes, motor skills, and spine
- Discussion of toilet training, social skills, and proper nutrition
- Review of sleep schedules and physical activity
- Review of behavior and discipline
- Counseling on safety practices and dental health
- Immunizations
- Urinalysis (depending on doctor)
- Counseling about outdoor protection from sun and bugs

Reflexes and Strength

- The doctor may check reflexes by tapping the knee with a rubber hammer and observing whether the leg swings up involuntarily.

- The reflex check determines whether nerves correctly carry messages from the brain and spinal cord telling the body what to do.

- Other common checks are asking a child to pull a doctor's index fingers or having a child push back a doctor's open hands with his own to check resistance and strength.

time, so make sure you make the most of it!

Your pediatrician may wish to discuss child safety practices, nutrition, and overall health as well as ask about behavioral and social development.

Physical checks will include vision and hearing tests, a dental evaluation (which doesn't replace regular visits to the dentist), and reflexes. The pediatrician may ask about your child's sleep schedule and about daily naps. Physical activity will also be discussed, and whether your child is participating in daily exercise programs—both structured and free.

Teeth

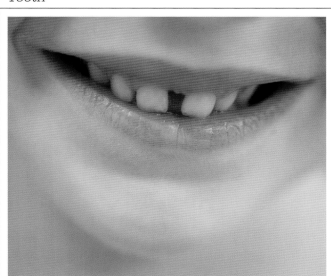

- Typical four-year-olds have 20 baby teeth.

- Children should see a pediatric dentist twice a year for cleaning and check-ups. Because permanent teeth may not come in for a while, cavities in baby teeth may need to be fixed. Otherwise, a child could be at risk of pain, infection, and more extensive dental work later.

- Teeth grinding in pre-schoolers is common, but the habit typically goes away by the time a child is seven or eight years old.

What Shots are Needed?

- At four years old your child will need the final dose in the Diphtheria, Tetanus, and Pertussis series.

- The final series of Inactivated Poliovirus will be administered.

- A Varivax booster will be given (if your child has not had the chickenpox).

- The Measles, Mumps, and Rubella booster will be administered.

- Depending on the time of year, an annual flu shot may be recommended.

SELF

Your preschooler oozes self-confidence and is proud of interests and passions . . . regardless of what others think

Your four-year-old knows who he is and typically has the self-assurance combined with a "whatever" attitude to flaunt it. At this age, while your youngster is increasingly influenced by other peers, she still likes what she likes, and that's that for the most part. A strong desire to fit in and be the same comes later. For now your preschooler thrives on being unique and

having strong passions about certain things.

You may notice your preschooler looking at himself in the mirror more and spending considerable time examining his body. Your child is quite curious, so it's only natural that he will delight in wiggling his toes or making funny faces at others. That's who he is, and it's quite normal. Many parents

Sense of Self

- Behaviors continue to be better controlled and reactions less spontaneous than in previous years.

- While preschoolers still have much maturing to do, parents typically delight in how their preschooler is starting to think about actions rather than just

- doing something without considering risks or consequences.

- Your child may begin to become more cautious and tentative.

- Your child typically feels good about himself.

Sense of Family

- Find ways to build strong family ties between your child and his grandparents or other extended family members.

- While younger children may have been more difficult to talk with, preschoolers' growing attention span and desire to hear about

- adventures and events from times past make them good conversationalists for older family members.

- Your child may delight in having an established role (such as being the older sister) within the immediate family, and having specific responsibilities.

give up on a "normal" photograph at this stage . . . your pre-schooler is going to be the one to stick his tongue out or otherwise be silly.

At the same time, your preschooler will be strongly attached and devoted to family, and he will typically openly embrace loved ones and still like to snuggle and hold hands. Four-year-olds cherish being a part of a family structure, which goes along with how they crave familiarity and sense of place at this stage.

Sense of Others

- Your child increasingly is showing intuitive behavior about how his actions or words affect others.

- Preschoolers at this stage can demonstrate a growing sense of respect for others, of personal space, and an understanding of why certain rules or protocols are necessary.

- Teach your child about ways to provide simple assistance to others, such as holding a door open, giving someone an object for comfort or convenience, or helping to carry in purchases from the car.

Time and Seasons

- Four-year-olds may increasingly remember details about events that occurred recently.

- They better understand yesterday, today, and tomorrow, and often can relate to expanded time passages such as recently or soon.

- They may understand a minute is short, an hour is longer, and have a general comprehension of time throughout a single day.

- Your child may begin to anticipate the changing of the seasons.

RULES

Your child may begin testing limits on rule-enforcement, so consistency is more important than ever

Rules and structure are different for preschoolers than they are for toddlers. When your child was a toddler, rules were quite simple: "Don't touch that" or "You may not go outside."

For preschoolers, however, increasing intelligence along with a better sense of judgment and ability to reason may affect the rules you establish. For the first time ever in your child's life, you may even begin to loosen the structure and provide greater flexibility … even if it's just a bit. That's because as your preschooler matures and gains better understanding of consequences and reasoning, you may use rules as a way to encourage appropriate behaviors and independence.

While parents should keep vigilant in enforcing rules about

Inappropriate Language

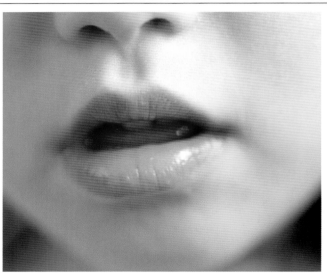

- Kids repeat what they hear and many a parent has been mortified over a child sputtering a profanity or using forbidden words.

- Before disciplining your child, first consider the source and circumstance. Preschoolers repeat what they hear and see. They then delight in using what they've learned—especially if they think it will incite a reaction.

- Establish rules that certain words or expressions are inappropriate and they should check with you if they aren't sure about a word choice.

Physical Restraint

- For the most part four-year-olds should be able to refrain from acting out physically, hurting either themselves or others.

- Set rules for which behaviors match family expectations and which are considered disruptive.

- Regularly reinforce which actions are appropriate.

- If your child continues to exhibit frequent and extreme physical reactions to rules, an evaluation should be scheduled to rule out any developmental problems.

safety and health (for example "You must sit in your car seat" and "Teeth must be brushed!"), other rules can be more flexible.

Preschoolers may begin pushing the limits and testing whether rules can be negotiated, however, so it is more important than ever for family members and caregivers to agree on rules—and to make sure they are kept and applied consistently. Food choices, snacks, television watching, and bedtimes are frequent sources of inconsistent rules, and preschoolers become adept at wrangling their own way if parents or caregivers waver.

TV Watching

- The average child watches television for three to four hours daily, despite recommendations from the American Academy of Pediatrics that children should watch no more than an hour or two per day.

- To help limit TV time, have your child watch a particular program. When the program (which is typically 30 minutes in length) ends, it is time for another activity—preferably one that is physical.

- Pre-record programs, if possible, and bypass commercials to minimize exposure to products.

Exposure to Violence

- Studies have suggested that preschoolers who watch violence on TV are more likely to exhibit aggressive behaviors and may have trouble sleeping or separating fiction from reality.

- Carefully select programs that emphasize interactivity so that your child doesn't just passively watch a program.

- Remember that the designation of "family film" doesn't mean it's suitable for your child.

BEHAVIOR

Cooperative play, a need for social stimulation, and desire for privacy are normal

By the end of their fourth birthday, children should be able, at least most of the time, to demonstrate behaviors that are pleasant and appropriate. Of course, slip-ups will continue to happen, but they will become the exception. Undesirable behaviors should be dealt with when they occur to discourage repeat offenses.

Friends and social activities rule a child's world at this stage, and much of your four-year-old's behavior is geared toward playmates. This is a prime age for children to truly master behaviors that are considered right and wrong, and preschoolers will begin learning about friendships, acting nice, playing cooperatively, and being fair.

Rule Changer

- Personality differences begin to emerge between leaders and followers, with some kids feeling a need to be in charge and to control games and play.

- Preschoolers are very competitive with their peers, and changing rules—to their advantage, of course—is a common behavior.

- Having rules that constantly change is frustrating to a child, so parents should help kids to understand and agree on rules up front when playing a game together.

The Shock Factor

- Preschoolers delight in shocking loved ones, but may not understand the line between what is funny and appropriate and what is not.

- You'll need to provide guidance to your child and help him understand that, for instance, while it may be okay to show his belly to someone, it is not okay to show his buttocks or genitals. Don't expect children to "just know" the difference.

- Kids are old enough to understand appropriate touching and modesty.

The not-so-nice behavior of "tattle-telling" has also been added to your child's repertoire. Kids this age love to "tattle" on others, and parents may find themselves being told, "He just did this," or "She just said that." The behavior is often exacerbated by a preschooler's inability to always separate imagination from reality, truth from lies. As a result, parents need to be aware that exaggeration and even wishful thinking may be coming into play, and should respond to their kids with that possibility in mind.

ZOOM

Parents try to keep things fair by equalizing expenses like gifts and activities, but may unwittingly engage with one child over another due to age or receptivity to talking. Try keeping your language similar and providing equal love and praise, even if a child seems disinterested—at least outwardly.

Boasting

- Boasting can become a behavioral problem at this stage, especially when combined with growing emotions of envy and materialism.

- Kids love to brag about new toys, planned outings, and even the size of their home and may not truly understand that it causes their friends to feel sad or jealous.

- Parents need to teach kids that while they have every right to be excited about something, they need to also consider the feelings of others.

Tattling

- Kids tattle because they are rule-oriented. They begin to "police" behaviors, and exceptions get reported to the nearest authority figure.

- Parents may unwittingly encourage tattle-telling by reacting strongly to information and quickly intervening.

- Encourage kids to work out their problems amongst themselves. Tell kids to "Play nice and quit coming to me or we will end the playdate and go home." Then, follow through.

FEARS

Increased caution and uncertainty may occur as preschoolers learn that they aren't invincible

Fears are a very normal aspect of childhood development, and the types of fears experienced may vary by age group.

Common fears for four-year-olds relate to anxiety over being separated from loved ones. Fear of being alone, fear of the dark, and even fear that something bad will happen to a parent are typically created out of a child's insecurity of being alone. Common fears include monsters, storms, and getting lost or taken away by a stranger. Preschoolers may also worry about fire, bugs or snakes, or even certain animals.

Four-year-olds are often attracted to scary things, yet it is the very activities they find so fun during the day that can lead to nightmares later. Preschoolers thrive on the sensation of

Fear of Separation

- For young preschoolers, the most common fears stem from anxiety over being separated from parents or loved ones.

- Having this fear does not mean a bad experience has happened to your child; rather, it may simply mean your child feels extra loved and comforted when you're around.

- Parents can help soothe separation fears by providing their child with a consistent reliable routine, by keeping their word about when they will return after scheduled time apart, and by offering continued reassurance.

Fear of Mortality

- Friendly ghosts and dancing skeletons are often depicted in kid-oriented movies and television shows, but children can become frightened of the images, especially when they realize their meaning.

- Kids may not totally grasp the concept of "dead" or "dying," but events in their personal life may expose them to this fact of life and make them fearful.

- Your preschooler may fear you growing old and dying as he becomes aware of the cycle of life. He may exhibit seemingly irrational fears of objects like balloons.

being scared, but only within limited boundaries. For example, a video with happy dancing skeletons may seem okay to watch at first, but later your child may begin to obsess about skeletons and the meaning behind them.

An overactive imagination, a love of pretend and fantasy, and even participation in events like trick-or-treating can be unsettling for some youngsters. Others may not show any signs of concern at all, so parents need to plan activities based on how they feel their child will most likely react.

Bedtime Fears

- Bedtime fears are usually the result of a child being insecure or nervous about being separated from their parents. Even children who have been sleeping well without incident may suddenly become fearful at night.

- Having an established bedtime routine that consists of ordinary activities helps to create a sense of calm and comfort.

- A family photograph or treasured memento can help a child to feel closer to you even when you are apart at night.

What to Do about Fears

- Most fears are temporary, and are outgrown as children mature.

- Acknowledge a child's fear instead of dismissing it. Talk to him calmly about his concerns—rational or not.

- Tell him you have confidence in his ability to work through his fears, but that you are always there if he needs you.

- If a fear affects your child's enjoyment of everyday life, schedule a visit with the pediatrician.

EXERCISE

As preschool obesity rates continue to rise, parents should focus on keeping their child active

Providing age-appropriate exercise for preschoolers is more important than ever, as the nation's obesity epidemic affects younger and younger children. Reports indicate that obesity rates are rising sharply among preschoolers. The American Heart Association has reported that about 14 percent of children between the ages of two and five years of age are overweight—compared with 10 percent just four years earlier—and the percentage continues to climb.

Why the spike in percentages? The United States has become a nation of fast food and super-sized portions, where even youngsters are tempted with "mighty-size" offerings of food that are high in calories and fat. But that's only

Recommended Activities

- A variety of physical programs geared specifically to preschoolers are offered through many community recreational programs or the YMCA.

- A growing number of daycare centers also offer daily exercise activities in addition to ample opportu-

nities for free play.

- Choose sports that encourage constant motion rather than just occasional movement. Soccer is often a better choice than T-ball, for example, if your child ends up only kicking the dirt in the outfield. Though any sport is better than none!

Building Exercise into Routine

- Parents should build physical activity into a child's daily routine.

- Avoid emphasizing structured learning at the expense of needed physical exercise. Remember that play is learning, too.

- Ask detailed questions

about what your child's provider or daycare center does to promote physical activity, including how often and how long each session occurs.

- Some children may need guidance on free play ideas, such as playing tag or learning to jump rope.

part of the problem. Children today spend less time outdoors engaged in unstructured free play just running around and being kids. Instead, in part due to safety concerns and hectic parent work schedules, children are more apt to spend their free time playing video games, on the computer, or watching television. That's where exercise comes in.

Look for structured programs such as soccer, dance, gymnastics, and swimming that are geared toward four-year-olds.

ZOOM

A child's ethnicity plays a role in body weight. Studies indicate that of the 14 percent of preschoolers who are overweight, 11.5 percent are non-Hispanic whites; 13 percent are non-Hispanic blacks; and 19.2 percent are Mexican Americans. Cultural food choices and activities play a role in a child's weight, although genetics determines body style and build.

Family Fitness

- Since children learn by example, the best way to encourage a healthy and active preschooler is by modeling a healthy and active lifestyle yourself.

- Many preschoolers enjoy activities like morning stretching routines alongside their parents and the ritual of daily walks to the park after dinner. Whatever your lifestyle or schedule, you can find something physical and fun to do with your child regularly.

- Gyms often have programs for kids while parents work out.

Calculating BMI

- The American Academy of Pediatrics recommends health care professionals calculate and record a child's body mass index (BMI) at annual well-child visits.

- BMI is a useful tool for determining whether a child is underweight, normal weight, or overweight.

- Parents can determine BMI by entering their child's height and weight using inches and pounds into a BMI table easily found on the Internet. Here is one option: http://pediatrics.about.com/cs/usefultools/l/bl_bmi_calc.htm

HYGIENE

Kids may have mastered the basics, but still need a parent's guidance

At age four, your child has now mostly-mastered using the bathroom without your help (although accidents may still occasionally occur) and can wash his hands, soap his body when taking a bath, and even get dressed and undressed by himself. For the first time, you may even begin to send your child into the bathroom by himself, and be mostly pleased with the results. Your child takes great pride in pleasing you and showing his independence, and hygiene is a way he can successfully demonstrate those skills!

At the same time, your child may become more opinionated and resistant to certain routines she deems unnecessary—leading to battles of the wills. Having fingernails and toenails

Bathroom Habits

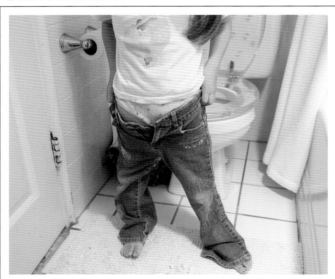

- While your child can typically go to the bathroom independently, wiping after bowel movements may still require parental assistance.

- Reinforce wiping from front to back for girls to prevent infection. Both boys and girls need guidance about how to wipe as well as how to avoid urine drips on underpants.

- Improper wiping can lead to rashes or infections—or a child who smells bad.

- Moist flushable wipes can help preschoolers do a more thorough job of wiping.

Independent Dressing

- Four-year-olds still do best with easy-on and easy-off clothing styles, especially since there are still possible last-minute runs to the bathroom.

- Your child can successfully navigate most zippers and snaps.

- Buttons can still present a challenge on waistbands or hard-to-reach places. Parents can help by loosening or stretching holes so the buttons go through easier.

- Many preschoolers become quite willful about what they do or do not want to wear at this stage.

trimmed and washing hair typically top the list of things that preschoolers don't like, and parents must be consistent in explaining why it is important to maintain proper hygiene.

A primary issue with preschoolers is having them keep their hands clean and preventing them from putting their fingers or hands in their mouths or around their eyes after touching something unclean. Other potential health and safety issues related to hygiene include proper wiping, drinking pool water, and even picking "boogers" from the nose.

Bathtime Battles

- Many preschoolers will continue to love baths, although some may begin to balk at bathtime routines.

- Parents must always directly supervise their preschooler in the bath but you can allow her to soap her own body or even wash her own hair.

- Some preschoolers may take showers—either with a parent or under direct adult supervision.

- Continue to use hypoallergenic and tear-free bath products. Adult shampoos are too harsh for children.

About Cryptosporidium

- Cryptosporidium is a waterborne illness carried by a chlorine-resistant parasite found in the fecal matter of infected humans and animals.

- It can cause diarrhea and dehydration.

- "Crypto" is found in many public swimming pools. It spreads when liquids or items that have been contaminated by an infected person are swallowed.

- Kids with diarrhea should not swim. And don't allow your child to swallow or scoop up water in the mouth when at public pools.

OCCASIONAL CHILD CARE

Finding a reliable, experienced, and trustworthy babysitter can be a challenge for protective parents

For many parents, finding occasional child care so they can attend adult-only outings or have a date night can be more stressful than choosing full-time care. That's because while full-time care options are typically more plentiful in most communities, parents may struggle to find reliable, affordable, and trustworthy occasional care for their children at times when they most need it.

Numerous options do exist, however, if you know where to look. Larger suburban and urban areas offer drop-in child care programs while so-called "convenience care" opportunities exist at local churches, schools, or youth programs. Teenagers often clamor for babysitting jobs as a way to pay

Drop-in Care

- Drop-in care centers are springing up across the country as a convenient option for parents who have problems finding a babysitter or don't want someone coming to their home to watch their children.

- Hourly rates tend to be higher, but perks may include meals and snacks, entertainment, and kid-friendly facilities.

- Many centers offer late-night hours and are open on weekends as well.

- Workers typically have similar training as daycare employees.

Convenience Care Programs

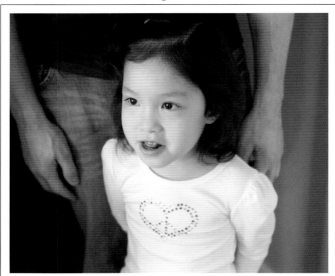

- Many churches, schools, and community organizations feature "parent day out" programs.

- Hours and days of services are often limited. These programs are usually geared to allow a parent to run errands or get a haircut, but are not typically offered for late-night outings.

- Programs are affordable and participation is extremely flexible.

- Be cautious about using "convenience care" programs, such as at gyms. Some caregivers there may not have any training.

for extras and to show responsibility. But these sources may or may not be available when you need them, and you may rightly have concerns about whether your child will be adequately cared for in your absence.

So what should you do? Finding an occasional babysitter is something that should be done when you don't already have an event you must attend. Check around and see whether there is drop-in care near where you live, and then try it for an hour or two with your child to evaluate the program. Ask your friends and others with similar-age children about any suggestions or who they use to babysit. Check with local churches and civic groups, but be sure to ask lots of questions about training, whether adults are supervising the babysitters, and whether background checks are performed on the volunteers before they are allowed to be around children.

Be sure to carefully check references, and choose a babysitter who has undergone basic first-aid training. If using a teenage babysitter, find out whether the teen's parents will be at home in case there is an issue that requires advice or immediate transportation (if the teen doesn't yet drive).

Teen Babysitters

- Using teen babysitters can provide an affordable child care solution for parents.

- Teen sitters should have completed a basic first-aid and babysitting course and should be able to correctly answer questions about how they would handle certain child care scenarios.

- Simply "loving kids" isn't a good reason to hire a sitter.

- Check references carefully.

- Consider using teen babysitters for short amounts of time or while you are at home until you are confident of their abilities.

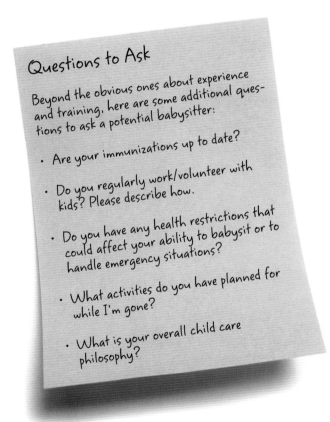

Questions to Ask

Beyond the obvious ones about experience and training, here are some additional questions to ask a potential babysitter:

- Are your immunizations up to date?

- Do you regularly work/volunteer with kids? Please describe how.

- Do you have any health restrictions that could affect your ability to babysit or to handle emergency situations?

- What activities do you have planned for while I'm gone?

- What is your overall child care philosophy?

OUTINGS

Managing expectations and maintaining rules for behavior set the stage for successful adventures out and about

Your preschooler most likely considers herself a seasoned "pro" at public outings—after all, you've most likely been taking her out and about to a variety of places since she was born! Many four-year-olds are outgoing and eagerly look forward to new events and experiences, so your job is to find ways to promote good behaviors and calmness rather than

build anticipation. While there are certainly exceptions to the rule, many four-year-olds operate on a "get ready, get set, go!" mentality when it comes to outings.

But that doesn't mean that all public outings go smoothly, however. Your child may quickly grow bored with the planned activity, or become fearful, shy, or even disruptive

How to Act

- Your child won't "just know" how to act appropriately when in public. Your constant guidance and reinforcement will help ensure success.

- Encourage your child to look people in the eyes when talking to them and

show him how to properly introduce himself to others.

- Show your child how to shake hands. Don't insist that your child hug people he doesn't know. If you wouldn't hug strangers, why should your child feel any different?

Discomfort or Fears

- Preschoolers can get scared by large crowds and fear becoming separated from loved ones.

- Many so-called child-friendly activities can actually be scary for kids, such as fireworks celebrations, carnivals, sporting events, and musical concerts.

Bright lights and loud sounds can overload the senses.

- Keep in mind that places like the zoo, circus, and theme parks can unnerve a child, who sometimes still has difficulty distinguishing between what is real and what isn't.

78

if the outing is too far out of her comfort zone or is not as expected.

In addition, parents have to worry about their child getting sensory overload from too much noise, excitement, or visual stimulation, which can result in an overtired child or a meltdown. Kids at this age think that they are invincible and that no harm can come to them, meaning parents have to carefully guide children's actions and keep careful structure and rules. It takes but a matter of seconds for kids to go missing, especially in crowded places.

Public Meltdowns

- At this age, public meltdowns are often due to discomfort—such as being too hot or cold—exhaustion, hunger, or boredom.

- Meltdowns may occur when a child is terrified. Avoid telling your child he is acting like a baby or making him feel guilty for being scared. Instead, provide comfort and try the activity again at a future time.

- Encourage your child to use his words next time to explain his feelings.

Safety Considerations

- Teach your child his full name, address, and phone number and review with him before every outing.

- Establish a meeting place in case you become separated.

- Avoid having your child wear or display items with his name on it in large crowds. Potential abductors often pretend to know a child by calling him by name.

SAFETY

Curiosity, mimicking parent's actions are among leading causes of accidents and injuries at this age

Preschoolers are often considered the highest-risk age group for getting hurt or worse from accidents. Insatiable curiosity, enhanced self-confidence, and the belief that no harm can come to them can have tragic results if children aren't adequately supervised. Many accidents result from a child's inability to fully understand the consequences of his actions.

Another factor contributing to injuries and accidents for this age group is youngsters emulating what they see their parents do without fully understanding the skill involved. Preschoolers may suddenly decide they want to cook breakfast for the family and turn on the stove just like they've seen adults do, to tragic results. That's why extra safety precautions—paired

Fire Safety

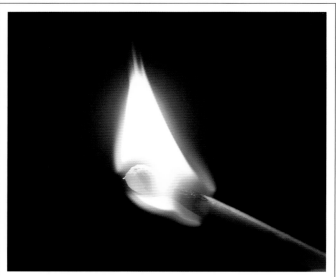

- Preschoolers are especially vulnerable to fire and burn injuries.

- Teach children the purpose of fire extinguishers and explain what a smoke detector does and what they should do if it goes off.

- Teach your child the basics of "Stop! Drop! and Roll!" and how to crawl low under smoke.

- Your child should be taught to go to a designated safe location and wait for you in the event of a fire in the home.

Sharp Objects

- Unintentional injuries account for between 20 to 25 percent of injuries for this age group. Many are severe enough to require medical attention.

- Many preschooler accidents involve sharp objects. Often, it is because a child runs or twirls while holding a sharp or pointed object such as a pencil and then falls.

- Never allow your child to run with a sucker, Popsicle, or similar object in his mouth.

- Projectile toys often have sharp ends and can cause injury if used improperly.

with repeated conversations about safety rules and expectations—are a must for this age group.

Parents should pay particular attention when doing something in front of their child that could be potentially unsafe. For example, parents may use a knife to cut apples without giving it a thought that their child may want to try cutting their own apple at a later time. Children are also attracted to fire, so matches and lighters must always stay out of harm's way.

GREEN ● LIGHT

Your four-year-old should know how to call 9-1-1 in the event of an emergency. Consider teaching a 911 song to reinforce the numbers (one option is sung to *Frère Jacques:* "There's a fire! There's a fire! 9-1-1! 9-1-1! Call the fire department! Call the fire department! 9-1-1! 9-1-1!"). Keep the number posted in plain sight and have your youngster practice on an inactive phone. Emphasize that they are never to dial 9-1-1 unless there is a true emergency.

Safety Precautions

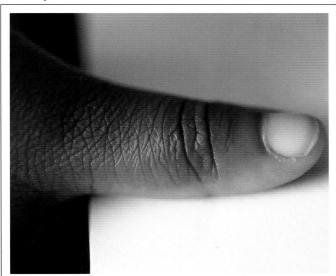

- Consider making a child-find kit as a safety precaution. You can do this yourself by getting your child's fingerprints on paper and then putting it in a plastic bag along with a recent photo and a hair sample. Some companies offer kits to schools and daycares, but often for a fee.

- Keep aware of your child's current weight and height so that you have the best description possible.

- Don't allow your child to stay at people's homes unless you feel totally comfortable with their safety practices.

Chemicals

- Common pesticides can accelerate aging of the immune and nervous system of some individuals.

- Parents who have a child with a weakened immune system should avoid using chemical products, and instead consider environmentally friendly and chemical-free solutions.

- New concerns about health risks from the chemical bisphenol A (BPA) used in plastics have resulted in new precautions about baby bottles, water bottles, certain toys, and even helmets and goggles.

SAFETY GEAR

Properly fitted gear and protection products help keep your preschooler healthy and safe

While many of the products and child gear on the market are nice but not really a necessity, some items are absolutely essential for keeping your preschooler safe.

Providing your youngster with proper protection from the sun's harmful rays, carefully fitting your child with a bike or sports helmet, using a Coast Guard–approved life preserver, and minimizing your child's exposure to ticks and bug bites are all key safety precautions. Yet, each year, tragedies occur because a parent or adult caregiver did not use proper safety gear.

Parents should consider quality over cost when choosing safety gear. While pricing may differ based on trendy styles

Sun Protection

- Proper protection from the sun is as important in winter months as in the summer.

- In addition to sunscreen, protect your child's delicate skin with hats that protect sensitive ears, face, and neck areas.

- Protect your child's eyes with properly fitted sunglasses, being careful not to choose "toy" glasses that offer no real UV protection.

- Consider investing in a sun shirt that contains materials that minimize the skin's exposure to the sun.

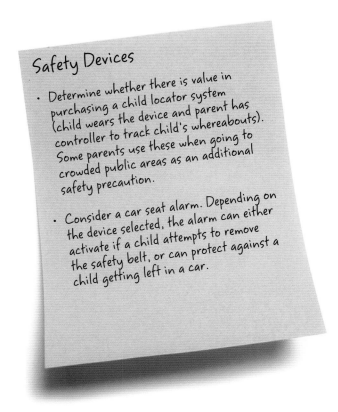

Safety Devices

- Determine whether there is value in purchasing a child locator system (child wears the device and parent has controller to track child's whereabouts). Some parents use these when going to crowded public areas as an additional safety precaution.

- Consider a car seat alarm. Depending on the device selected, the alarm can either activate if a child attempts to remove the safety belt, or can protect against a child getting left in a car.

or colors, make sure the product you pick meets appropriate safety guidelines and will provide the protection you are seeking.

Some parents make the mistake of buying safety gear in a size that is too big—with the idea that it will allow longer use. While "buying for growth" is okay for certain products, safety experts advise buying the size that fits your child properly when the item is to be worn. Too-big helmet, pads, or life jacket may mean the gear won't properly protect your child in an accident.

Personal Floatation Device

- Choose a U.S. Coast Guard–approved jacket, preferably with at least three buckles and a strap that goes between the legs to prevent it from slipping off.

- Don't let your child rely on beach toys such as noodles; they are not designed to save lives.

- Water wings (floaties), rings, and rafts are not intended to save lives and can provide your child with a false sense of security. Only use these when you are with your child in the water.

Bug Exposure

- Disease-carrying ticks and mosquitoes are strong reasons to keep your child as protected as possible from bugs.

- Dress your preschooler in high socks, closed-toe shoes, and long-sleeved shirts and pants when participating in activities where the risk of bug bites is high.

- Bug sprays containing the chemical DEET are fine for use on any child over the age of two months. Consider bug repellant bracelets and other wearable devices for additional protection.

EARLY LEARNING

Your child may begin to show interest in learning concepts and more structured ideas

While most early childhood learning up to this point has been associated with play and sorting out how to do things using growing brain power and motor skills, four-year-olds often express interest in more structured learning. Early education helps preschoolers develop a strong foundation for future learning and overall school success.

Early learning takes place in many ways, and most educators agree that simply providing preschoolers with exposure to a variety of activities and promoting curiosity, exploration, and hands-on learning fun is enough to begin to gain skills that will be needed for school.

If your child attends daycare or any type of program where

Letters

- Four-year-olds can learn to write their first name. Most children use all capital letters initially because they are easier to write.

- Your child may enjoy tracing letters. Start by having him trace the letters with his finger, and then let him try while holding a pencil.

- Promote letter recognition by making a game of pointing out letters on things you see and then having your child identify the letter.

Spatial Learning

- Encourage your child to show you the way to familiar places and to navigate which direction to go in.

- Begin to talk to your child about "left" versus "right." Have her pretend she is a taxi driver and either direct her to turn left or right, or have her tell you which way the car is turning.

- Emphasize the spatial concepts of up and down, back and forward, high and low, and so on.

other similar-age children are grouped together, he'll also be learning about appropriate behaviors and typical expectations. Many activities are based around so-called learning centers or small-group clusters, where a larger group of youngsters is pared down to smaller, more manageable groups to promote more constant and interactive learning experiences.

Most child programs feature kid-friendly crafts and activities already, and parents can incorporate basic memorization, early reading, and body coordination skills within the daily routine without making it a formal process.

ZOOM

Areas of study in typical four-year-old classrooms revolve around weather and the seasons, transportation (planes, trains, and automobiles), self and family, health and nutrition, and even the rituals and routines of school. Art is incorporated into daily activities and more and more pre-kindergarten and daycare settings offer formal physical activities as well.

Sight Words and Symbols

- Begin to incorporate the teaching of sight words into daily reading and into your child's regular routine.

- Most preschoolers can begin to recognize simple one- and two-letter sight words and their meaning, such as "I," "A," and "is."

- Introduce your child to symbols that are commonly used in public, such as the signs for restrooms by gender or what a circle with a line drawn through it diagonally means.

Counting

- Your four-year-old may like to count just about anything and everything, and it's a great way to memorize the number sequence.

- Encourage your child to count cars, seats, plates, or whatever provides him with the opportunity for rote memorization.

- Introduce your child to the symbols used for single-digit numbers (e.g., 1, 2, 3) as a way to visually recognize the numbers as well as being able to count out loud.

- Your child may begin to understand simple math.

CURIOSITY

Preschoolers' desire for exploration and experimentation makes it a challenge to stay a step ahead

It's a common—and only half-joking—complaint by parents of preschoolers: Their child NEVER seems to stop asking questions and scrutinizing every aspect of just about everything. While at times charming, a precocious preschooler's constant barrage of questions can torment busy parents. But, then again, that's the way kids learn.

Watch how your child studies and inspects even the most miniscule of objects. Note how she becomes utterly transfixed over a detail you find absolutely routine and ordinary. While you can't always stop and let your child smell the roses, so to speak, you can encourage moments of unhurried exploration as a way to celebrate your child's inquisitive spirit.

Exploration

- Some of the most memorable times are those in which your child discovers something on his own, and marvels at his findings.

- Slow down the pace whenever possible and let your child spend leisurely time examining the blades of grass or feeling various fabrics and textures within your home.

- Be extra careful of lapses of judgment or a false sense of security when on-the-go. Close supervision is still a must!

Experimentation

- Show your preschooler safe and child-friendly concoctions and experiments.

- Demonstrate how food coloring can change the color of food or even the petals of flowers when the stem is set in colored water, or any other interesting facts that captivate your child's sense of discovery.

- Children may like to dump and pour water into measuring cups or similar containers. Have them see how many cups of water it takes to fill a pitcher, for example.

Take advantage of an increased attention span and focus on details to show your preschooler things he may totally ignore or overlook when older. There is no better time to show your child the infinite wonders of nature and his ever-expanding world.

Utilize items around the house to encourage curiosity without spending money. A paper towel holder can become a telescope; a small plastic container can be used for experiments. Kids marvel about how hot and cold water mixed with flavored powder can transform into tasty gelatin and how mud turns back into dry dirt after baking in the hot sun.

Let your child know that no question is too small, and use magazines, family walks, the computer, and even journeys of the imagination to search for answers together. Be daring and set up a science lab in your home to pique a love of science. Your child will find it amazing that a potato grows roots when left in water or that a lima bean sprouts when given soil and water. Who knows what wonders and experiments you and your child can imagine or create together?

If This, Then What

- Encourage "If this, then what?" type of thinking with your child.

- Four-year-olds can become intrigued with trying an action and then observing the resulting reaction. Rather than just doing the same thing again and again, they may begin to use logic to vary their actions to get a different reaction.

- Mischief may ensue as your preschooler begins to try things simply because he can (e.g., boys urinating on a surface other than in the toilet).

Mother Nature

- Let your child learn about nature by providing ample unstructured time to explore in the backyard. Let him dig to find worms, do a leaf rubbing using chalk and a piece of paper, or collect acorns, for example.

- Use a bug jar to temporarily capture a bug so that your child can closely examine it, and then teach her how to appreciate life by letting the bug loose.

- Teach your child how to respect our Earth's resources and habitat.

GAMES & CHALLENGES

Incorporate challenges into your preschooler's daily life to encourage problem solving and creative solutions

Life is a game for four-year-olds, and half of the fun of parenting them is developing new challenges and teaching skills while providing entertainment at the same time.

Rarely will a day pass without your preschooler challenging you to a new contest or wanting to play a new game—often one that he has just made up and one in which he will

certainly win! The best part is that games for kids this age are easy, and many simply involve guessing or nothing more than something readily available or just using a pencil and paper.

Parents often delight in creating simple "thinking games" for their child, such as "I love you because" and then providing an answer and then having the child do the same. Other

Problem Solving

- Ask your child to problem solve with simple scenarios such as, "How many forks will we need to set the table for our family?" This encourages your child to recall family members and then to count how many will be dining.

- Encourage your child to collaborate with you on working out issues or potential problems.

- Allow your child the ability to resolve problems by himself—even if the answer he comes up with is different from yours.

Obstacle Courses

- Instead of hitting the playground, try creating exciting obstacle courses using safe and simple items already in your home as a way to boost coordination and challenge skills. Be sure to explain rules and directions up front.

- Have your child then build

an obstacle course for you using the same materials. It's a great way to encourage creative thinking.

- Have your child demonstrate alternate ways to accomplish the same thing. "Show me three ways you can jump over the spoon on the floor," for example.

thinking games include drawing a full-length person but leaving out an essential part (for instance the ears, fingers, a foot) and then having your child guess it.

More active games such as indoor treasure hunts, bean bag tosses, red light/green light (in which kids can move forward when the light is green but must stay in place when the light is red) allow physical fun, while hand puppets or silly creatures made from pipe cleaners and googly eyes can bring out the creativity.

Stacking Games

- Use shoe boxes and other unbreakable and light-weight household items for stacking. Colorful plastic toy blocks provide hours of stacking fun.

- Stacking helps preschoolers learn what will logically stack onto another surface and to begin to sort things by weight, size, and shape.

- Use disposable cups to show your child simple cup stacking. A four-year-old may enjoy building patterns and then slamming them down (by putting cups into each other) in a rapid motion.

First Board Games

- Board games are a fun way to spend time with your preschooler and help teach the concepts of rules, taking turns, and good sportsmanship.

- There are countless preschool-age board games on the market for under $10. Games that may seem overly silly to you can provide hysterical entertainment to your four-year-old.

- Consider classic games like "Chutes and Ladders" or fun ones like "Hungry, Hungry Hippos."

- Show your child how to roll and count dice.

89

FAMILY FUN

Forget the fuss and overlook the mistakes; focus on ways to build memories and laughs

There's no magic formula for family fun. The simplest approach is usually the best: Involve your precocious preschooler in your daily routine. It's pretty much that simple. Four-year-olds love doing whatever it is that you're doing—that's why they typically hover over your every movement and constantly ask, "What are you doing?" Come on, parents!

That's your cue to show them, taking time to explain things at a level they'll understand. Remember that preschoolers even think taking out the trash is a blast!

While many parents worry about providing their children with ample enrichment and early learning opportunities, most educators agree that daily reading combined with

Art

- Try making handprint art: Trace a child's hands in cookie dough, or press them into clay or cement to create hand impressions, or press hands into water-based paint and then onto paper.

- Make mud castles by adding water to dirt until it has the consistency of dough.

- Expose your child to sculptures or other nearby art works. Don't expect your child to become an art aficionado at this age; however, your child may appreciate the use of colors and images.

Science

- Capture your child's interest in space by stargazing in the backyard or away from city lights. Most preschoolers love watching the changing phases of the moon.

- Concepts such as what makes liquids transform into solids may be fascinating to your child.

- Encourage your child to create a weather chart that tracks sun and rain. Temperature can be shown with different colors (for example, "cold outside" can be a blue mark and "hot outside" can be depicted in red).

appropriate daily connections between parents and kids is all that they really need.

So, for now, forget about preparing for school and simply prepare to have fun! Look for spontaneous moments to wage a friendly pillow fight, play a game of kickball in the backyard, share a bowl of ice cream, or craft a handprint masterpiece. So what if more icing ends up on the kitchen counter than on the cupcake? Forget the fuss and overlook the mistakes and you both will have so much fun that you won't even notice the minor messes that come from little hands.

Drama

- Have your child act out her favorite cartoon character.

- Switch roles: Have your child be the parent and you be the child, and both act accordingly.

- Explore different voices, tones, inflections, and silly made-up accents. Ask your child how a mouse might talk as compared with an elephant, for example.

- Develop your own secret handshake, pet name, or silly dance move that you perform whenever you say hello or goodbye.

Silly Fun

- Get everyone's shoes and hide them around the house (don't make it too hard), and have your preschooler find, and then match, shoes.

- Play games like "Simon Says" or make your child think about how to act like an animal or object.

- Switch mealtime routines, such as having breakfast at lunchtime, or eating dinner in pajamas—anything that will provide some silliness and family time together.

ENRICHMENT

Behavior, interest can determine when your preschooler is old enough for team sports and group classes

It's tempting to enroll your four-year-old in an enrichment class or two or perhaps a team sport consisting of pint-size players. After all, many parents rationalize that sampling as many different activities as possible at a young age will help youngsters determine their true areas of interest.

In addition, many school and community programs today are extremely competitive about who makes the team, especially in larger urban areas. Some parents may even begin to plan activities for their child early in hopes of landing a coveted college scholarship or professional career. But hold it! We're still talking about four-year-olds here!

While many preschoolers this age are indeed ready to take

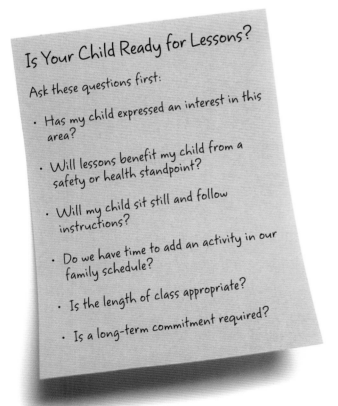

Is Your Child Ready for Lessons?

Ask these questions first:

- Has my child expressed an interest in this area?

- Will lessons benefit my child from a safety or health standpoint?

- Will my child sit still and follow instructions?

- Do we have time to add an activity in our family schedule?

- Is the length of class appropriate?

- Is a long-term commitment required?

Group Classes

- Small-sized group classes of like-age preschoolers work best for this age group. Look for instructor-to-child ratios of 6 to 1 or less.

- Classes should typically last an hour at most, because preschoolers will lose interest for any longer than that.

- Ask if you can observe a class or have your preschooler try a class before signing up.

- Make sure your child is interested in the class itself, and not just the dance shoes or tutu, for example.

a music exploration, art or body movement class, and even begin learning the basics of soccer, others simply aren't ready yet. Putting a preschooler into a class in the hopes that they will show interest and focus can set the stage for an unsuccessful experience.

And just because classes for preschoolers are advertised as being age appropriate, it doesn't mean the instructors truly understand what is needed to motivate and keep little ones focused on the activity at hand. So instead of promoting new interests, some well-meaning parents actually accomplish the opposite in that their child doesn't want to participate in a particular activity ever again.

Consider enrolling your child in a short-term or even single-day class first and see how he does. Separation from parents, hesitancy about trying something new and unknown, being in a strange environment, and even being worried about finding the bathroom are typical preschooler concerns. Your child may also love attending a program for a time or two, only to lose focus and not want to go back later. Avoid pressuring your child; she may change her mind later

Sports

- An increasing number of youth organizations and community recreation leagues are offering sport programs for preschool-age children.

- An emphasis should be on having fun and exercising, with a little bit of learning about a particular sport

thrown in.

- Look for programs that don't keep score; avoid competition-based programs at this age.

- Make sure safety and health considerations are a priority, and that practices are kept short and motivational.

Private Lessons

- Certain activities, such as learning to play the piano, are best accomplished through private lessons.

- Lessons should be kept to 30 minutes and should be planned so that the child stays busy and interested.

- Avoid pressuring your child to achieve a certain level or to practice much at this stage.

- Make sure your child—not just you—really wants to learn more about an activity before signing up for (often expensive) private lessons.

EQUIPMENT

Consider safety, interests, and appropriate age when buying toys and gear for your four-year-old

Motion-driven toys to go along with motion-driven kids are popular purchases for parents of four-year-olds, with a bike topping the list. There are numerous varieties and styles of riding toys; however, most kids this age can successfully learn to ride a two-wheeled bicycle with training wheels. Later, training wheels can be removed.

Preschoolers also like push scooters, skates, and just about anything that lets them be on the go. Safety-conscious parents should make sure that safety gear comes with the package, so that their child clearly understands that helmets, pads, and even face shields are a requirement, and not merely a suggestion.

In keeping with their love of constant movement, kids may

Trikes and Bikes

- Your four-year-old is most likely ready for a move up from a tricycle to a bike with training wheels.

- Insist your child wear a bike safety helmet—even if only riding in the backyard driveway. No exceptions should be the rule.

- While cheap bikes are readily available, choose one with quality construction. If in doubt, have the bike professionally assembled to minimize any safety risk.

- Regularly check the bike's brakes, handlebars, seat area, and spokes.

Interactive Toys

- Four-year-olds love the appeal of pop-up books that add an element of surprise—even after looking through it endless times.

- Consider interactive books made of durable materials as protection from excessive wear and tear. Your child may pull tabs or play

- with the three-dimensional pop-up portions a little rougher than you'd like, so teach your child how to properly care for cherished books.

- Computer games feature interactive learning that are geared toward your child's age and interests.

enjoy pop-up or interactive books where they pull a tab or push a button to hear or see extra features related to the story itself. If your child has access to a computer, interactive preschool readers are also available where kids can learn to point and click to see characters in the book come to life on the monitor!

As your child becomes more mobile, consider investing in additional child safety devices, such as a child locator system. Some parents place a locator beacon on their preschooler's bike or helmet, for example.

An increasing number of parents who use child care providers in their home are considering use of a so-called "nanny cam"—an in-home surveillance device. But the wireless devices available at costs ranging from inexpensive to excessive aren't without controversy. Many child care providers caution parents to purchase the spying devices if they like, but make sure they disclose their use so trust issues and feelings of deception won't arise later.

Helmet Safety

- If your child rides a trike or similar riding toy, then a bike helmet is a must. Studies have clearly shown that bike helmets reduce a child's risk of death by more than 50 percent.

- Universal bike helmet use would prevent about 40,000 head injuries and

50,000 scalp and face injuries each year.

- Ensure proper fit and make sure the helmet's chin strap fits snugly.

- Don't allow the helmet to be pushed back on the head.

Safety Gear

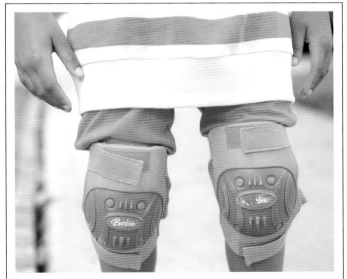

- In addition to a helmet, outfit your child in appropriate safety gear to protect elbows, knees, and other areas.

- Broken bones are common childhood injuries resulting from falls from bicycling or other movement-oriented activities. Knee pads, wrist

and elbow pads, and shin guards can help protect against broken bones when worn properly.

- Since choking or gagging can still be a problem, mouthpieces are generally not worn by children this age with rare exceptions. Face shields may be used.

SOCIAL

Having friends and playing cooperatively with peers guide the busy social lives of most four-year-olds

What's it like to be four years old? Most likely, your child is now quite social, having lost much of the shyness and inhibitions around strangers exhibited in earlier years. Your child's social life, more than anything else, is what guides his activities and playtime, as preschoolers crave friendship and cooperative play with peers.

Strong friendships can be formed at this age, and your child may love to hold hands or put his arm around a friend, as well as try to comfort a friend who is hurt or soothe a peer who is upset. Your child may like to talk—a lot—about friends and their likes and dislikes, and even begin to want to be just like them at times. Comparisons may also start to creep in, as

Cooperative Play

- Your four-year-old is mostly able to take turns, share toys, and wait in line.

- Bossy behaviors may emerge during periods of cooperative play. Most kids want to be the leader yet many resist being the follower, even when taking turns. Parents can help kids work through a desire to always want to be in charge.

- If your child doesn't want to share a particular toy, require that it be put away and not taken out while a friend visits.

Social Enjoyment

- Most preschoolers crave playtime with similar-age friends.

- Daycare and parents' day out programs provide ample time for playing with peers. If your child doesn't participate in child care, be sure to provide opportuni- ties that allow playtime with other preschoolers as a way to build social skills.

- Always carefully supervise your child in larger group settings such as at parks, where emotions and physi- cal behaviors can quickly get out of control.

your child will want something "just like" his friend.

While your preschooler may enjoy sharing secrets with a friend or establishing a private club or special greeting, true loyalty may come and go. Your child may have a "best friend forever" up to the point that the friend gets a preferred seat or reaches the slide first. A typical short-term reaction can very well be that your child "no longer likes her" and that they "aren't friends." Within minutes, however, the best-friend status is renewed.

Emotional outbursts and hurtful words such as stomping out while screaming "I don't want to play with you ever again!" are not unusual occurrences. While parents should correct bad behaviors and require respect of people and property, resist the urge to serve as referee. Instead, ask your child (privately) how he would "feel" if someone said something negative or hurtful about him.

Temperament

- Much of the time, you'll enjoy your fabulous four-year-old who is more often than not joyful, positive, and easy-to-please.

- Four-year-olds can also exhibit extreme mood swings. It's not unusual for them to be happy one minute and then angry or sad the next.

- Provide comfort as needed, but avoid "playing up" to moody behaviors so your child doesn't begin to use them as a way to manipulate you or others to get what she wants.

"I Want It Now"

- Patience requires continued practice, as preschoolers still struggle with a desire for immediate gratification.

- While parents should be empathetic to a child's wants or desires, overindulgent adults actually do a disservice to their children when they respond to their every whim.

- Remember that kids are still struggling with self-control and that mastery over emotions requires more maturity and time.

PHYSICAL

Kids love showing off mastery of gross motor skills with increasingly complex motions, flexibility

You'll marvel at the growing repertoire of physical skills and abilities of your four-year-old. Now, your child can demonstrate mastery of her body and showcase agility and flexibility. Skills can also be performed in combinations ... your child may not think twice about hopping, jumping, twirling, doing a front roll, and then striking a pose. She's got movement down pat, and loves to show off emerging skills every chance she gets!

Encourage your child's love for constant motion and need for exercise by consistently introducing new physical activities. Parents may also consider placing their child in a simple tumbling class or "stretch-n-grow" style course that promotes

Physical Motion

- Teach your child varied jump patterns such as left foot hop, two foot jump, right foot hop. Hopscotch is a fun way to promote that skill.

- Some kids may be able to learn how to do jumping jacks or skipping but many still find the motions too complex at this stage.

- Play "Follow the Leader" and teach your child skills such as galloping, twirling, and so-called "bear walks" with hands and feet on ground.

Climbing

- Kids may be fearless with climbing, which is why lines at the tallest slide in the neighborhood park can be among the longest.

- Kids love to climb stairs, ledges, playground equipment, and just about anything that can be scaled—which means close supervision is a must.

- Don't just assume your child knows not to climb on something. You'll need to specifically tell kids what they cannot climb and why it would be unsafe and inappropriate.

stretching exercise, flexibility, and ways to keep the body healthy. The same skills can be learned at home with adult supervision.

While the use of gross motor skills (large muscles) still plays a major role in an active four-year-old's lifestyle, interest may heighten in the use of fine motor skills (small muscles). But that's only when you can slow your preschooler down long enough to sit still.

Continue to boost hand-eye coordination by playing basketball, catch, or backyard bowling with your child. Many preschoolers are quite flexible at this age and may even be able to do the splits or other extreme stretches. A few may even begin to perform more complex physical skills such as doing a cartwheel, although that is more the exception than the norm at this age.

Your child still doesn't understand many of the limitations of her body, and accidents and resulting injuries may occur. Keep a careful eye on your child during physical play and watch for any unsafe activities that could cause harm to her head, back, face, or neck, or result in breaks and sprains.

Complex Combinations

- Some kids are beginning to successfully put together increasingly complex skills. For example, a cartwheel is essentially a multistep physical skill involving hands, legs, body motion, and momentum.

- Most four-year-olds are capable of memorizing and repeating a series of steps or motions (such as in dance)—if they choose to do so!

- Sports ability and coordination markedly increase although wavering attention and focus may limit an ongoing interest in a particular activity.

Fine Motor Skills

- Fine motor skills are emerging, and you'll notice marked improvement in a child's ability to hold a pencil or crayon and to use them correctly.

- Look for activities that promote BOTH gross motor skills and fine motor skills. Performing the popular "Chicken Dance" or "Hokey Pokey" is an example of using big muscles along with more intricate hand movements.

- Have your child draw a picture and then act out the character.

- Teach your child to wink.

INTELLECTUAL

Meaningful conversations and following unrelated directions are signs your four-year-old is gaining intelligence

Preschoolers typically make great intellectual strides during their fourth year. Your child has a much clearer understanding of directions—even a series of unrelated ones—and is able to remember sequences and events better than ever. Logic is increasing, and your child may begin to rationalize behaviors and justify actions. It's quite obvious that "brain power" is fully engaged as reasoning and articulation of wants and needs continues to increase.

While nurturing interests and intellectual development, be sure to avoid adding pressure or requiring advanced tasks at this stage. It's great that your child may want to read more or learn ballet or soccer; it's another thing to begin pushing her

Bodily-Kinesthetic Intelligence

- This intelligence is characterized by using the body to solve problems and express ideas and feelings.

- Signs can include excelling in several sports and physical activities, having the ability to mimic others' body movements, and being well-coordinated.

- This intelligence can also be seen through enjoyment of disassembling things and putting them back together, showing skills that require fine motor development, a desire to touch things all the time, and speaking with hands or using body gestures.

Interpersonal Intelligence

- Signs of this intelligence include a strong desire to be with friends and peers, wishing to join groups, and being viewed as a natural leader.

- Your child may demonstrate this intelligence by enjoying teaching other kids new skills, giving advice, and showing self-confidence and natural street savvy.

- Kids with this intelligence seem to serve as a magnet for other similar-age kids, who want to become their friends and play.

to do so. Applying pressure to do something or manipulating a child at this age may result in frustration and resistance.

The best way to boost a child's intelligence is continued exposure to new experiences along with encouraging questions and time to see processes and how things work and grow. You may also begin to notice particular strengths in differing areas of intelligence as demonstrated through your child's natural interests, temperament, and skills. Your preschooler will most likely guide the way in terms of how he naturally prefers to learn and explore—so pay attention!

You've undoubtedly heard about the premise of the so-called "Mozart effect," a theory that early exposure to classical music can develop a child's spatial and mathematical reasoning. While the theory has met with numerous critics, it's indisputable that most children love and respond to music, and can develop a sense of musical intelligence at a very young age.

Intrapersonal Intelligence

- This intelligence is defined as a well-developed sense of self and ability to look inward. Kids may be referred to as "deep thinkers" or "loners."

- Signs of this intelligence may appear as independence or strong will, with kids being comfortable playing independently rather than always with others. They may study objects methodically as a way to learn.

- Kids with this intelligence may sometimes be described as "marching to their own drummer" and not following others.

Linguistic Intelligence

- This intelligence is associated with mastery of words and language, and can be visual or auditory.

- Preschoolers with well-developed linguistic intelligence may enjoy reading books and can write, speak, and spell better than similar-age peers. They may like hearing stories without seeing the book.

- Kids may be able to tell jokes and stories better than most, and be able to successfully tell rhymes and tongue-twisters.

- This child may excel at articulating ideas and feelings.

CREATIVE
Elaborate plans and detailed specifics show your four-year-old's maturity and emerging sense of creativity

There's absolutely no shortage of creativity when it comes to four-year-olds. While your child most likely has already been demonstrating bursts of creativity and imagination, you may be astonished at just how elaborate and detailed your four-year-old can be!

Younger preschoolers may begin dramatic play and mimicking by playing "house" but as your child matures, the plots become quite specific. Now, playing house may mean developing a shopping list and going to the grocery store and even pretending to cook dinner once home. Or, your child may visit the shoe store and spend time trying on various "new" shoes to see which pair to purchase for a special occasion.

Drama Queen and King

- Encourage your child to spend time and energy building elaborate stages or sets from things like empty boxes and fabric.

- Help your preschooler think of props and costumes using existing materials around the home instead of going out and buying costumes. Not only is it more fun to make a costume, but the result will be one of a kind!

- Show your child how imagination can be an exciting way to have fun.

Tall Tales and Exaggerations

- Have fun with silly exaggerations, such as "I caught a fish so big that . . ." Take turns inventing opening lines and topping each other's idea.

- Be sure to emphasize the difference between having fun with silly stories and trying to pass something off as real when it isn't.

- Encourage lively conversations and inventive descriptions. Ask your child what made-up word or color he would create for a new color, and help guide him through the creative thinking process.

There are countless ways parents can help to raise a child who is creative—and the best part is that encouraging creativity doesn't have to cost a penny.

Although we are inundated with commercials showing the newest toys on the market, studies have shown that kids are typically fascinated for a longer period with items found around the house than those purchased from the store. Why? Many commercial toys only have one way to be played with in order to work or function properly whereas items around the house can be utilized in countless different ways.

Enhanced Drawings

- During your child's fourth year, you may begin to notice that her drawings are showing increased details.

- Encourage your child to draw what he observes. Ask him to draw your face, and note how many features he includes without prompt-ing. A child's attention to details is often demon-strated in early drawings and even color choices.

- Don't dictate what colors your child should use. It's really okay if your child wants the ocean to be pink!

Assembling

- Four-year-olds may enjoy learning to cut, glue, and assemble simple projects.

- Encourage creativity and the learning of basic school skills by planning simple projects such as decorat-ing paper bag puppets with yarn for hair and using markers to create facial expressions.

- Your child may enjoy making simple cards with cut-out shapes glued into colorful patterns.

- Let your preschooler add glitter to glue—if you don't mind the mess!

EMOTIONAL

"Magical" tendencies of how things work can confuse and overwhelm even savvy four-year-olds

There's no doubt that your child thinks of things differently than even kids only a few years older. For example, as four-year-olds observe things happening in their environment, such as you turning the lights on or off or going somewhere in the family car, they associate it with magic, not understanding the mechanics or science involved. These beliefs,

especially when coupled with a preschooler's sense of how they fit in their ever-expanding world, can contribute to an increasingly wider range of emotions.

Four-year-olds also have trouble understanding relationships of objects or people to one another—an intuitive thought process called conservation. Your child will think

Possessiveness

- It's normal for your four-year-old to be fiercely protective of prized objects, which can include toys, possessions, and even you! While your child has gotten much better at sharing, discuss expected behaviors before every playdate to help reinforce positive behaviors.

- Jealousy (a.k.a. the green-eyed monster) can begin to take hold of your pre-schooler, especially when coupled with the natural inclination to brag about things.

- Provide your youngsters with positive ways to deal with jealousy.

Escapism

- Many young kids have difficulty separating reality from make-believe, especially since they believe everything they see in the media.

- Kids who are struggling with making friends or who have an unsettled home life may prefer a pretend world to their real existence, and

- may increasingly escape to their own world with their own rules.

- Consult with your child's pediatrician if you feel the lines between fantasy and reality have become too blurred or if you are worried about your child's imaginary life.

that there is more ice cream in a big cup than a little cup—even if you used the same scoop to put the same amount in each. He also doesn't associate that grandma is his daddy's mother or that Aunt Lois is his mother's sister.

New details and a lack of understanding of how they all fit together can be somewhat overwhelming and stressful for youngsters. Be patient with your child, and explain how things work in a kid-friendly way. Give it a few years, and they'll put it all together as they begin to make sense of their world.

YELLOW ● LIGHT

Studies show that stressed-out parents often result in stressed-out kids, even ones as young as preschool age. Because youngsters typically don't understand the reason behind stress-induced behaviors such as impatience or being snappish, many internalize the stress and think that they have somehow caused mommy or daddy to be unhappy and that it's their fault. The key is communication and reassurance that it has nothing to do with them and that you love them.

Self-Confidence

- Most four-year-olds exhibit a healthy self-confidence and may even flaunt their emerging abilities to other friends and adults.

- As children gain independence, they begin to separate from their parents and caregivers just a little, although they will typically remain quite loving.

- Youngsters readily and openly express love, fear, and uncertainty of others.

- A shy child doesn't mean she lacks self-confidence; it could simply be her style of temperament.

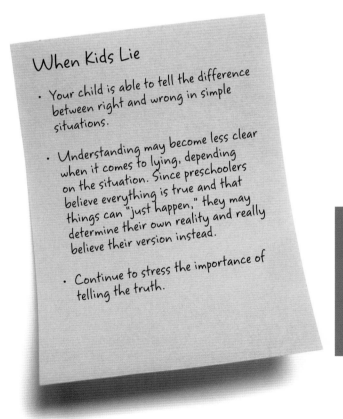

When Kids Lie

- Your child is able to tell the difference between right and wrong in simple situations.

- Understanding may become less clear when it comes to lying, depending on the situation. Since preschoolers believe everything is true and that things can "just happen," they may determine their own reality and really believe their version instead.

- Continue to stress the importance of telling the truth.

LANGUAGE

Your child can adapt language to a listener's level and apply past tense to words

The early childhood years are a critical time for language development. At age four, your child should be able to carry on an extended conversation using short but complete sentences and utilizing a diverse word bank. While grammatical mistakes and improper word choice is to be expected, most preschoolers no longer stumble over a lack of words. In fact, you may wonder if your child will ever stop talking!

In order to promote continued language development, provide your child with ample language-rich experiences. In other words, your child already has the basics. Now, it's time to emphasize the details by discussing an array of colors, textures, numbers, and movements.

Words and Associations

- The number of words your preschooler knows may vary greatly, and can range from the high hundreds to the thousands. Parents should focus on continued language growth as an indicator of language success.

- Four-year-olds should know what a letter is and be able to point out some and call them by name. They should be able to pretend to read and understand that words carry a message.

- They should be able to describe the meaning of simple words.

Active Language Exchange

- Four-year-olds should be able to initiate and maintain an active conversation using the right inflection.

- Your preschooler should be able to speak in complete sentences, although he may still use abbreviated phrases at times—especially when tired or uncomfortable with the conversational setting.

- When prompted, most kids this age can complete an incomplete sentence with the proper word.

- Preschoolers should be able to repeat a sentence of six to eight words successfully.

Instead of talking more simply to your child, boost vocabulary skills by using more descriptive words and then explaining to your child what they mean. For example, go ahead and teach your child that the blue precious stone is called a "sapphire" and the green one is an "emerald" rather than just saying "a red stone." Your child may or may not remember the names, but frequent exposure to proper terminology will provide your child with a vocabulary advantage.

Encourage complete sentences instead of relying on phrases or single words.

ZOOM

In many countries, it is normal for people to speak two or three languages; half of Europe is multilingual. Raising kids to use at least one other language does not result in language or speech problems, although kids may learn at different rates. In fact, some studies show kids may learn a second language easier when learning it along with English at the same time.

Adaptive Language Usage

- Your child will be able to tailor his speech depending on who he is talking to. Observe how your child adjusts word choices and uses different intonations when talking to adults or babies, or even the family pet.

- Let your child take the lead in conversations and ask follow-up questions to spur additional details and explanation.

- Explain something to your preschooler and then ask him to share the information with someone else as a way to boost listening and adaptive language usage.

Adding Past Tense

- Four-year-olds will typically begin adding past tense to words, although often not correctly.

- Your child may tell you he "runned to the corner" or "goed to his friend's house." The use of past tense is a positive language development, although it will still take time for your preschooler to change words like "run" into "ran" and "go" to "went."

APPEARANCE

Facial features, body show five-year-old's transition from preschooler to that of a school-age child

At age five, your child may weigh between 31 and 57 pounds and be between 39 and 48 inches tall. Boys may weigh slightly more and be a bit taller than girls, although genetics and overall health affect a child's height and weight more than gender at this stage.

Your child is energetic and enthusiastic, and these high activity levels mean that about 10 to 11 hours of nightly sleep is still needed for optimal performance!

Expect continued physical changes that show your child transitioning from a preschooler to a school-age child in the coming year, with a more "grown up" look.

Kids may become more contentious about their appearance

Up Close

- Your child's face may continue to slim down along with the rest of his body.

- Head size may increase about an inch over the course of the year.

- Many five-year-olds will express a strong preference for a particular haircut or style. Some may begin to spend time on getting their hair "just right" while others could care less.

- Children may begin to lose their teeth at this age, and so-called "snaggle-tooth" appearances are common.

Growth

- Five-year-olds may grow between 2 and 3 inches in height and gain 4 to 6 pounds on average. Spurts in growth will vary by child and are largely based on genetics.

- If he hasn't already before now, expect your child to make the transition from toddler- or preschool-sized clothing to the boys or girls department.

- Clothing options may now be available in "slim," "regular," and "husky" or "plus" sizes.

at this age, and begin comparing themselves to others. Your beautiful brunette-haired daughter might suddenly want to become a blonde like her best friend or your son might prefer curly hair or freckles, or even brown eyes instead of blue.

Episodes like a child cutting his own hair or asking whether he "looks good" in a particular outfit may occur. Be on the lookout for youngsters who become somewhat obsessive about their looks. You want your child to work on behavior and internal beauty rather than focusing on what's on the outside.

Body Image

- Five-year-olds' body shapes can vary significantly at this stage and your child may become aware of his body and how it compares with others.

- Some children may flaunt their body while others may become self-conscious.

- Talk to your child about positive body image, and how the goal is to eat properly and get enough physical exercise on a daily basis.

- Teach kids to avoid judging others by how they look or commenting about size.

Hands and Feet

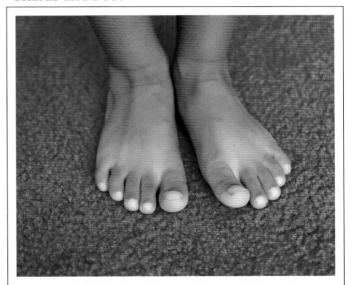

- Just as a child's body and face begins to slim down, so do his hands and feet. While your toddler may have had fat feet, you may notice that your preschooler's feet have slimmed down and an arch is developing.

- Kids may become interested in jewelry and rings, and girls may like to have their fingernails and toenails painted—just like mom.

- Shoe sizes typically range from around 11 to 13, but genetics play a major factor.

WELL-CHILD CARE

Physicians may ask additional questions to help gauge a child's readiness for kindergarten

At the five-year visit, your child's pediatrician may ask additional questions about your child's development and behaviors as well as conducting a thorough physical checkup. That's because your child may very well be among the preschoolers who will start kindergarten in the coming year.

Expect questions about overall eating habits, including nutritional choices, how often, and how much. Your doctor may talk about your child's socialization with other kids, ability to focus, gross and fine motor skill development, and ability to follow rules and respect the authority of adults. Your doctor may also ask about your preschooler's sense of responsibility, and whether he is showing signs of increased independence—good readiness

What to Expect

- Measurement of height and weight
- Blood pressure check
- An examination of growth and development
- Check of reflexes, motor skills, and spine
- Discussion of social skills and school readiness
- Review of eating and sleeping schedules
- Review of behavior and discipline
- Counseling of safety practices
- Immunizations, if not up-to-date, and possible flu shots
- Vision and hearing check
- Urinalysis may be attempted, depending on doctor

Additional Physical Checks

- The pediatrician may examine your child's spinal alignment by having him bend down and touch his toes.

- Vision and hearing screenings are typically conducted. Your doctor may urge a more comprehensive eye exam with an ophthalmologist to ensure your child has a proper range of vision for school success.

- Coordination, balance, and flexibility may also be checked.

- BMI percentage is now typically calculated, results and their meaning shared with parents.

signs for beginning kindergarten.

Since five is a milestone year for your child, think about any questions or concerns you may have to discuss with the pediatrician at your child's well-child visit. You may be wrestling with whether your child should begin school or wait, and the doctor may be able to offer some advice or resources to consult while making this important decision.

Some doctors may ask about family medical history, including high cholesterol and heart attacks, or whether your child is exposed to cigarette smoke or at risk for lead poisoning.

Dental Health

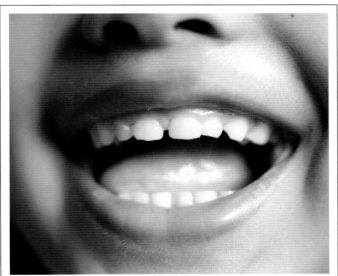

- Typically the first baby tooth lost is one of the lower front primary teeth. This may occur in the child's fifth year, although it can be later.

- The first permanent tooth to erupt is usually the first permanent molar.

- Sealants may be recommended for baby molars and then any permanent molar to protect them from cavities. Sealing teeth is quick and painless, but insurance may or may not cover the process, depending on your plan.

Safety Considerations

- Today's flat-screen televisions and wall-mounted designs can pose safety hazards for kids if not properly installed or secured.

- Make sure that cords from home exercise equipment are kept out of reach. Never let your child play on exercise equipment.

- Keep knives out of your child's reach.

- Personal guns should be kept in a locked cabinet.

BEHAVIOR

Five-year-olds act properly more often than not, but become more sensitive to what friends think

Five-year-olds are quite the charmers: They know how to engage adults with their wit and sense of humor, and don't hesitate to resort to cute antics or tender gestures with loved ones. Kids typically demonstrate a greater degree of politeness, cooperative play, and overall agreeable behaviors than ever before—welcome news for parents!

Growing maturity of the mind and body, coupled with a greater understanding of expectations and that the world doesn't revolve around them, makes for more pleasant conversations and activities and far fewer meltdowns. When things aren't going the way a five-year-old wants, your child may have the skills needed to calm down or resolve

Accomplished Behaviors

- Your child loves to please adults, and is usually quick to offer assistance with chores or wherever help is needed.

- Five-year-olds will ask "please" and say "thank you" at appropriate times, but may still need prompting.

- Your child may be eager to show off emerging responsibility, and can be depended on to do expected things like putting her toys away.

- Most five-year-olds can handle changes in routine and unexpected schedule variances without fuss.

Social Behaviors

- Your child can take turns and share, but might complain about it sometimes.

- Most five-year-olds are bossy. However, an understanding of the need for "fair play" typically means that disagreements get worked out without parental intervention.

- Preschoolers this age often brag and boast, although kids may recognize when they begin to hurt someone's feelings.

- Your child may at times become argumentative and insist she is right (even when she isn't).

the situation himself—although a hug and reassuring comments from parents are still appreciated!

At the same time, five-year-olds may become sensitive to the opinions and comments of their friends, and get their feelings hurt more easily. They may feel embarrassed about things that never bothered them previously; they can also become critical of others. While these behaviors need to be properly managed, they are experienced as a normal part of understanding where they fit into their world and reinforce what a child feels or believes.

ZOOM

Public behavior versus private behavior: Is there a difference? Yes, there is, and five-year-olds are able to distinguish between the two. As social acceptance and opinions of others becomes increasingly important to your child, a division may form between how your child acts with family and with friends. Your child may no longer want to dance or sing in public, but will in private.

Behaviors to Watch

- Your child may still express anger physically (such as kicking something when mad).

- Emotional or physical outbursts may occur when a child becomes jealous.

- Preschoolers may attempt to use sulking or isolation to get their way.

- Kids may become highly critical or use mean words to kids they don't want to be around. Parents need to provide their child with acceptable ways to respond, such as saying "I don't feel like playing now."

Self-Esteem

- Your child may become embarrassed by mistakes she makes in front of others or by perceived differences between herself and others.

- Kids may begin to compare their body shape, hairstyle, height, or abilities and skills, and either be critical or braggy depending on how they feel about the comparisons.

- Preschoolers may begin to resist doing something if they don't think they will be the best at it.

- Your child may positively support the esteem of others.

AGE 5: MILESTONES

CAUSE & EFFECT

Begin providing your preschooler with the ability to make independent decisions and to consider the consequences

Your child is becoming keenly aware of how his actions and words affect others. Start spending more time emphasizing the "cause and effect" outcomes that are influenced by decisions, behaviors, and even responsibility (or lack of). Consider it more practice for expected school behavior!

Parents can help children understand that they are accountable for their own actions by reviewing expectations and detailing appropriate behaviors before events, and then praising self-control and demonstrations of responsibility.

Increasingly offer your child choices in decision-making to help boost this level of understanding. If you are taking your child on a road trip and you expect him to entertain himself,

Actions

- Kids like small groups of friends (usually one or two) and may begin to say mean things to other children outside their preferred group or attempt to exclude others.

- Parents should ask kids about "how they would feel" if the tables were turned and others were treating them the same way. Engage your child in coming up with a better course of action.

- As youngsters become more understanding of feeling and emotions, they may become more empathetic.

Decision Making

- Five-year-olds should begin making their own simple decisions without parental interference. Parents often make the mistake of telling their child to make his own decision, but then hovering, expressing disappointment, or trying to force the child to change his mind afterward.

- The more decisions you can allow your preschooler to make now, the more independent and responsible he will become.

- Don't offer choices that you can't live with if chosen.

for example, ask what items might be brought along.

Many five-year-olds begin performing chores in conjunction with being a contributing part of the family. Providing an allowance may be appropriate at this stage as long as parents use it to reinforce that the money is for nonessential items that the child may want, and that saving up money may be required.

At the same time, parents should begin letting children make their own mistakes, rather than hovering over their every decision.

Learning Consequences

- Your child may resist rules or ignore recommendations in certain instances, for instance refusing to bring a jacket to daycare on a chilly day. If the consequence is not one that causes health or safety concerns, parents should let the child learn from his mistake. He will learn from the experience and know that it was a consequence of not listening to advice or taking the appropriate action.

Beginning an Allowance

- Providing your child with a small weekly allowance is a way to help kids learn about money and saving for special items.

- Try starting with an allowance that is half the child's age. So a five-year-old would receive $2.50 each week.

- Avoid rescuing your child from purchasing mistakes. If your child buys a toy and later wishes he bought something else, don't give in to his whines for the other toy.

115

GENDER ISSUES

Kids typically prefer same-sex friendships, but different genders may require different parenting approaches

While most preschoolers play nicely and appropriately with kids of both genders, typical friendships at this age are with kids of the same sex. Kids are relating to others of the same gender and in doing so learning more about themselves and about physical, emotional, and social similarities and differences.

Make sure your child doesn't have such a strong same-gender preference that he becomes mean toward kids of the opposite sex. Since most kids regularly interact with either siblings or family members of the opposite gender, this typically isn't a problem. In fact, unless your child attends a single-sex preschool, most all activities and programs consist of mostly equal boys-to-girls ratios. Teachers talk about mutual

Hygiene Issues for Girls

- Encourage girls to separate their legs while wiping from front to back for thorough cleaning.

- Cotton panties help protect against bacteria and infections because the fabric breathes. Some panties feature lacy trim, which can rub and cause rashes.

- After a bowel movement, girls should reach around their bottom to wipe instead of reaching between their legs.

- Discuss public toilet practices (such as what to do if there are drips on a toilet seat).

Gender Preferences

- Children may naturally prefer the same-gender parent over the opposite-sex parent at this stage, but try not to feel left out or rejected. A child may prefer mom one week, and then shift to dad the next.

- Same-sex friendships are most common as most kids relate best to kids who are most like them in interests, abilities, and gender. However, this doesn't mean that opposite-gender friendships should be discouraged.

respect and how kids should get along and value all differences, including size, shape, color, and gender.

At the same time, you may notice that your children are starting to play favorites, with daughters tending to favor mom and sons favoring dad. Kids are interested in what others of the same gender do, and it may translate into clothing styles, career, hobbies, and even hygiene. Kids may also begin stereotyping that "only" boys play football or "only" girls take ballet. Parents should have frequent discussions about various activities that are offered to both boys and girls.

Using Public Restrooms

- It's a safety dilemma for many parents with opposite-gender children as to when a child can use a public restroom without direct adult supervision.

- Many parents opt to take the child with them into the restroom that is appropriate for the parent's gender. The reality is that it's easier for women to take their son in than a man to take a daughter into the men's restroom because of public urinals.

- Look for unisex bathrooms, or even better, stick to establishments that have designated family bathrooms.

Hygiene Issues for Boys

- Uncircumcised boys should be taught to retract the foreskin back when they urinate.

- Both uncircumcised and circumcised boys should be taught how to properly wash their penis.

- Boys should be taught sanitary and thorough wiping techniques after defecating.

- Boys should learn urinal etiquette versus using private bathroom stalls. Boys may need to be taught about different types of urinals and how to use them correctly.

AGE 5: MILESTONES

SKILLS

Enhanced dexterity, coordination, and confidence set the stage for an abundance of new abilities

Five-year-olds just seem to have their act together. For the most part, parents can introduce their older preschoolers to a variety of new skills, and their focus, interest, motivation, and enhanced dexterity all seem to work together so that the mission gets accomplished.

Not only can your five-year-old now remember what you've

told him and perform gross and fine motor skills successfully, she may now know her letters and be able to write most of them. By the end of the fifth year, most parents have no doubt that their preschooler is ready for the learning experience that waits at school.

Look for new ways to challenge your child and prepare her

Tying Shoes

- Have your five-year-old practice tying shoes privately when other kids aren't around so your child doesn't become self-conscious or embarrassed about early attempts.

- Don't let your child wear laced shoes until she consistently ties her shoes

at the appropriate tightness and without taking too much time.

- Educators don't have time to retie shoes all the time, and dangling laces can become a safety issue.

- Some kids may still prefer Velcro or pull-on styles.

Riding a Bike

- Some five-year-olds may learn to ride their bike independently, but many may still require a little extra time to become better coordinated.

- Never allow your child to ride alone, and always require a bike helmet.

- Teach your child all bike safety rules, and go over them before every bike ride.

- Make sure your child can start and stop her bike independently, and can get off and walk with it across the street safely.

for needed independence when away from home by asking her to help lead the way home from the park, or to decide where you should ride bikes, or to help set a schedule for the day's activities.

Your child may excel at new challenges such as learning to tie her shoes, and will take great joy in choosing a new pair of sneakers with laces. Some kids may learn to ride their bikes without training wheels and even begin to ride scooters, skateboards, or use electronics efficiently.

Multistep Tasks

- Five-year-olds can typically remember up to three-step directions correctly, and parents can help promote this skill by having their child recite back instructions as additional reinforcement.

- Your child may have the ability to memorize details and the order of things quite well at this stage.

- Folding towels or unloading silverware from the dishwasher and then sorting them are examples.

- Some kids can successfully recite the alphabet and count to 10 or 20.

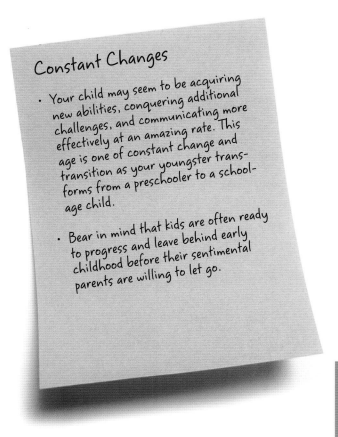

Constant Changes

- Your child may seem to be acquiring new abilities, conquering additional challenges, and communicating more effectively at an amazing rate. This age is one of constant change and transition as your youngster transforms from a preschooler to a school-age child.

- Bear in mind that kids are often ready to progress and leave behind early childhood before their sentimental parents are willing to let go.

AGE 5: MILESTONES

119

ALL IN THE FAMILY

Birth order, household dynamics, and even gender play a role in how preschoolers view family

Today's family unit is more diverse than ever. No longer is a family only defined as two parents, two kids, and a family pet. Many kids today are raised by single parents. Others are part of a blended family and have to adjust to suddenly having other kids in the home. Some are co-raised by parents who share responsibilities, and an increasing number of children are raised by grandparents or other extended family members.

Whatever the configuration is within your home, your preschooler is trying to sort through the constantly evolving roles and figuring out where he fits into the mix.

Preschoolers may also deal with transitioning from being an only child to being an older sibling when a new baby is

New Baby

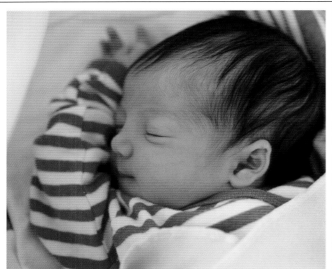

- Toddlers are more apt to have difficulty adjusting to a new baby than preschoolers.

- Preschoolers can be tremendous helpers and may like doing things for the baby.

- Jealousy can still occur at

this age, but parents are typically able to provide adequate reassurance about their love.

- Provide additional areas of responsibility and special privileges to your preschooler to let him know he is valued and a special part of the family.

Siblings

- Parents should seek out ways to balance family activities so that each child has some one-on-one time.

- Realize that preschoolers may begin to compare themselves with older siblings and may become critical of their own abilities

due to a lack of understanding about how skills relate to age.

- Your preschooler will most likely relate better to younger siblings than older ones and may enjoy "teaching" a younger child skills he has mastered.

added to the household. Or, your preschooler may be one of several siblings, each with their own personalities and particular interactions. There's no doubt that where children fall in birth order has an effect on their overall behavior and perception of themselves. Gender of other siblings also may play a role.

Since family structure is extremely important to most preschoolers, it is vital that you help your child to understand the dynamics of your household and that you reassure him that he is an integral part of your home.

ZOOM

Studies have shown that first-born children may be the most responsible and are most likely to attend college. Middle children often feel caught in the middle and may rebel from expectations and feeling they never get attention. The youngest wants to do things the older ones do. Parents should emphasize uniqueness and individual strengths and avoid comparisons.

Pets

- Preschoolers can successfully care for a household pet, with supervision and reminders from parents.

- Do not allow your child to leash walk your pet. If your pet suddenly startles or tries to run off, your preschooler won't be able to provide adequate restraint.

- Child-animal interactions should still be supervised, and your preschooler should be taught how to avoid acting in ways an animal might find threatening.

- Your child should be taught to never approach other animals—even if they appear friendly.

The Only Child

- If your preschooler is an only child, does that mean he is spoiled? Typically, the answer is yes, but studies show that he is probably also self-confident and may be more mature than his peers.

Typical characteristics of the only child include:

- Is often the center of attention, and may grow up expecting that to continue even when with others.

- Relies on the service of others rather than doing something himself.

- May be a natural leader, but can also pout more than other kids when he doesn't get his own way.

GROOMING

Expect some battles as your child asserts her independence in personal hygiene matters

A battle of wills may begin to develop as parents are more anxious for their kids to have clean hair and bodies than kids are to have them. Resistance to baths, haircuts, brushing teeth, going to bed, waking up, washing hands, and even getting dressed mean that routine tasks—which had previously been conducted with minimal fuss—can sometimes be a challenge. Clothing styles, especially choices of appropriate wear for certain occasions, can also result in frustration for parents and preschoolers alike.

Why the resistance? Five-year-olds have a growing need for independence and a strong desire to be in control. Taking care of personal hygiene is a very normal first proving ground

Hair

- Your child may declare that he wants a specific type of hairstyle, when previously he never had an opinion.

- Resistance to certain hairstyles or even getting hair cut at a salon may occur. It is often due to a child wanting a hairstyle like a friend has.

- Your daughter may start rebelling over having hair rolled or styled in looks she considers babyish, such as pig-tails, curls, and big bows. Or, she may have a particular "look" she insists on wearing.

Body

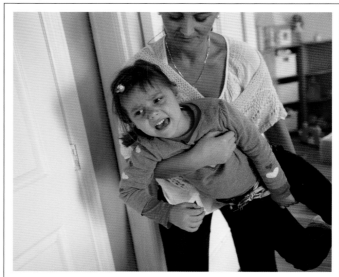

- Just when kids are getting dirtier and smellier from increased activity levels, baths may suddenly become a battleground.

- Some five-year-olds may prefer showering over bathing, although parents need to closely supervise their cleaning efforts and rinsing.

- Parents need to keep a close watch on nails, and make sure that they are kept clean and clipped or filed to an appropriate length. Unkempt nails can cause minor injuries to your child or to others during active play.

122

for your preschooler to express that he is in charge. After all, five-year-olds consider themselves "big kids now" and view parental assistance as being for babies.

Parents can work around this by providing kids with some flexibility as to when, or even how, certain things get done. Or, they can allow their child to brush teeth independently and then conduct a quick parental review and cleanup brush if necessary, all the while praising a child's efforts. If you provide sticker rewards or similar for jobs well done, your child may become even more eager to do a thorough job.

Dressing

- Choose play clothes that your child can put on and take off without any adult assistance. Remember that emergency dashes to the bathroom are still quite common at this age, and clothes that are difficult to remove may result in an embarrassing accident for your child.

- Also choose clothing for practicality and comfort, so that you aren't constantly worried about stains or tears that will undoubtedly occur during normal play.

- Let your child have input into acceptable styles and colors.

Style Preferences

- Five-year-olds often have strong preferences about what they will—and won't—wear.

- Don't make needless rules about clothing. At the same time, don't give in and allow your child to wear something inappropriate just because you want to avoid conflict.

- Make sure your child's choice of shoes works for the activity planned. Don't let your child go to the mall wearing princess dress-up shoes, for example.

TRANSITIONS
Seeking adult approval, finishing tasks, and demonstrating being "all grown up" are signs of maturity

Expect to see a number of behavioral and physical transitions this year as your five-year-old makes the move to school-age readiness. Parents can't help but note the many changes in how their preschooler acts, thinks, communicates, and even reasons. Almost gone are the out-of-control and irrational actions and reactions to things. Your preschooler is now beginning to understand that certain things are simply beyond her control while other things may be maneuverable.

Five-year-olds often seek the approval of loved ones. Whether it is helping with household chores or learning how to count to 10, your preschooler will take the time needed to get something right—as long as it is something that is of interest. You

Approval and Opinions

Maturing Outlook

- Ask your child's opinion on things and discuss how differing opinions should always be respected, even if a person says something contrary to personal beliefs.

- Five-year-olds crave adult support and approval, so offer appropriate praise and feedback whenever your child is trying something new or shows responsibility.

- Teach your child that her opinions are valued, but that there are times when expressing them is inappropriate (such as remarking on a person's attire your child finds ugly).

- Children may ask for apparel or accessories similar to those used by their same-gender parent. A girl might want to begin carrying a purse, and a boy might want to have a wallet. These items can help a five-year-old learn responsibility for personal possessions.

- A watch may be of interest and kids begin to track time and to associate their schedule with time of day.

- Some five-year-olds become embarrassed over wearing clothing with characters, designs, or even colors they deem "babyish."

might be amazed at your child's growing patience and attention span. Mealtimes and other sit-down as well as quiet times may now become more relaxing and even enjoyable, as your child can contribute appropriately to activities and usually refrain from excessive wiggling and fidgeting. Of course, having a silent activity your child can participate in during quiet time, such as coloring, can also help, especially if the duration will be more than about 30 minutes. This ability is a great sign of school readiness in the coming months or year!

Relationship Dynamics

- Your child may begin to ask more questions about relationships, including ones that may require thoughtful responses, such as why mom and dad sleep together and even how babies are born.

- Parents should provide preschoolers with enough information to satisfy their curiosity without going into extended detail. Short and simple yet truthful responses are all that is needed now. Keep in mind that these questions may have been prompted by what your child has been exposed to in the media.

Giving Up Naps

- Age five is when most preschoolers typically give up naptimes, although some may still take them up until they start school.

- If your child still takes naps and will begin school in the fall, gradually transition naptimes out of your preschooler's routine and add extra quality sleep time at bedtime.

- Your child may occasionally still take naps when extremely tired.

- Kindergarteners may crave downtime after school to rejuvenate for the rest of the day.

PEER INFLUENCES

Your child may begin caring what other friends think and do as conforming becomes important

While you may have learned to love your preschooler's "do your own thing" mentality, don't be too terribly surprised if your five-year-old starts wanting to do what everyone else does. While your older preschooler often has a unique sense of style or extreme interests, he may increasingly start caring what other peers do, think, wear, and even like. For

the first time ever, you may see your child experience emotions relating to being like others and wanting to "fit in" with peer groups.

Your five-year-old may also be establishing a stronger awareness of who he is and his various so-called strengths and weaknesses. There's no surprise here: If he is really good

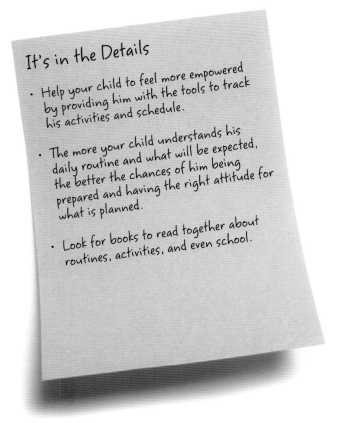

It's in the Details

- Help your child to feel more empowered by providing him with the tools to track his activities and schedule.

- The more your child understands his daily routine and what will be expected, the better the chances of him being prepared and having the right attitude for what is planned.

- Look for books to read together about routines, activities, and even school.

Conformity

- While your child still may not care what others think, many begin to look to peer approval and acceptance on an increasing basis.

- This is a good time to talk with your five-year-old about conformity and why it's okay to like certain

things, but that it shouldn't be just because a friend does.

- Teach your child coping mechanisms for when she gets teased by peers or how to stand up for something she believes in.

at running fast and is nervous about navigating the obstacle course at the playground, then he will want to challenge his friends to running races while avoiding the playground. It's a normal reaction as your child wants to always showcase his best! Parents will also have to emphasize to their child that certain skills may take extra practice or time to accomplish, as many five-year-olds can be pretty hard on themselves when they can't do something as well as others.

Help your preschooler better understand his schedule by avoiding springing something unexpected on him whenever possible. While certain surprises (such as a special reward, for example) are always fun, many preschoolers don't like changes to their schedule. Rather, they are at their best when they are able to think through a new activity or to plan how they want to do something—even planning out a playdate with a friend.

Many five-year-olds want to be able to track what day it is, which month, and may incessantly ask "Are we going to do anything?"—not necessarily because they are bored, but because of their desire to plan and control their day.

Self-Esteem

- Your child may begin to change his opinion of himself either becoming extra critical of himself or having an inflated view of his abilities.

- Avoid comments about skills (or lack thereof) that your child can use as comparisons.

- If your child starts talking about what he "can't" do, provide alternatives with things he can do.

- Kids who are overly "braggy" about their abilities may have that attitude because adults have over-hyped their achievements.

Stopping the "Shock Talk"

- Five-year-olds may repeat inappropriate things they hear because they like getting a reaction from others—even when they don't understand the meaning behind the words they are saying.

- Kids may also use "bathroom humor" for similar reactions.

- Parents should avoid overreacting to these comments. Privately explain why certain words are inappropriate and encourage your child to discreetly ask you when he's unsure whether a word is okay to say.

ON-THE-GO

Prepare for possible motion sickness, stomach ailments, and safety concerns when taking kids out

As your child becomes more used to traveling and his interests grow, so may the frequency of your family's outings. Five-year-olds are typically a traveling delight; they are able to remain calm and keep themselves mostly entertained, can navigate public restrooms, and practice proper bathroom hygiene, and can follow rules. Plus, five-year-olds are genuinely interested

in going to new places, and look forward to opportunities to travel by car, plane, train, or even boat.

This isn't to say that it will all be easy; advanced planning is a must when traveling with your five-year-old. Parents should take precautions against motion sickness and other types of childhood illnesses as well. Parents also need to make

Motion Sickness

- Motion sickness is common in preschoolers and toddlers.

- It can be hereditary. If either parent had motion sickness as a child, your kid might, too.

- Make sure the car is kept at a comfortable temperature.

- Hunger can also contribute to a feeling of nausea and headaches.

- Provide healthy snacks, water, and a battery powered fan to help alleviate queasiness. Looking out the window and frequent stops can help.

Stranger Danger

- Emphasize that all family members must pay particular attention to staying together while traveling.

- Though you should be careful not to overly worry or scare your youngster, make sure she understands that she should not talk to or go with people she does not know.

sure that their child is kept safe, and rules should be regularly enforced and reviewed in terms of what to do in public, stranger danger, and what to do if your child gets lost.

Many child care providers begin taking five-year-olds on field trips. While kids may greatly anticipate the trip itself, you want to make sure that your preschooler comes back from the outing healthy and happy. Don't hesitate to ask what safety precautions are in place, how children are chaperoned and accounted for at all times, and what training staff and parent volunteers have.

Field Trips

- Just because your child is invited on a field trip doesn't mean it is appropriate for her to go.

- Determine whether your child is truly even interested and able to participate in the activity. For example, if your child has never rollerskated, she may not be ready for an afternoon at the roller rink.

- Make sure your child is comfortable with being on a bus and away from a familiar setting. Remember that one child can ruin it for everyone.

Supervision on Outings

- Before sending your child on a field trip (even if you're going with him), make sure that all safety guidelines are in place and that you are comfortable with the activity.

- Ask about adult-to-child ratios and what safety plan will be followed to keep kids together.

- Determine what types of communications among adults are used and whether someone in attendance has proper first-aid training.

FAMILY FUN

Special interactions and meaningful traditions create magical childhood memories

Some of the best family times can be as simple as a spontaneous interaction with your five-year-old. Or, with planning, special outings and excursions can be every bit as exciting for you as they are for your child. Your preschooler understands and follows rules, behaves in accordance with expectations (at least most of the time), and enjoys trying out new things

and going to new places. These qualities make your five-year-old a fun traveling companion, a special shopping assistant, and a valued helper. Let's hear it for the five-year-olds!

They are also a blast around seasonal celebrations and family outings, although they can easily get caught up in the commercialism. Even museums and child-focused events

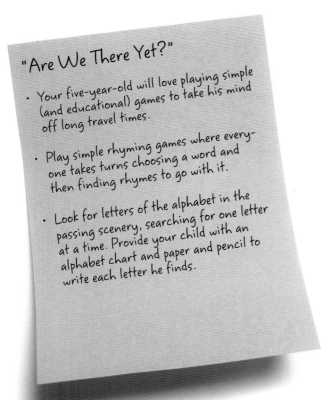

"Are We There Yet?"

- Your five-year-old will love playing simple (and educational) games to take his mind off long travel times.

- Play simple rhyming games where everyone takes turns choosing a word and then finding rhymes to go with it.

- Look for letters of the alphabet in the passing scenery, searching for one letter at a time. Provide your child with an alphabet chart and paper and pencil to write each letter he finds.

Adventures

- Turn beloved activities into opportunities for sharing information. While out on a walk, ask your preschooler to find you three items from nature and then have him "teach" you everything he knows about it. Or show your child how to help out in the kitchen.

- Look for ways to pique your child's curiosity. If your child likes gazing at stars, make a family project out of researching interesting facts about constellations and our solar system.

- Plan "discovery days" where your preschooler takes the lead and you follow.

often have gift shops and snack bars, which can set the stage for wanting to buy something instead of enjoying the experience. Look for ways your child can enjoy various holidays and teach him the meanings behind each one.

Family traditions or rituals are also exciting for your child, who will now want to be a busy participant rather than just an observer. Let your child play a role in celebrating the arrival of spring or observing Hanukkah, for example. Your child's perspective on special family times and seasonal events can add cherished meaning to togetherness for everyone!

ZOOM

Interfaith couples have extra challenges when determining how to celebrate religious holidays. Couples should decide early on (when the children are still young) whether one faith's traditions will be followed or whether both holidays will be incorporated, and how. Communicating your plans establishes expectations and minimizes potential conflicts.

Family Rituals

- Rituals and celebrations often revolve around the holidays, but they don't have to. Create some rituals that are unique to just your family, such as staging a Friday Family Night, a First Day of Summer party, a Family Snugglefest, or regular celebrations to honor family members for good deeds.

- Create a unique tradition kids can look forward to each year. One example is taking a photo each year of your child in the same birthday hat and then placing the photo into a birthday scrapbook for future comparisons. The sillier, the better—and certainly more memorable.

Holiday Observances

- Choosing how—and even if—you want your child to participate in holiday happenings can be tricky.

- Creative alternatives can be substituted if you wish to opt out of certain traditions, such as trick-or-treating, for example. An afternoon spent at the pumpkin patch

can be just as fun.

- Parents should communicate with their child's caregiver about holiday preferences to minimize mixed messages. In daycare settings, however, parents should understand that not all individual preferences can be met.

ACTIVITIES

Five-year-olds may start categorizing and organizing objects and even themselves

While imagination and exploration still rule at this stage, you may find that your child is also becoming more interested in organizing and categorizing things. That's because your preschooler is beginning to exhibit school readiness through associating time of day, schedules, how things fit into the scheme of life, and even determining his place in daily life.

While some five-year-olds could care less about room organization or matching clothes, others do. Parents may find that their kids actually want to have designated places for personal possessions. An example of this is keeping all the parts of a game together and put away in the box to avoid losing them. The same concept of "everything in its place"

Categorization

- Encourage your child to categorize her surroundings by turning it into a game or a friendly contest.

- Ask kids to categorize clean and dirty, big and small, socks and shirts, living and not living, and by shape and color. Help your child think about more catego-

ries by posing open-ended questions about how they would separate or categorize certain things and why.

- Use books and reading to discuss how they should be categorized (whether they are factual or fiction, for example).

Organization

- Being organized helps many youngsters with expectations and sense of place.

- Help your five-year-old to organize his room. While you should guide placement of certain items ("clothes go into these drawers," for example), let

your child lead the way. It's okay if he wants his underwear in the top drawer and socks in the bottom.

- Show your child how to organize clothing by season and how to keep toys and other items properly stored away.

may begin to manifest itself with clothing organization, supplies, and learning concepts of how much time it takes to get a particular task accomplished.

Parents can encourage the building of these skills through simple activities, such as sorting laundry, putting away dishes, and organizing clothes by tops and bottoms and by seasons. Using flashcards and asking kids to categorize persons, places, and things, for example, are also ways to boost this skill.

Encourage your child to time certain things to see how long it takes, such as getting ready in the morning.

YELLOW ● LIGHT

Some kids are organizers and others are not. However, if your child seems unable to recognize simple things like the difference between a cat and a rock, for example, or is unable to concentrate on a single activity for more than five minutes, you may want to request an evaluation from the pediatrician. Keep in mind that kids develop at different paces and milestones are more general guidelines than absolutes!

Spatial

- Five-year-olds should mostly understand the meaning of yesterday, today, and tomorrow but may still struggle with weeks, months, and years.

- Your child should understand morning, afternoon, and evening. Often, kids make the association through mealtimes, such as breakfast is in the morning.

- Review spatial concepts with your child regularly, including in between, behind, far and close, near and around. Hide an object and have your child find it based on your directions only.

Telling Time

- Many five-year-olds can learn to tell time. Provide your child with access to a digital clock that is easily viewable to help promote basic time concepts of hours and minutes.

- Show your child how a stopwatch works and let her time things as a way to increase understanding of seconds and minutes.

- Provide your preschooler with an inexpensive watch for tracking time and promote associations to schedules related to the hour of the day.

ARTS & CRAFTS

Ability to concentrate and complete multistep processes helps creativity to blossom

A five-year-old's emerging art skills can be quite impressive. Since your preschooler now has an adequate attention span and mastery of fine motor skills, projects that involve multiple steps to prepare and then assemble are now feasible.

Parents, child care providers, group leaders and coaches alike may find that they now spend less time trying to keep kids focused and on task and more time truly enjoying children's creativity.

Don't make the mistake of providing your child with a fun arts and crafts project and then setting a short timeframe for completion. Providing a leisurely experience where your child can explore using paints, scissors, glue, assembly, and

Cutting

- Your child should be able to use scissors correctly and cut along basic line patterns. Cutting a star shape, however, may still be tricky!

- Have your child draw simple shapes and then practice cutting them out.

- Don't jump to conclusions about which hand your child favors, although most will use right-handed scissors. Many school groups use "community scissors" but if your child needs a separate left-handed pair you may need to buy those and have them kept separately.

Gluing

- While many preschoolers are restricted to glue sticks to minimize messes, teach your child how to use school glue and rubber cement as well.

- Preschoolers love cutting out and then gluing pieces together. Make a festive jack-o-lantern using orange construction paper for the pumpkin and then black shapes for the eyes, nose, and mouth. Have your child draw the shape first, then cut and glue it together.

- Teach your child the importance of putting paper underneath a gluing project.

even the ever-important glitter is a way to encourage creativity. Kindergarten is filled with creative projects that coincide with early learning, so look for ways you can get your child a head start in these areas. Copying and tracing are also popular projects, especially when combined with early letter or word associations.

If your child doesn't seem too interested in art projects, there's no cause for concern. As long as your preschooler is able to focus on and complete projects when required, it's okay if art is not his favorite thing. Not all kids are art aficionados!

YELLOW ● LIGHT

While praise and positive reinforcement may help your budding artist explore creative outlets, avoid the common mistake of over-hyping your child's talent. Some parents are so quick to heap on extreme accolades that kids begin to think that their simple finger painting is a magnificent work. Having a false sense of extraordinary talent may backfire with kids who do not see a need to practice or improve their already "perfect" technique.

Coloring

- Go ahead and spring for a larger size package of crayons and let your child explore the many different colors.

- Your child should be able to use regular-size crayons now (rather than the larger-size ones).

- While some kids may love to color in coloring books, others prefer blank sheets of paper on which they can do their own thing.

- Let your preschooler experiment with washable markers, glitter pens, and other coloring tools as well.

Assembling

- Your child has the skills to assemble projects with minimal adult help.

- You may need to pre-punch holes or do prep work but most five-year-olds can use most materials needed to successfully create and complete projects.

- Encourage your child to watch what you do and then do it herself with her own materials rather than having you help with each stage.

- Avoid complex projects that may be too challenging or cumbersome.

MUSIC & MOVEMENT

Encourage active music participation, not just listening or observing, for heightened focus and control

Silly songs using rhyming words and movements are not just fun, they are educational as well. That's why so many preschool and kindergarten teachers utilize them! Songs help preschoolers to learn word associations and meanings, and are easy to memorize. Movements paired with songs help promote gross motor and fine motor skills and coordination,

and are great social ice breakers as well. After all, who can't help but giggle while performing the "Hokey Pokey" or singing "Old MacDonald!"

Many early educators use familiar melodies with custom lyrics to teach kids about color choices, shapes, and even emotions. Another tactic is taking a popular preschooler

Singing

- Singing can be incorporated formally and informally into a preschooler's normal daily routine.

- Sing silly made-up songs when you awaken your tot in the morning, and then sing about getting dressed, putting on shoes, hygiene, breakfast, and even brush-

ing teeth. The sillier you are, the more fun your child will have and the more apt he'll be to sing along.

- Teach your kids the lyrics to popular preschool-level songs but also encourage made-up melodies and even nonsense tunes to promote creativity.

Balance and Coordination

- Movement to music is a terrific way to provide youngsters with an outlet for their endless energy. If your child starts acting restless or bored, bring out some music with movements to go along with it and ward off the wiggles.

- Add moves that promote physical skills and balance such as hopping on one foot, twirling around, or imitating animal walks.

- Consider teaching your child exercises (such as jumping jacks) to music.

song and letting kids act out certain parts through dance or signs only. Keeping beat to songs is another way to foster a love of music. Even kids who are more resistant to singing or dancing may enjoy keeping beat to songs, and supplies can be as easy as an empty container and a wooden spoon!

Music provides youngsters with so-called "rich sensory experiences," which simply put means that kids are exposed to a variety of sensations. Researchers believe that active participation in musical experiences helps to create neural connections, or pathways, between the cells in the brain.

Musical Instruments

- A few kids may begin learning to play formal instruments, such as the piano, at this stage. For most kids, however, formal music lessons are still years away.

- Some programs teach preschoolers musical fundamentals using inexpensive recorders. They also show them the basics of reading music.

- Most kids enjoy musical instruments of the home-made variety. Kids enjoy learning to follow (or create their own) beats using their hands or rhythmic spoons on a tin can or similar "drum."

Musical Styles

- Expose your child to different music genres such as country, rock, popular, classical, religious, and ethnic.

- Talk to your preschooler about the sounds different instruments make in a song and whether a particular song features only instrumentals or includes vocal accompaniment. Ask your child what she likes or doesn't like about certain music and how listening to it makes her feel.

- Make sure lyrics are age-appropriate.

SCHOOL PREP

Introduce classroom concepts such as learning centers, circle time, and raising a hand before speaking

Having your five-year-old know common kindergarten procedures certainly isn't a must. In fact, most preschoolers who attend preschool, daycare, or even a parent's day out program already know about learning centers, circle time, and raising hands before saying something. At the same time, many parents want their children to know basic school rules

ahead of time so they can practice skills and be better prepared for the school year.

What are some things your five-year-old might need to know about school? Many kindergarten teachers indicate that a child's understanding of basic social behaviors and classroom expectations can be more important than

Learning Centers

- Many kindergarten programs utilize rotating centers where kids participate in a certain activity for a designated amount of time.

- While most child care programs allow kids to choose what they want to play with, in kindergarten par-

ticipation in centers may be required and not optional. Make sure your child is prepared for this change.

- Help your child understand the importance of trying new things and doing what the teacher says.

Cooperative Play

- Your child is most likely already doing this naturally, but you should still continue to encourage ways to play cooperatively with others and taking turns. It's one thing for a child to play with another friend, but it can be a bit more challenging when there are four or five kids in a group.

- Many programs pool common supplies and youngsters may initially struggle with items not personally belonging to them. Discuss how using a favorite color of scissors, for example, is unimportant.

knowing academics at this point.

Why? Kids beginning formal schooling come from a wide variety of readiness levels, with some already knowing how to read, others knowing most of their letters and how to spell their name, and a few only knowing very rudimentary basics. Regardless of where they are when they start school, skill levels typically equalize within a few years.

Early childhood educators say they most want to see a child who comes to school eager to learn and able to demonstrate self-control and age-appropriate social behaviors.

Classroom Behaviors

- Kindergarten teachers will spend a lot of time during the first part of the school year reviewing appropriate classroom behaviors with students.

- A big adjustment is not blurting out comments or answers. Raising hands rather than shouting as a way to get the teacher's attention will take some getting used to.

- Not touching other kids (hugging, grabbing, poking, and tapping others are common behaviors) is a behavior to work on. Teach your child what is considered personal space.

Number Sense

- While counting will be taught in kindergarten, parents can give their kids a head start with basic math by promoting counting, grouping, sorting, and organizing.

- Ask your child to count out how many grapes he eats or how many rooms are in your home, for example. Show your child how counting is used in everyday life, such as how many napkins should be put on the table so that every guest will have one.

READING

Choose concept and pattern books to promote school readiness and ask questions about story

Hopefully, you've been reading to your child since birth. It's never too early to introduce reading and foster a love of learning with your child. If you haven't already been reading daily to your child, now's a good time to start!

Earlier reading with your child focused more on you reading aloud and pointing things out to your child. As your preschooler

has grown and matured, you've most likely been engaging your child in some open-ended questions about the book or asking your child to identify characters or objects. That's great! But as your child begins to prepare for school, there's more you can do to help encourage language and pre-reading skills.

Concept books, or books that teach educational elements

Choosing Books

- Choose books about subjects your child is interested in, or better yet, let your child pick books out himself.

- Simple stories with predictable plots work well with older preschoolers.

- Many preschoolers will

want to read and re-read the same book over and over again. While you may tire of it, your child will love the familiarity of knowing what comes next.

- Look for books that promote the ABCs, numbers, and life skills such as managing emotions.

Identifying Story Structure

- Talk about a story's beginning, middle, and end. After reading a book, ask your child what he liked best about the ending and how it was different from the beginning.

- Ask your child who his most favorite and least favorite characters are and why.

- Show your child the book's title and the name of the author and illustrator and how this information typically appears on all books.

such as the ABCs or counting, don't have to come across as academic. Often, they are written in a way that is fun and inviting and encourage interactive listening and fun responses. Pattern books using rhymes and repetition are also highly recommended.

While sound-effects and pop-up styles are still popular with your preschooler, they are not used as much in kindergarten, in part because they can be disruptive to others nearby if the sound effects are activated. Interactive books where tabs are pulled or three-dimensional objects appear when the pages are turned are also more fragile, and can get torn more easily through frequent and rough use.

Rather than just reading to your child, you'll want to read in stages, letting your child join in or even take over. Kids often love reading a cherished book over and over and can recite the words accurately, even though they aren't truly reading them.

Pause during reading to let your child fill in the blanks about what happens next or to discuss a character or scene. Ask your child why she thinks a character did something or even why the artist chose to illustrate the book in a certain way.

Living Books

- Ask your child what a character from a book should sound like and then use that voice. Have your child also "read" parts of familiar books.

- Act out what you are reading using props from around the home, if desired.

- Let your child dress up like a character from a favorite book. Or, create a silly tradition like using an "imagination cape" or wrapping up in a particular "reading blanket."

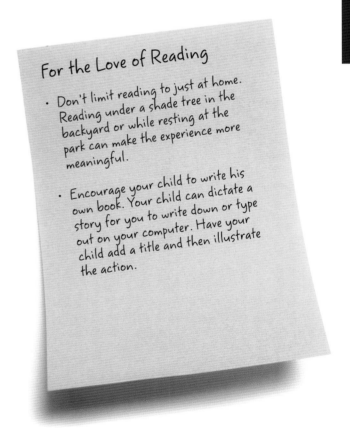

For the Love of Reading

- Don't limit reading to just at home. Reading under a shade tree in the backyard or while resting at the park can make the experience more meaningful.

- Encourage your child to write his own book. Your child can dictate a story for you to write down or type out on your computer. Have your child add a title and then illustrate the action.

141

MANIPULATIVES

Most kids learn best through hands-on experiences and exploration that uses multiple senses

It's one thing to tell your child about a fact and quite another to let him learn it for himself through exploration. Most children process and remember information best when they are able to use multiple senses at the same time. The best part is that using so-called manipulatives—considered a highly effective way to promote learning—is fun and engaging at

the same time! Manipulatives generally refer to an object that a child uses to build, practice with, or examine to correlate a meaning to something else.

Manipulatives take many forms and the same manipulative can often be used for differing concepts. For example, construction-style manipulatives can teach preschoolers

Flash Cards

- Using flash cards offers simple fun and learning at the same time. They can be used while out and about or whenever a quiet activity is needed.

- Parents can adjust the use of flash cards based on a child's particular skill level.

- Involve your child with making flash cards by having them write the letters themselves or illustrate the words. Cut out pictures from a magazine on particular topics, and then glue them on the index cards.

Building

- Stacking, sorting, and building skills become increasingly complex as kids mature. Ask your child to build something that cars can go through or a home for a favorite stuffed animal, for example, as a way to encourage creative thinking.

- Provide your child with household items, such as blankets, shoe boxes, and plastic containers.

- Many five-year-olds begin preferring more intricate and challenging projects and may like step-by-step processes.

about colors, shapes, size, compatibility, sorting, counting, and even how things work. Other types of manipulatives are geared toward a specific purpose, such as tying shoes or telling time.

A common manipulative for this age group involves the use of flash cards for letter and number recognition, matching, word and picture associations, and even simple board games and puzzles. Your child's interest in manipulatives and their level of complexity changes along with her skills. Keep in mind that you may not need to change out a toy as your child gets older; your preschooler may simply begin playing with them in a more complex fashion!

There's no need to buy a certain type of manipulative toy for your child to have fun. Common household items such as playing cards, dominoes, a calculator, or index cards (where you draw in what you want) work well and are friendly toward the family budget at the same time. A favorite with many educators is using plastic letters (or index cards with one letter per card) and showing preschoolers how the letters are placed in a particular pattern to form words.

Games

- Bingo games, especially ones that have been modified to reflect a special interest or holiday, can be particularly entertaining to five-year-olds.

- Your child may also enjoy the challenge of simple tic-tac-toe or even dot games, but may not demonstrate strategic thinking yet at this point.

- Many five-year-olds like simple follow-the-number projects that result in familiar objects. Paint-by-number sets can also provide enrichment if the projects are designed for preschoolers and not older children.

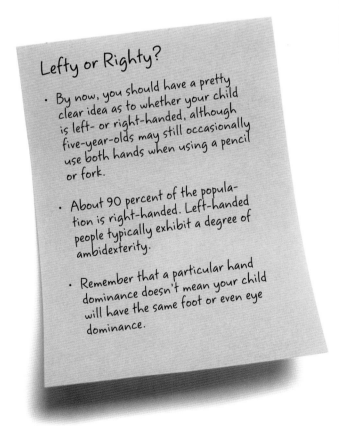

Lefty or Righty?

- By now, you should have a pretty clear idea as to whether your child is left- or right-handed, although five-year-olds may still occasionally use both hands when using a pencil or fork.

- About 90 percent of the population is right-handed. Left-handed people typically exhibit a degree of ambidexterity.

- Remember that a particular hand dominance doesn't mean your child will have the same foot or even eye dominance.

SOCIAL
Your child should be able to act appropriately most of the time, especially around friends

It usually comes as a big relief to parents that most five-year-olds possess a fairly clear understanding of appropriate social behaviors and for the most part don't require constant adult supervision. They know the fundamental differences between right and wrong, and understand why behaviors such as hitting or biting are hurtful and must not ever occur. While

slip-ups (both unintentional and deliberate) will still occur, less parenting time is being spent on correcting behaviors and more on encouraging friendships and trying new things.

Your five-year-old may likely enjoy energetic play with others and simply chatting with friends. Interactions may involve inventing games with simple rules, pretend play, and

Empathy

- Your child may become sensitive to the needs and desires of others, especially children who are younger.

- Traits such as compassion and the desire to comfort others who are sad or hurt are signs your child is becoming more aware

that there are needs and feelings of others outside of himself.

- Your child may become concerned about the plight of others in need or of animals and may want to do something to help out.

Right from Wrong

- Your child's moral compass is developing quickly, although many five-year-olds don't yet fully understand accountability for their actions.

- It is common for a child to try and hedge the truth to avoid getting in trouble. However, when your child

outright lies, he now knows it is wrong and may feel guilt or remorse.

- Parents can help their child to develop a sense of ethics and beliefs by posing questions about situations and providing positive ways to deal with them.

challenging others to contests. Keep in mind, however, that most five-year-olds only want to stage contests and competitions when they have the clear advantage. After all, most still don't know how to lose with grace at this stage.

Friendships rule your child's world at this stage, and five-year-olds typically prefer playing with one or two special friends. Parents and adult caregivers have to keep watch, however, that cliques don't form that result in hurt feelings when others are left out or excluded from play.

While youngsters typically desire close friendships with select friends, playing together doesn't always go smoothly. Some kids may exhibit extremely bossy behavior and the need to always be right. Parents should have frequent conversations with their child to discuss how to be a good friend to others, being nice to everyone, and avoiding hurting others' feelings.

The good news is that preschoolers at this age are increasingly able to work out small squabbles by themselves. Learning how to compromise and make up so that playtime can continue is a skill they will be working on in the coming years of childhood.

Manipulation

- Your child may still struggle with certain concepts about what is real and what he would like to be real.

- Five-year-olds may try and manipulate circumstances to be in their favor even though they typically do not intend to be dishonest.

- Kids may struggle more with authority and try to talk their way out of situations or rules that they don't agree with. However, they still wish to please and will do what is asked.

Friends

- Most five-year-olds actively seek out friendships with at least a best friend or two.

- Friends made at this stage, especially those attending the same kindergarten and primary school as your child, can be long-lasting and continue throughout a child's school years—and beyond.

- Expect kids to squabble and bicker, but help them find solutions to end disagreements and prevent reoccurrence of the argument.

145

PHYSICAL

Increased endurance and mastery of body control signifies a readiness for sports and physical activities

When it comes to overall coordination, your five-year-old seems to have it all pulled together. Gone are the clumsy movements and gawky attempts at complex gross motor skill actions. Your child's attitude concerning physical skills has also improved, and you'll most likely note fewer whines that something is too hard. Your preschooler is a walking, jumping, leaping, and running ball of energy, and you may be quite amazed at her burgeoning speed and grace.

In addition to enhanced body control, your five-year-old is also showing a marked increase in stamina. Sports hold more appeal now and your child's ability to focus, willingness to learn, ability to execute new skills, and desire to please the

Sports Skills

- Five-year-olds can learn to jump rope and even hula-hoop with practice.

- Many can throw a ball, catch it, and kick it.

- Most sports involving a ball of any kind hold special appeal to youngsters, especially baseball, football, basketball, soccer, and kickball.

- Tennis and golf may be too complex to do successfully at this point.

- Be wary of pushing competitive sports on kids at too early an age.

Gross Motor Skills

- Your child should be able to walk down stairs putting one foot in front of the other on separate steps without having to double-step.

- Your child can skip with some practice.

- Encourage your child to try new physical skills, such as walking backward, twirling, and even walking while balancing on a surface that is slightly raised. Be sure that the new physical skills your child is trying out are safe!

coach makes being on a team a more positive experience than ever before.

Physical milestones aren't limited to just gross motor skills. You'll notice achievements in other areas as well, including being able to button and unbutton clothing better and being able to get dressed in more complex clothing by themselves. Fine motor skill mastery is seen through improvements in holding a pencil or crayon and in writing, using child-size prongs or small tools to pick up, turn, and grasp things, and with tying shoes.

ZOOM

What should you do if your child hates sports? Peer pressure can be persuasive, and your child may initially be interested in a sport simply because a friend is, only to hate it once the season actually begins. Since physical activity should be encouraged, let your child try new sports until she finds something she likes. Don't get locked into activities just because everyone else does them.

Multi-step Skills

- Many youngsters can begin performing increasingly complex tumbling skills, such as multiple cartwheels in a series, a handstand to a forward roll, or even a round-off.

- Both boys and girls typically enjoy basic tumbling classes at this stage.

- Your child may begin to show off some multiple-step dance moves involving feet, body, and hands.

- Consider letting your child participate in kid-friendly activities like tae kwon do that teach body movement and control in conjunction with kicking skills and flexibility.

Strength and Agility

- Many five-year-olds begin testing their physical strength and agility. Arm-wrestling competitions and running races are common.

- Encourage your child to test his strength through helping you unload groceries and carrying items.

- Many five-year-olds can now successfully support their body weight and navigate the monkey bars and other playground apparatus that utilize arm strength.

- Begin to talk to your child about the importance of stretching first to keep muscles healthy.

INTELLECTUAL

Your child's preferred style of learning and "intelligence strengths" begin to emerge at this age

All individuals have multiple intelligences—areas of special skill or strength. Children are no different, and at this age many of the natural characteristics of their so-called "brain power" begin to emerge.

While your five-year-old is far too young for you to determine traditional intelligences in verbal and math skills, you undoubtedly are beginning to note areas to which your child gravitates or seems to excel. While we all have abilities to a greater or lesser degree and can foster certain areas to strengthen them, our nature is what often determines overall interests and eventual careers in adult life.

Aside from the theories of bodily-kinesthetic, interpersonal,

Logical-Mathematical Intelligence

- This intelligence is associated with an effective understanding and use of numbers and the ability to reason well. Kids with this intelligence may have fun with numbers and how things work, enjoy math and computer games, and excel at strategic games like checkers, puzzles, and brain teasers. They are often described as logical.

- Children may enjoy discovery-style museums and exhibits and actively desire to learn about history and science.

Musical Intelligence

- This type of intelligence is broader than having a love of music. Kids may relate to music in different ways, either as a performer, a music critic, or as a composer.

- Kids may easily remember lyrics; be constantly singing, humming, or tapping out rhythms; and may respond emotionally—positively or negatively—to music they hear.

- They may show sensitivity to noises in their environment, and often recognize and even critique music that seems off-key.

intrapersonal, and linguistic intelligences discussed earlier, there are four additional intelligences. They include logical-mathematical, musical, naturalist, and spatial.

Genetics play a role in how your child thinks and processes information. But your child may also have many unique processing skills as well. Finding ways to develop dominant tendencies while nurturing areas that could use some extra support is the balancing act that parents and eventually teachers will have to navigate in the years to come.

ZOOM

Common types of "learning styles" or approaches include visual learners, who learn through seeing; auditory learners, who learn through listening; and tactile/kinesthetic learners, who learn through doing. Visual learners need to see facial expressions and body language while auditory learners flourish through discussions and listening. Kinesthetic learners have a hands-on approach.

Naturalist Intelligence

- This type of intelligence marvels at the wonders of nature, and children may be fiercely protective of plants, bugs, and nature.

- Children may enjoy collecting leaves, watching birds, and gardening. They greatly enjoy animals, and pursue hobbies involving nature.

- Kids may seem more at ease in nature settings versus cultural attractions and enjoy visiting zoos, aquariums, and parks.

- They may have an environmental consciousness beyond other same-age peers.

Spatial Intelligence

- This type of intelligence involves perceiving the visual-spatial world in an accurate and effective way.

- Skills may manifest themselves in various ways, such as by accurately understanding charts and graphs; through art projects such as drawing, painting, and sculpting; and even with the ability to remember directions.

- Kids may like visual presentations, study the illustrations in books they are reading, and arrange their rooms and even "decorate" by individual preference.

CREATIVE

Five-year-olds may exhibit self-direction, self-sufficiency, and a strong confidence in creative abilities

Your child is naturally creative, and many early childhood education experts maintain that creativity is at an all-time high right around the time your child enters school. That's because your child uses imagination and pretend to create the world that he wants around him.

Most five-year-olds exhibit strong confidence in their abilities

to sing, dance, draw, and pretend. But it may come as a surprise to many that a preferred way to encourage creativity is by providing some structure to what you want your child to do creatively. In other words, rather than just saying to "draw whatever you like," ask your child to draw a particular topic, such as his family. Why? We are creatures of habit, and often

Inventors

- Most kids are inventors of some thing or another at this stage. Many like to invent things (in their minds) that will make their lives easier or more fun, such as a spaceship they can drive to the toy store.

- Kids often enjoy making up new games with rules of their choosing.

- Capitalize on your child's learning style to have him find new ways to organize his room or set the table, for example.

Tracing and Copying

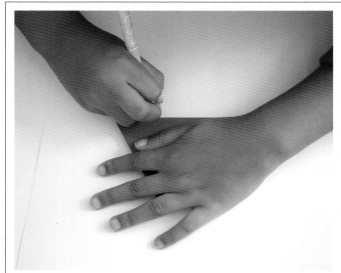

- Your child may like copying basic shapes or objects as a way of learning patterns.

- Tracing over more complex shapes, even just using a finger, can help your child to better associate lines and curves to a finished object.

- Discourage your child from only relying on copying and tracing objects, however. Encourage your child's sense of imagination and free-thinking by also asking what he thinks the perfect car should look like, for example.

repeat the same creative projects again and again based on previous success. Asking your child to do something differently or new can actually help generate creative ideas.

While following a teacher and mimicking a certain move or sequence can be a starting point for certain creative outlets, doing only that and that alone can be boring to some children. Others, however, may thrive following patterns. Learn what makes your child blossom and regularly set aside time to encourage those experiences.

ZOOM

Some parents think kids should be doing something at all times in order to learn. But don't be afraid of having absolutely nothing to do. Being bored can actually promote a child's sense of creativity by forcing them to come up with something that is self-directed or even self-taught. A child who is able to keep himself entertained is more likely to be self-sufficient and satisfied.

Innovative Thinking

- Innovative thinking is essential for success in school and work, and parents should promote their child's creative desires.

- Imaginative play helps to foster original thinking and problem-solving abilities, which can be an asset when children face new or even uncomfortable situations.

- Provide your child with ideas for interesting activities and creative outlets, and then support her as she adds her own flair or version of fun.

Creative Projects

- Have your child make a montage of things found in nature, like grass, leaves, and nuts. Items can be organized and then glued on paper.

- Work together to construct creation stations that the family can participate in at designated times. Projects can be as simple as decorating cookies, having a costume contest, playing charades, or creating an art gallery.

- Plan a scavenger hunt around the house.

EMOTIONAL
Balancing social and alone time, and wanting to help others are signs of maturity

You may find that your five-year-old alternates between playing with peers, conversing with adults, and wanting to be alone. Finding a balance and having time to think and spend some "me time" is a positive step toward maturity and is a way many youngsters keep an emotional check on themselves.

While younger preschoolers often gravitate toward a same-gender parent when possible, you may notice that your child is becoming more curious and receptive to the opposite-gender parent or caregiver. He may begin to ask more about similarities and differences among people, not just with gender, but height, family background or lifestyle, and hair or skin color, just to name a few.

Emotional Sensitivities

- Even the slightest perception of criticism can send your youngster into an emotional huff or sulking fit.

- Your child's feelings may get hurt more easily now, especially by another peer, in part due to your youngster's better grasp on emotions in general.

- Teach your child that words can be weapons, and that there is a lot of truth in the adage, "If you can't say something nice, then don't say anything at all."

Similarities and Differences

- Your child's awareness of how individuals and lifestyles are similar as well as very different begins to emerge.

- It's typical for your five-year-old to begin to want to be "just like" a friend and want to buy clothing and even wear her hair just like friends.

- Encourage your child to find ways to feel part of the group while maintaining her own unique identity. The issue of "fitting in" will be one that your child faces throughout school.

This is a good time for dads and male figures to become more actively involved in their child's life—if they haven't already been doing so all along. While an increasing number of single dads are raising their children, moms still comprise the majority of single households. And having both a mother and father in the home doesn't necessarily mean active parenting is occurring either.

Regardless of your family's structure, seek out quality ways to engage your child with positive role models and caring adults and family members of both genders.

Your child may begin reaching out to others more and searching for ways to connect. An understanding of similarities and differences in other families, combined with more complex emotions such as compassion and empathy, may mean your child wants to begin advocating for others.

Look for ways to help promote your five-year-old's spirit of generosity and caring, being careful not to overemphasize how big of a deal it is. You want your child to grow up thinking that charity and helping others is a way of life, and not a reason for being rewarded.

Temperament

- Your child's overall temperament is now an influencing factor on friendships and activities.

- You may be able to let your child make her own decisions about social circles and trying new things, but extremely timid or cautious personalities may still require additional coaxing and parental assistance.

- Regularly talk to your child about what behavior is expected in situations, and techniques for calming herself down when angry or sad.

Teaching Sportsmanship

- Teaching kids to do their best at a sport or activity and to win or lose with grace can be a challenge.

- Talk about good sportsmanship and what it means before every game or event.

- Be a good role model when cheering on your child, and support other teammates and players as well. Keep in mind that kids often learn bad behaviors from watching how adults act.

153

LANGUAGE

Your child understands a larger vocabulary and knows how to properly use words in sentences

By most estimates, your five-year-old understands about 13,000 words, with more complex words and meanings being added to his vocabulary all the time. Your child's word choices and syntax more closely mimic that of an adult, with complete sentences consisting of five to ten words on average. Parents may also notice that their child is able to use the

power of words to his advantage. The ability to reason, persuade, and even argue through language is a newly developed skill.

Incessant questions of "why" are now being replaced with "because," typically used in matter-of-fact responses. At times, your five-year-old may seem like a know-it-all, as he

Recognizing Rhyming

- Rhyming is an early reading and language skill that is used to help youngsters identify sounds and letters.

- Most five-year-olds enjoy rhyming games.

- Parents can promote rhyming skills by taking turns

- with their kids coming up with words that rhyme with "sun," for example. When options are exhausted, the other person chooses a simple word and the rhyming begins anew.

- Rhyming can also promote simple spelling as well.

Being Understood

- Others should now be able to understand what your five-year-old is saying. While occasional mispronunciations or similar speech slip-ups may still occur, your child should be evaluated by a speech therapist if people constantly indicate that they can't understand what is being said.

- Your child should now be able to speak using proper inflection and tone most of the time.

- Kids should be able to use their voice properly when asking questions, making a statement, or issuing an exclamation.

takes great delight in spouting out facts and opinions every chance he gets.

Your child's good memory means he has stored a significant amount of information, which he draws on to make a point or debate why something is the way it is. Having a command of language means that he is also able to describe things in detail and do some extended creative storytelling. Riddles and jokes are now more fun, as your child is able to recall the joke and share it with others for shared laughs.

Your child's use of grammar may still be incorrect much of the time, although he will often be able to catch what he says and then correct it on his own. Frequent mistakes should still be expected with more complex word choices and appropriate tenses.

Help foster your child's mastery of language by using bigger words and showing your youngster how there are many word choices that can be used to say similar things. Your child may also like learning new words for color variations, such as peach, beige, neon, and what it means when something shimmers.

Word Banks

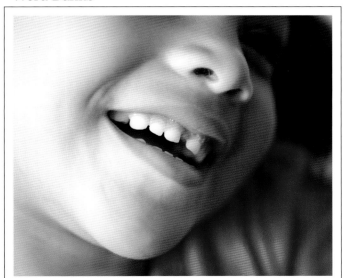

- Encourage your youngster to use different words that have the same or similar meaning by making a game out of it.

- Ask your child how many ways he can describe a "cat," for example, without using the actual word.

- When you use a larger or more complex word when speaking to your child, make sure you explain what the word means and how it is used in a sentence. Then ask your child to repeat it back to you.

Language-Building Skills

- Continue to read with your child on a daily basis. Kids who have an interest in reading and how the written word is used to express ideas will typically be more fluent in language.

- Explain the relationship between oral and written language.

- Ask your child to explain what a story is about, what the main ideas and characters are, and even how the story is structured.

WHAT TO EAT

Promote healthy eating choices that include enough calcium and iron for your child's growing body

Proper nutrition is vital to your child's overall health and well-being. Preschoolers should eat three healthy meals a day and two nutritious snacks. Her diet should include fruits and vegetables, lean meats, and low-fat dairy products, including a glass of low-fat milk at every meal. Limits should also be placed on high-fat and high-sugar foods, often found in fast foods or "convenience food" packaging.

Preschoolers, when given the choice, will quickly learn to prefer foods that they are served regularly, and parents often err in feeding kids "junk-style" foods because they are afraid they are not getting enough to eat otherwise. Kids given choices to eat what they want will quickly learn to bypass

Portions

- Portion control, combined with adequate physical activity, is one effective way to keep your child at an age-appropriate weight.

- Restaurants continue to "biggie-size" portions as a means to entice patrons and to market extra value. Parents often push too-big portions on their children and then push them to clean their plate.

- Keep mealtimes positive and don't force your child to eat something he doesn't want or to eat when he isn't hungry.

Healthy Options

- Provide your child with healthy choices and allow your child to experiment with various foods. Keep in mind a child who may not like something one day may love it a few months later.

- Don't focus too much on your child having a balanced diet at every meal, but rather whether he is receiving a balanced diet over an entire week.

- It is not necessary to feed your child a grain, vegetable, fruit, dairy, and meat each and every meal.

nutritional foods in favor of ones that are laden with calories, setting the stage for weight problems later.

When choosing what to serve your preschooler, make sure your child is receiving enough calcium, not just from milk, but from yogurt and cheese; is served plenty of grain products, vegetables, and fresh fruit; and has a diet that is moderate in sugars and salt and low in fat, saturated fats, and cholesterol. Don't forget to make sure that she gets enough iron for her growing body's requirements. What you eat should set a positive example as well.

ZOOM

Your child should consume about three servings of low-fat milk daily. And, while juice is okay, it should be 100 percent pasteurized fruit juice and not fruit drinks and should be limited to only four to six ounces daily. Drinking water should be encouraged for all other times, although a sports-type drink after playing soccer or other physical activity is okay.

Picky Eaters

- Most preschoolers go through bouts of picky eating, and parents may unwittingly exacerbate the situation by fussing over what their child eats.

- Your child should be served whatever the family eats. If your child won't eat what is served, then offer a piece of fruit or other healthy snack only until the next meal. Your child won't starve.

- Don't make the common mistake of becoming a short order cook for your child's dietary preferences.

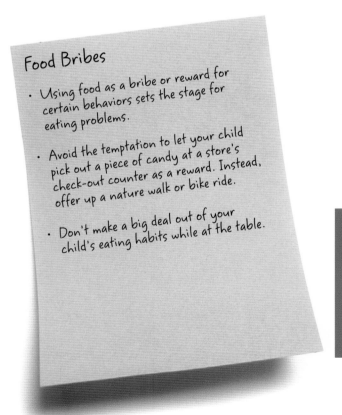

Food Bribes

- Using food as a bribe or reward for certain behaviors sets the stage for eating problems.

- Avoid the temptation to let your child pick out a piece of candy at a store's check-out counter as a reward. Instead, offer up a nature walk or bike ride.

- Don't make a big deal out of your child's eating habits while at the table.

NUTRITION

EATING OUT

With proper planning and nutritional choices fast food doesn't have to mean bad food

If you're like most families, you feel like you're constantly on the go, and life is all about getting from destination to destination. If you work outside of the home in addition to raising kids, you're caught trying to balance work and family life. Most often, that means your preschooler attends daycare or a similar caregiver setting while you're on the job. If your child

has begun participating in an enrichment activity, you have that to coordinate as well.

Today's hectic lifestyles often mean that nutritional meals sometimes get bypassed in the attempt to get everything done in a given day. The quickest solution is going through a drive-through and eating on the run. While that is fine on

Fast Food

- Preschoolers can sometimes be such picky eaters that parents push fattening foods on them initially to get them to eat. That notion backfires later!

- Having fattening, salty, or high-calorie food is okay at times, but look for healthier options that don't involve frying or sugar.

- Avoid feeding your child while in the car except in extreme situations. Potential choking risks can occur plus you're creating some bad eating habits that will be hard to break later.

Junk Food

- It's called junk food for a reason: These foods feature so-called empty calories or have very little to no nutritional value whatsoever. They might also be foods that are laden with salt, oils, and sugar but don't meet the nutritional needs of a growing child.

- Pre-packaged snack foods are often the worst, and serving sizes can be misleading. What appears to be a single serving is often two or more servings of foods packed with preservatives and almost unidentifiable ingredients.

occasion, nutritionists are increasingly becoming concerned that eating a nutritious meal is becoming the exception instead of the norm. So, what to do?

Eating on the go doesn't have to mean eating unhealthy, although additional planning may be needed to ensure proper nutrition. While an array of poor food choices are offered at every popular kid-friendly fast-food restaurant, healthier choices are also being offered. A junior hamburger or chicken nuggets can provide food basics when you're in a hurry, and aren't considered nutritional no-nos. It's what you order with them that can cause the problems.

While you may not be voted favorite parent, you'll be doing your kids a favor by requiring low-fat milk instead of juice, a soft drink, or a high-calorie milkshake, and fruit instead of French fries.

Packing a lunch doesn't always mean good nutrition is being served up either. Carefully read labels and look for nutritional value before choosing convenience-packed single-serve items that preschoolers often love. You'll always want to be sure you keep food at appropriate temperatures.

Brown Bagging It

- A low-fat meat-and-cheese or peanut butter sandwich, carrots and celery, fresh fruit, and perhaps a low-fat dessert can provide your child with a tasty and nutritional lunch. Add a carton of low-fat milk and your child's lunch is ideal!

- Caregivers indicate that much of what a parent packs for their preschool-age child's lunch is thrown away because portions are too big. Or, kids will eat their dessert and bypass the sandwich and fruit if given the option.

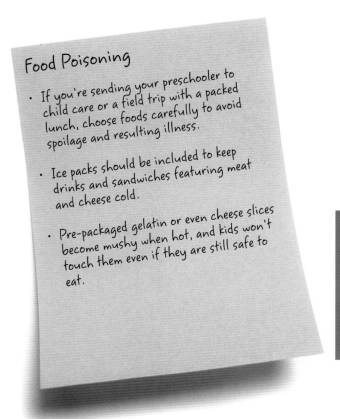

Food Poisoning

- If you're sending your preschooler to child care or a field trip with a packed lunch, choose foods carefully to avoid spoilage and resulting illness.

- Ice packs should be included to keep drinks and sandwiches featuring meat and cheese cold.

- Pre-packaged gelatin or even cheese slices become mushy when hot, and kids won't touch them even if they are still safe to eat.

TABLE MANNERS

Now is the time to teach proper mealtime behaviors to avoid embarrassment later

Early childhood educators commonly report that preschoolers have not been taught how to eat properly or how to behave while eating. The time to teach your child proper table manners—at home as well as out in public—is now . . . before school begins.

Why is it that so many parents haven't yet done so? Parents often point to the fact that their child has to be coaxed to eat and that short attention span, food pickiness, and clumsy use of utensils all contribute to putting off teaching table manners. The argument is that it is a big enough battle just to get their child to eat, so they've saved etiquette for a later lesson.

The truth is, however, that even very young children

Eating in a Group

- Mealtimes are very much a social time for preschoolers. It's a time for talking with friends but also presents opportunities for mischievous and inappropriate food behaviors.

- Continuously reinforce that talking with a mouthful of food, playing with food rather than eating it, and getting up from the table during mealtimes is not allowed.

- A common practice is for children to raise their hands if they need assistance with something when eating.

Preschooler Etiquette

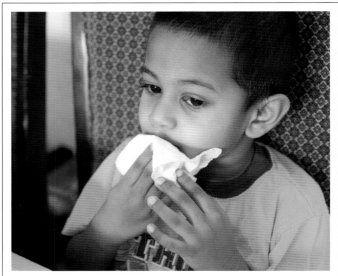

- Social eating behaviors— good and bad—are typically learned in daycare and similar settings. Ask your child's provider what rules they set for mealtimes, and if you like what you hear, make sure you reinforce those same behaviors at home.

- While many families bless each meal before eating, this is not a common practice at many daycare settings due to diverse religious observances. Your child can be taught that there are different rules in different situations.

typically behave in accordance with the expectations that are put before them. If your child knows that you'll let him eat with his fingers even when a fork or spoon is called for, then by all means he will do so. Playing with food, not sitting still, getting up from the table before everyone is done, and putting elbows (or other body parts) on the table are common offenses.

If you set the stage now for what is expected—such as joining the family for meals, saying "please" and "thank you" and other signs of respect, and keeping hands and feet to herself—you'll have a well-behaved child at holiday meals and when eating out in public. While you're at it, show your child how to properly place a napkin in her lap, to actually use it when needed, and to chew with her mouth closed. Mastery of mealtime basics now will save embarrassment later. Plus, your child's kindergarten teacher will thank you . . . again and again!

Independent Eating

- Parents provide their children a disservice by not encouraging independent eating at as early an age as possible.

- Don't hover over or nag a child who is attempting to use eating utensils correctly. Overlook small messes that may come from buttering bread or getting a serving from a bowl. That's how kids learn.

- When packing a lunch, don't use containers or pre-packaged foods that your child is unable to open by himself.

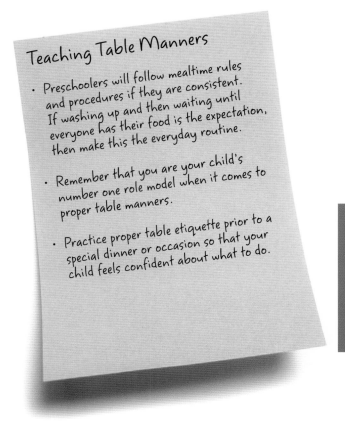

Teaching Table Manners

- Preschoolers will follow mealtime rules and procedures if they are consistent. If washing up and then waiting until everyone has their food is the expectation, then make this the everyday routine.

- Remember that you are your child's number one role model when it comes to proper table manners.

- Practice proper table etiquette prior to a special dinner or occasion so that your child feels confident about what to do.

FOOD ALLERGIES

"Big 8" foods cause most allergic reactions; parents and caregivers need to know what to do

Food allergies affect about 5 to 8 percent of young children. Infants, toddlers, and preschoolers are more likely to develop food allergies than older children because allergies typically occur early in life when digestive and immune systems are still immature.

Developing food allergies is greatly influenced by your family's medical history. Research has shown that children with an allergic parent have twice the risk of developing a food allergy than children without an allergic parent.

Ninety percent of all food allergy reactions are caused by the so-called "Big 8" foods. These include: eggs, fish, milk, peanuts, shellfish, soy, tree nuts, and wheat. Children sometimes

Food Intolerance

- Food intolerance (in contrast to food allergies) is a reaction that does not involve the immune system. Milk, chocolate, or monosodium glutamate (MSG) are common problematic foods.

- A child with lactose intolerance lacks the enzyme necessary to digest milk

sugar, and as a result he may experience abdominal pain, gas, or bloating.

- If your child starts exhibiting symptoms of food intolerance, begin tracking his reactions after consuming foods with food coloring, preservatives, and sulfites.

Food Allergy Testing

- Allergy shots don't usually work well for food allergies, so the best treatment is learning which foods to avoid.

- In addition to avoiding foods that cause those allergic reactions, a more thorough evaluation may be recommended.

- Allergists may conduct skin testing to determine reactions. Typically, parents prefer to wait until children are older.

- Another option is a radioallergosorbent test known as RAST. It checks for antibodies against certain foods your child may be allergic to.

outgrow allergies to certain foods, while others may stay allergic throughout their lifetime.

Food allergies are the result of the body's immune system believing that certain food is harmful. In order to protect the body, the immune system makes IgE antibodies. When the offending food is eaten, these antibodies and the chemical histamine are released, triggering allergic reactions that can affect the respiratory system, gastrointestinal tract, cardiovascular system, and skin.

Living with Allergies

- Children with severe allergic reactions, including life-threatening breathing difficulties, should wear a medical alert bracelet to notify others of this health condition.

- Parents should educate all family members, caregivers, and teachers about their child's food allergies.

- Teach your preschooler about his food allergy and that he must avoid foods he is allergic to.

- Your child (or teacher) may need to keep an epinephrine autoinjector (like an EpiPen) nearby at all times.

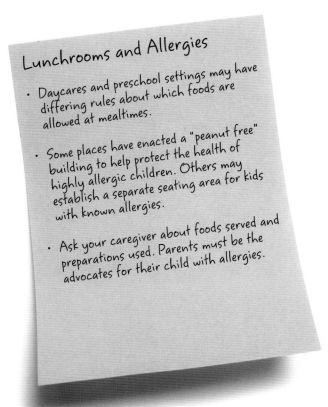

Lunchrooms and Allergies

- Daycares and preschool settings may have differing rules about which foods are allowed at mealtimes.

- Some places have enacted a "peanut free" building to help protect the health of highly allergic children. Others may establish a separate seating area for kids with known allergies.

- Ask your caregiver about foods served and preparations used. Parents must be the advocates for their child with allergies.

NUTRITION

FOOD FUN

Fun in the kitchen helps promote math, logic, problem-solving skills, and a sense of contribution

Stir up some fun in the kitchen with your preschooler. Don't mind the mess; your child will delight in participating in meal preparations. Let him help to select and shop for food, measure and pour in ingredients, and then serve up the result.

Early childhood educators agree that cooking can help to promote essential skills of math, logic, problem-solving, and togetherness. So, go ahead, and show your child how to crack an egg or use an electric mixer—under close supervision, of course! At the same time, maintain a focus on safety as well as proper food handling procedures. Do not let your preschooler anywhere near a hot stove or oven until he is older—most kitchen-related accidents involve scalding or

Young Cooks

- Always insist on proper hand-washing and clean food surfaces. It's a habit your child will hopefully keep in later years.

- Provide your preschooler with his own cooking utensils, such as a spatula and spoon, and even a child-size apron.

- Purchase a nonslip step-stool so your child can be at the right height for helping and observing you in action at the counter.

- Avoid overreacting to spills or messes. Accidents will happen!

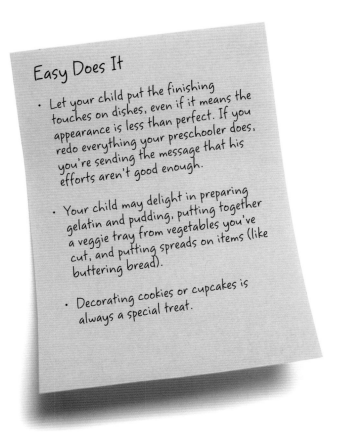

Easy Does It

- Let your child put the finishing touches on dishes, even if it means the appearance is less than perfect. If you redo everything your preschooler does, you're sending the message that his efforts aren't good enough.

- Your child may delight in preparing gelatin and pudding, putting together a veggie tray from vegetables you've cut, and putting spreads on items (like buttering bread).

- Decorating cookies or cupcakes is always a special treat.

164

burns. A second kitchen no-no for this age involves knives or sharp utensils. There's plenty to do in the kitchen without having your child attempt to cut or chop.

Studies have shown that children really like the rituals and together-time that come with cooking and eating together. Not only is cooking fun and tasty, but it is a lifelong skill that promotes nutritional and positive eating experiences later.

Family cooking can also be a relationship-builder between a grandparent and grandchild, especially if the elder member reveals some family cooking secrets!

Holiday Recipes

• There's a kid-friendly recipe available for practically every holiday. Half the fun is using your imagination to personalize it.

• Look for fun and easy food crafts like red and green gelatin squares with whipped topping for Christmas, eggs cooked in a heart shape for Valentine's Day, or putting popcorn into a plastic glove and decorating it with a spider ring and fingernails for Halloween.

• Food coloring can make ordinary edibles extraordinary and requires very little effort.

Healthy Delights

• Healthy foods can also be creative and fun. Let your child "decorate" a morning pancake by adding strawberry and banana slices or blueberries to make a smiley face.

• Use cute names for prepared dishes to promote experimentation with new foods. Topping a rib of celery with peanut butter, cheese or even low-fat dressing and then decorating with raisins, for example, is typically called "Ants on a Log."

• Most kids love making—and then drinking—healthy fruit smoothies.

NUTRITION

LUNCH BOXES

Safety, environmental-friendliness, and convenience are all factors worth considering with lunch boxes

Food is a big deal to most preschoolers. Just as important for many kids is the gear that holds the food. For a variety of reasons, the disposable brown bag simply won't do when packing meals for field trips or daycare. Preschoolers want a lunchbox that reflects the latest colors, designs, or even action heroes with matching ice packs and kid-friendly containers.

In most cases, parents are quick to oblige, as lunch carriers are typically inexpensive and last a long time.

Parents may also want the latest container products for different reasons. A paper lunch bag stuffed with food in plastic sandwich bags is certainly not eco-friendly, a concern of many environmentally conscious families. At the same

Lunch Boxes

- Do your homework before choosing a lunch box for your child. Safety should overrule any trend or character design.

- Determine whether your child's lunch will be refrigerated each day until mealtime. Not only will the answer influence what you

- pack, but what container or bag it should be packed in.

- Juices, liquids, or even food messes can create health and safety issues, and parents should not expect their child's caregiver to wipe out and clean up a lunch box after every meal.

Snack Containers

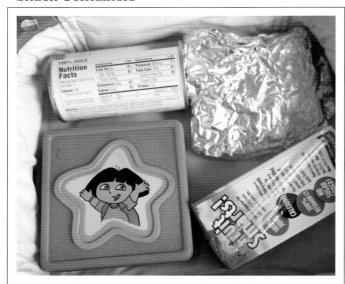

- Despite what she says, your youngster most likely won't eat anything that becomes melted, bruised, squished, or too hot or too cold. As such, having the right type of container for foods is extremely important.

- Finger foods in appropriate-size portions are convenient for kids to eat.

- Avoid lunches that have to be assembled, though simple foods like baby carrots with a side of low-fat ranch dressing can easily be packed and opened.

time, parents want the lunch bags to be safe and to be light enough for young hands to carry. Luckily, there are seemingly endless options on the market.

Look for waterproof sandwich and snack bags that can be simply wiped clean or laundered as needed, bags made from vintage and reclaimed fabrics, or ones that have a built-in place for a drink for added convenience.

Parents should also determine whether a food container is truly safe. While you may like the nostalgia of your child carrying your old metal lunch box or using soft insulated styles that were made even a few years ago, don't. Many of these styles have been tested and found to have unsafe levels of lead. Until recently some of the convenient hard plastic storage products have contained the chemical Bisphenol A. While BPA is still in use and is considered safe, there are still concerns and questions about its safety. The safest bet is to buy new products with labels that state they are lead-free and BPA-free or to pack lunches in canvas or similar bags.

Ice Packs

- Ice packs are considered a lunch box staple if your child's lunch isn't refrigerated. You may need more than one each day: one for your child's drink and one to keep food at proper temperature (such as a meat and cheese sandwich).

- Consider plastic containers featuring ice-pack lids that keep foods cool and safe from spoilage. Not only is a warm sandwich or melted cheese unappetizing, it may not be safe.

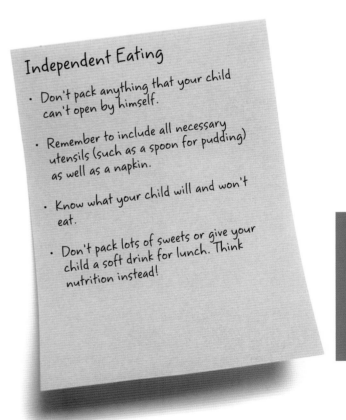

Independent Eating

- Don't pack anything that your child can't open by himself.

- Remember to include all necessary utensils (such as a spoon for pudding) as well as a napkin.

- Know what your child will and won't eat.

- Don't pack lots of sweets or give your child a soft drink for lunch. Think nutrition instead!

TYPICAL BEHAVIORS

Milestones vary greatly, but growing independence, sociability, and exploration are considered norms

When talking about "typical" behaviors of preschoolers, it's important to note that a wide variety of behaviors are considered normal milestones. The range of typical preschooler behavior is extremely diverse, especially when considering the development and maturity that occurs between when a child is three and five years of age.

Some traits, however, are considered relatively common. Some include egotism, where your child still thinks that he is in more control of people and his life than the other way around; pretend or fantasy; and how wishing something were a certain way is all that is needed to make it come true.

Many preschoolers are also quickly learning sociability,

Making Decisions

- Preschoolers can at times both strive and struggle when learning about appropriate choices, often depending on their attitude at the time.

- Offering choices teaches life skills and provides preschoolers with a desired sense of control.

- Parents should offer simple choices in which either option is acceptable. Avoid encouraging one selection over another.

- Preschoolers should be taught that they have to accept the choices they make.

Cooperation

- Cooperation—or lack of—is a typical behavior cited by many parents. Usually your preschooler isn't trying to be particularly unco-operative; it's just that he has other things he would much rather be doing.

- Parents can encourage cooperation by talking

to their child about why something is important and how everyone's help and participation is needed. In other words, the more you can tell your child about "why" something is needed, the greater the likelihood of acceptance.

listening, and language skills, and are constantly asking "why" in order to learn all about their world. They are heavily influenced by what they see and often relatively uninhibited. It is normal for your preschooler to have a sexual curiosity. As with danger and unsafe behaviors, parents will need to serve as guides for children to determine the differences between right and wrong, and which actions are considered inappropriate.

Find ways to boost your child's self esteem and confidence, especially when it comes to fostering a new skill or potentially natural talent.

Active Listening

- Parents may lament that their preschooler tunes them out. Active listening is a two-way process, and many parents nag, lecture, command, or yell at their child—resulting in a child getting turned off to listening.

- Engage in silly listening games, such as telling a secret, turning chores into a friendly contest, and utilizing "if and then" whenever possible. For example, say *if* your child will pick up his toys, *then* you'll go for a walk to the park.

Fantasy

- Fantasy and pretend most likely rules your child's life. Dramatics, costumes to some degree, and make-believe typically play an important role in your child's daily life.

- Parents should remember that their preschooler may truly believe that she is a fairy, a rock star, or race car driver, and that make-believe is a healthy and normal way to explore the world.

- Parents should balance teaching kids the difference between reality and pretend and letting them have magical moments.

INAPPROPRIATE BEHAVIORS
Kids have to learn the difference between right and wrong and what is considered appropriate

While there is significant leeway in acceptable behaviors for preschoolers, there are some actions that are always inappropriate. Inappropriate behaviors doesn't necessarily mean "bad"; keep in mind that preschoolers have to learn the boundaries of what is acceptable and appropriate, and the differences between right or wrong. When it comes to

teaching preschoolers the virtues of good behaviors versus ones that are considered selfish, embarrassing, antisocial, or even dangerous, parents should know that it is a continuing journey . . . and that every child makes mistakes or occasionally demonstrates inappropriate behaviors.

Inconsistency also contributes to a child's confusion over

Embarrassing Behaviors

- Parents find certain behaviors more embarrassing or unacceptable than their children. It is your job to help teach your child why certain actions should be considered inappropriate.

- Common embarrassing behaviors that require conversations include pick-

ing the nose, playing with the genitals, being gross in some way, and belching on purpose.

- Kids should also be taught that they shouldn't comment about others (such as, "She is fat!" or "He looks funny!").

Antisocial

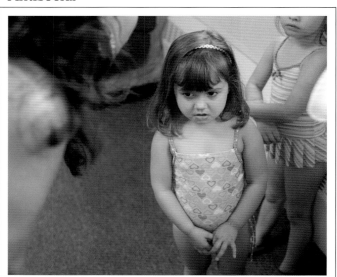

- Many preschoolers adopt a huffy or pouting behavior, often dramatically running away from the group with the expectation that someone will seek them out to comfort them and eventually give in to their wish.

- Some preschoolers may "diss" peers they don't

feel like being social with by ignoring them or not acknowledging greetings or conversations.

- Parents must continuously stress the importance of being polite and respectful to others.

when something is considered acceptable and when it is not. Parents sometimes have differing standards between behaviors at home versus ones out in public. A common example of this is a child running around in his underwear at home but not being allowed to do the same at daycare. From a child's point of view, why not? If you think about the number of "exceptions" we allow our kids to make (often due to circumstances that benefit parents or are considered critical), then it's easy to understand why kids don't pick up the nuances of why situations might differ, and along with them, the rules.

Aggression

At the same time, extremely aggressive behaviors (such as physical actions or bullying) or highly inappropriate ones (such as spitting on another child) can never be condoned. Parents and caregivers will need to take swift action to prevent future incidents. Many times, behaviors can be corrected with adult intervention.

The worst things adults can do when it comes to a preschool-age kid exhibiting inappropriate behaviors, are to explain them away, ignore them, or somehow justify a child's actions as acceptable when they aren't.

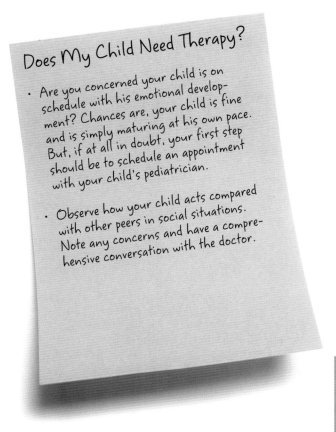

Does My Child Need Therapy?

- Are you concerned your child is on schedule with his emotional development? Chances are, your child is fine and is simply maturing at his own pace. But, if at all in doubt, your first step should be to schedule an appointment with your child's pediatrician.

- Observe how your child acts compared with other peers in social situations. Note any concerns and have a comprehensive conversation with the doctor.

- By age three, your child should understand that biting, hitting, or other aggressive behaviors like kicking or scratching are never acceptable.

- Be on the watch for bullying behaviors that begin to emerge during the preschool-age years.

Whether your child is the one bullying or is being bullied, immediate intervention is a must. Remember that girls are as apt to be bullies as boys.

- Teach your child ways to "work off steam" or calm down without using aggression.

171

BEHAVIORAL MANAGEMENT
Avoid inconsistencies about what you find acceptable, discuss expectations, and heap on the praise!

What is the most successful way to motivate and encourage preschoolers? That's easy: Kids learn best and try hardest when they are recognized for doing things right. Usually, kids aren't naughty on purpose. Rather, they typically misbehave because they don't truly understand that what they are doing is considered inappropriate, or they lack self-control or maturity, or use certain behaviors as a way to get attention.

Parents sometimes set their kids up for lapses in acceptable behavior because they are inconsistent with their parenting approach. Parents may laugh at something their child does at home and then become appalled when the child exhibits the same behavior at daycare or while out in public.

Positive Reinforcement

- There's a fine line between positive reinforcement, deserved praise, and letting your child think that everything she does is a masterpiece or practically perfect!

- The key is offering encouragement without being overly complimentary of your child's first attempts at something—not always an easy balancing act.

- Give your child your full attention. Don't look at your cell phone or read something at the same time. You want your child to feel his efforts are valued.

Modeling Expectations

- Don't expect your child to do something that you can't do yourself . . . unless it pertains to an athletic skill or similar that you just don't know how to do. In those cases, once your child learns something, ask her to teach you related skills!

- Don't fib or say not-so-nice comments in front of your child and then tell her that she should always tell the truth and never talk about others. Your child will quickly pick up on the double standard.

Kids also are quick to pick up on a parent's eye contact and whether a loved one is truly paying attention to what is being said. Preschoolers can have their feelings hurt quite easily by a parent who isn't truly listening, and may act out as a result.

Parents should be consistent with their expectations and in discussing and outlining rules that can help a child succeed socially and emotionally. Have heartfelt discussions in private about proper ways to act before each social setting. Don't wait until others are around or after a misdeed has occurred to correct or admonish your child.

Taking time to answer any questions or addressing any concerns beforehand is also recommended. Establish what the consequences will be if your child doesn't act appropriately, and then follow through with what you say. If you continue to give your child second chances, he will learn to push to the limit and go as far as he can before he gets in real trouble.

Peer Appropriateness

- As your preschooler enters preschool or daycare, ask about any particular rules that your child may need to know about that could be inadvertently broken.

- Many child care settings have a "no touch" rule so that actions are not misconstrued. Your child may have to lighten up on the friendly hugs and hand-holding that are common at this stage.

- Other behaviors such as sticking a tongue out at a peer are always no-nos.

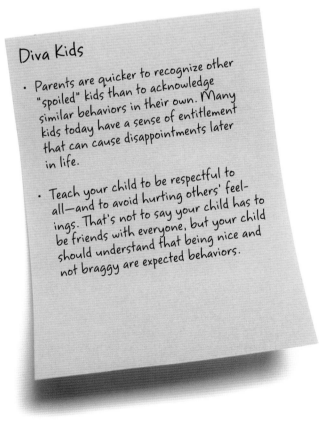

Diva Kids

- Parents are quicker to recognize other "spoiled" kids than to acknowledge similar behaviors in their own. Many kids today have a sense of entitlement that can cause disappointments later in life.

- Teach your child to be respectful to all—and to avoid hurting others' feelings. That's not to say your child has to be friends with everyone, but your child should understand that being nice and not braggy are expected behaviors.

DISCIPLINARY APPROACHES

The goal of discipline is to teach a lesson while maintaining positive interactions with your child

Knowing how to effectively discipline your child should be well thought out beforehand, and not something you do as a heated reaction or on the spur-of-the-moment. It's how you respond and what they take away from the particular experience that sets the foundation for loving interactions later.

While there are many touted or preferred approaches to discipline, there really is no single one that works above all others. No matter which approach you choose, the key is consistency. That should apply to everyone who cares for your child, if at all possible. If you do it one way and your partner does it another, or if you have certain behavioral expectations with designated consequences and a grandparent

Time-Outs

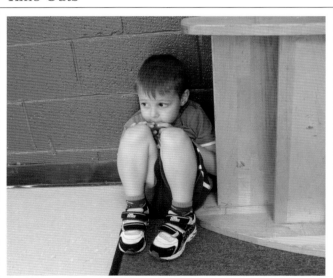

- The popular time-out disciplinary method removes a child from inflammatory situations to allow him an opportunity to calm down and regain self-control.

- A time-out location should be chosen ahead of time and should be a place that is uninteresting but not scary to a child.

- Time-outs should be kept brief: one minute for each year of age is recommended.

- Consider using a timer. If your child leaves the time-out area, reset the timer.

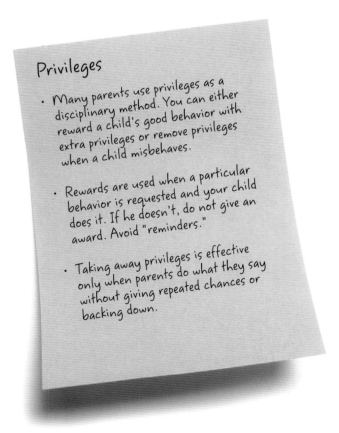

Privileges

- Many parents use privileges as a disciplinary method. You can either reward a child's good behavior with extra privileges or remove privileges when a child misbehaves.

- Rewards are used when a particular behavior is requested and your child does it. If he doesn't, do not give an award. Avoid "reminders."

- Taking away privileges is effective only when parents do what they say without giving repeated chances or backing down.

doesn't enforce them, that also sets the stage for conflicts.

Parents also need to exercise care that they don't use hurtful words, yell, or physically grab onto a child and yank their small bodies around, potentially causing injury. If you feel like your child has pushed your buttons to the point that you're about to lose control, then put your child in her bedroom and take a few minutes to calm down and regain control of your own anger and emotions before re-engaging with your child.

 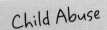
Spankings

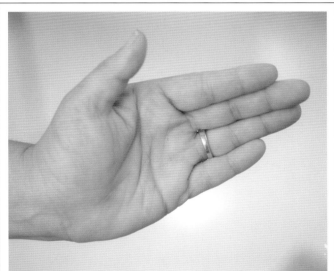

- Spankings are not recommended, although studies show more parents spank than will admit it. Spankings may encourage aggression in your child and result in behavioral and psychological issues later.

- "Swatting" a child's hand or rear end occurs more frequently and usually is the result of a defiant or unsafe action that needs to cease immediately. If you do this, be sure to talk calmly to your preschooler about his undesired behavior immediately afterward so your child can learn from the experience.

Child Abuse

- An action doesn't have to be intentional to be considered child abuse.

- Child abuse doesn't have to be physical or result from neglect. Words just as much as actions can inflict lasting wounds.

- According to studies, incidents of child abuse are reported an average of every ten seconds and three children die every day as a result of such abuse.

- Support groups and help are available in most communities.

PARENTING TIPS

Teach your child about individual rights but also that your rules and expectations are absolutes

An important lesson parents should teach their preschoolers is to know their individual rights. Child abuse can potentially occur in any situation where an adult figure has responsibility over a child. A kid who is taught that he is unique, that he has a right to be safe, and that certain things are considered acceptable while others are not is more likely to tell someone about uncomfortable or dangerous situations.

Kids always need to know that they have a loved one who they can trust to care for them and keep them safe. They should feel comfortable discussing anything without fear of judgment or punishment. They should also know that their parents and caregivers also have rights and responsibilities

Giving In

Resistance

- Parents often admit that they give in to their child's incessant requests, especially if it avoids the dreaded tantrums or whining behaviors. What they may not realize, however, is that they're creating a hard-to-break cycle of relinquishing control to their child.

- Before a situation arises, strategize ways to prevent your child from becoming a so-called egomaniac. Calmly discuss expectations and rules with your child in a calm and positive way, and then hold firm when the inevitable occurs.

- Some kids resist doing anything new or different, and as a result may miss out on new experiences or opportunities.

- Kids need to be taught that not every activity, errand, or chore is fun, but that many are necessary nonetheless.

- Avoid asking your child if he wants to do something or help, when you don't really mean to give her a choice. If she says "No," you've set up a potentially confrontational conversation.

as well. The more a child understands the roles of others and expectations of himself, the less likely that there will be conflicts and power struggles.

Parents should make sure a child understands the difference between being cared for and being entitled to anything he wants, however. A child needs to know that adults are in charge, that it's not all about him, that your rules and expectations are there for a reason (such as safety), and that your job is to keep everyone healthy, active, and protected from harm.

Household Pets

- Most households have some type of pet. The most common are dogs or cats.

- Don't expect your preschooler to truly be in charge of caring for an animal. While he may enjoy giving food or water to the pet (usually with prompting), he is too young to have full responsibility.

- Teach your child how to act around animals, and to never approach or pet animals he doesn't know.

Overscheduling Kids

- Kids who are too busy to enjoy some unstructured play or down time are typically less happy and well adjusted than those who do.

- Kids can become stressed and overloaded from hopping from one activity to another, especially if they attend a daycare or similar child care on most days.

- While your child may be ready for an enrichment program, limit it to one activity at a time.

PARENTING OTHER PEOPLE'S KIDS

Knowing when to speak up or intervene presents challenges for parents with differing styles

Who hasn't observed out-of-control or unsupervised kids at a party or playgroup, and nobody seems to be doing anything? This is a common lament of parents of young children. Too often parents wait as long as possible before taking any corrective action in the hope that the child settles down or that the kid's parent intervenes. But waiting and hoping can

actually allow the bad behavior to spiral even more out of control. So, what should you do?

Since many frenzied behaviors can quickly escalate and become potentially harmful situations, most early educators recommend that parents take swift and calm action as soon as a problem develops. If the adult in charge is present, speak

When You're in Charge

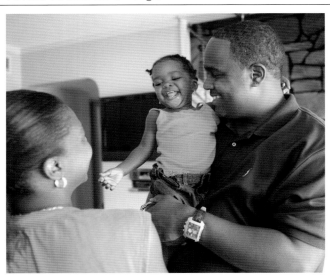

- Before entertaining other kids at your home (as in a playdate), consider having a conversation with the other parents to outline expectations and approaches first.

- Talk about discipline tactics you use, food that you will

be serving (to avoid any allergy concerns or restrictions), and what you will do if kids begin to misbehave.

- Keep initial playdates short and have the other parent's cell phone number in case you need to call.

When Your Child Is a Guest

- Make sure you are comfortable before leaving your preschooler with anyone else. If in doubt, plan to remain at the event.

- Don't be afraid to ask questions. Ask which movies or shows will be watched, whether firearms are kept

at the home, and about any pets or other health or safety factors.

- Don't leave out details about your child that are important, such as your kid often forgets to go potty when he is having too much fun.

up and ask them to do something in the interest of all kids. If not, be prepared to step in.

Usually, simply removing the child from the situation and presenting him to the parent or caregiver with a simple explanation of what was happening is all that is needed. Be prepared for tears or a tantrum or even a parent who becomes upset over your involvement.

The situation may become trickier if a caregiver has a different set of expectations and parenting approach than you do. For example, you may not allow your child to throw rocks at the playground while other parents don't mind their child doing so as long as they are not thrown at kids directly. Or, a parent may turn a blind eye to their child who keeps cutting in line, explaining it away as a "typical kid thing."

While you should choose your battles wisely, it is important to maintain consistency with your own child, even if it involves a conversation about not doing certain things you find unacceptable, even when other parents allow it. It's a lesson your child will learn over and over.

Disciplining Other People's Kids

- If a playdate is at your house, talk to your guest about your "parent rules" and expectations as soon as they arrive.

- Other kids may try and challenge you, saying they are allowed to do something at their home that you don't allow, or even using the "You're not my parent!" excuse.

- If the situation cannot be resolved, end the playdate calmly, and talk to your child about why after his friend leaves.

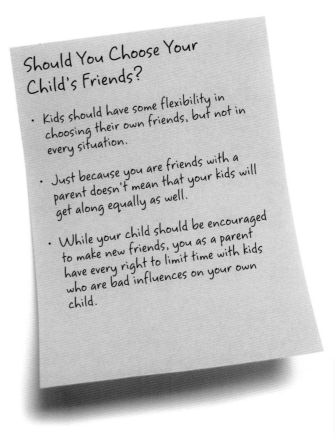

Should You Choose Your Child's Friends?

- Kids should have some flexibility in choosing their own friends, but not in every situation.

- Just because you are friends with a parent doesn't mean that your kids will get along equally as well.

- While your child should be encouraged to make new friends, you as a parent have every right to limit time with kids who are bad influences on your own child.

179

EUROPEAN LEARNING PHILOSOPHIES

Preschool pedagogies often focus on the unique gifts of each child through arts and exploration

Most early childhood education philosophies are influenced by innovative ideas and learning philosophies from European teachers.

Maria Montessori was an Italian physician and educator who developed her method of teaching youngsters in the early part of the twentieth century. A great many preschools still follow the "Montessori method" of preschool today. The Association of Montessori Internationale adheres to the traditional Montessori program teachings while the American Montessori Society incorporates more recent materials and methods. Montessori emphasizes a child's exploration of knowledge at his own individual pace and encourages the

Montessori

- This philosophy emphasizes individuality combined with self initiative and independence, regardless of ability level, learning style, or maturity.

- Preschoolers are able to initiate, explore, and progress through an ordered series of structured or spontaneous learning activities at their own self-initiated pace.

- Manipulatives emphasize the use of all senses for learning.

- This discipline utilizes true-life situations in preparation for the future.

Reggio Emilia

- This whole-child philosophy of early childhood education encourages the building of thinking skills and collaborative problem solving while retaining each individual's "voice."

- The name refers not to a person, but to a city in northern Italy. Parents in surrounding villages established this philosophy after World War II with the belief that children form who they are as individuals in the early years of development.

- The program is based on principles of respect, responsibility, and community.

use of senses to learn along with initiative and independence.

The Reggio Emilia preschool philosophy also originated in Italy. This whole-child system emphasizes art, creativity, and the child's interests and overall environment.

The Waldorf program is based on the principles developed by Austrian educator Rudolf Steiner. Many Waldorf programs begin in preschool and may continue through graduation. It focuses on developing a child's intelligence in harmony with natural aspects of the world and environment. Creativity and use of natural materials are emphasized.

ZOOM

Most preschools have a written philosophy statement, which lets prospective families better understand the center's learning environment and goals. Look for phrases such as "theme-based," "individual-paced," or "cooperative learning" along with how curriculum may be aligned with recommended standards. Most preschool programs have a daily schedule, so ask to see it.

Waldorf

- This pedagogy emphasizes a child's intellectual powers in harmony with emotions and physical aspects of his nature.

- The typically group-oriented programs include much creative activity and emphasize use of natural materials in the classroom.

- The program encourages the development of children's sense of truth, beauty, and goodness.

- The aim is to inspire a lifelong love of learning so that students are able to fully develop their unique capacities.

Ensuring a good fit

- Just because a particular preschool program is considered renowned in your area doesn't mean it will be right for your child.

- A positive experience at preschool is more likely if your child's particular learning style is compatible with a program's philosophy.

- An important consideration is whether your child likes learning independently and at his own pace or prefers a more structured, active approach.

DEVELOPMENT STYLE

Look for programs that offer age-appropriate instruction and whose philosophies meet needs of your child

Development style just refers to what many preschool programs determine to be developmentally appropriate for the kids in their care. Don't think that common terms such as "child-centered" or "play-based" means unstructured or unorganized. Many preschools use these descriptions to mean a developmental approach, which is perhaps the most

common style of instruction for early childhood education.

While general philosophies of learning may seem similar, parents need to probe into a program's particular style and approach to determine whether its overall classroom and learning environment is a match for their child.

An important consideration is the role that educators play

Classroom Groupings

- Classroom organization doesn't have to be determined by a child's age, although this is the most common way.

- Many centers cluster kids by interests, learning preferences, and even how they respond to varying teachers' styles of instruction in order to provide the maximum potential to learn.

- Some preschools establish "family groups" with children of multiple ages, similar to a home setting, rather than having only same-age peers. The belief is that it encourages cooperative learning and helping others.

Bank Street

- New York's Bank Street College of Education was founded in 1916 with the belief that learning through experience and utilizing a child-centered and developmental approach with teachers as facilitators provides the best opportunity for kids to learn.

- The name is considered synonymous with being a leader in early childhood education. Today, Bank Street College offers a spectrum of education ranging from a school for children and family center, a graduate school, a division of continuing education, and a publications and media group.

in the teaching environment. These roles can differ greatly.

Ask how instructors are utilized and what the instructor-to-child ratio is for each classroom. Don't settle on the center's overall average ratio; you want to know specifically how many kids to how many trained educators are in the classroom your child would be in. If the program uses aides, ask about their purpose. Extra helping hands can be great, but you want to make sure a fully qualified early childhood educator is actively engaged with students. Ask about the average tenure of instructors as well.

Head Start

- Head Start is a federally funded child development program of the U.S. Department of Health and Human Services. It began in 1965. Programs for children ages three to five are free and are primarily for qualifying low-income families and homeless children. Services are also offered to children with disabilities.

- The program's purpose is to provide education, health, and social services with the goal of ensuring participants are ready to start school.

- Local Head Start programs can be found throughout the country.

HighScope

- The HighScope educational approach was founded in 1970 and is perhaps best known for its research on the lasting effects of preschool education and its preschool curriculum approach.

- HighScope emphasizes direct, hands-on experiences with people, objects, events, and ideas. Its mission is to lift lives through education.

- Active learning—whether planned by adults or initiated by children—is the central element of the curriculum. It includes a balanced approach to adult-child interaction, called "intentional teaching."

PARENT PARTICIPATION

Your availability to volunteer time and efforts may influence choice of early education program

Of course you want to be involved in your child's life. What parent doesn't? Other demands on your time, however, such as employment outside of the home or balancing family needs overall, may impact the level of participation and influence child care.

Parental involvement is always encouraged and often requested with any activity involving preschool-age children. Having a small adult-to-child ratio helps keeps everyone safer, focused, and overall happier. While most daycare centers, preschool programs, and other child care facilities invite parents to help out as often as they like, other programs require a certain level of parental participation in order for a child to attend.

Co-op Preschools

- The first parent co-op preschool was founded in 1916, and the concept remains popular today. It is an organization that is owned or managed by members of the group.

- Parents don't just drop their kids off with a professional staff member for care. In co-ops, parents must take responsibility for the school and are required to work regularly in the classroom.

- Parents may also perform other tasks, ranging from building maintenance, doing laundry, and preparing snacks.

Home Schooling

- Some parents opt against choosing a preschool-age program to meet their child's educational and social needs and provide that instruction themselves.

- While the term "homeschooling" primarily refers to school-age children, there is an array of curricula for parents to utilize to efficiently prepare their child for kindergarten at home.

- Homeschooling support groups often coordinate field trips and other enrichment-style activities to provide additional parent help along with social opportunities for children.

Some programs assign parents duties that may or may not involve their child's classroom directly. The notion is that it takes everyone working together and having a personal stake in a program to truly make a child's overall experience there successful.

When considering an early education program for your child, begin by being honest with yourself about your availability to help out. Are you going to be able to volunteer to chaperone field trips, work in the classroom, and do whatever is needed or are you barely able to adjust your schedule in order to make it to your child's special production? It's no reflection on your individual parenting skills if your job or schedule doesn't allow frequent participation, but it can influence which type of program you should consider.

Parents should also plan to stay on-premises and available when their preschooler begins enrichment-style activities. Typically, programs such as dance, sports, music lessons, or similar are less than one hour in length. Also, if your child chooses not to participate or becomes disruptive, you may be asked to remove him from the class.

Enrichment

- While not considered child care per se, many preschoolers are under the care of trained (or not) individuals who serve as their coach, leader, teacher, or supervisor in enrichment-style activities.

- A person may have training in the skill being taught but may have only basic parenting skills in terms of watching over kids.

- You should plan to stay with your child during these activity periods, not only from a safety perspective, but to lend a helping hand.

Parent Days Out

- These programs were formerly called "Mom's Day Out," but most are now generic in recognition that primary caregivers may also be dads.

- Programs are typically operated by churches or community-based groups. Adults usually possess basic child care skills but may not be educators by profession.

- This type of care gives parents a chance to run errands, go to appointments, or take a break, child-free. It is usually at a set rate for a few hours at a time on designated days.

PRESCHOOL PREP

Parents seeking enrollment in coveted primary schools often turn to academic prep programs

In addition to early education programs that follow ascribed philosophies such as Montessori, there are numerous other preschool prep centers that emphasize academics and kindergarten readiness in a more formal structure.

Often, these programs have a particular area of focus that parents want their children to begin learning at a young age.

Some preschool prep programs are religion-based so kids learn about their particular religion and beliefs along with academics before beginning primary school. Some focus on immersion skills, such as learning two languages. Typically all prep programs are academic-oriented.

Most early educators maintain that rigorous preschool

Academic

- Academic-focused preschools tout that they prepare youngsters for kindergarten in all aspects.

- Routine and structure is more common, but learning is typically still presented in an interactive and engaging fashion.

- A primary focus is on reading skills. Many preschoolers who attend an academic preschool begin kindergarten possessing strong pre-reading skills.

- Math is another focus, with counting as well as basic addition and subtraction skills taught and practiced.

Religious

- Parents who want their child to begin religious instruction along with learning academic skills often turn to religious preschool programs.

- Enrollment in a private faith-based program provides for greater religious freedoms and practices—

such as bible study and formal prayer—than when a child attends a public preschool.

- Nutritional needs and holiday observances based on religious practices can be better met and potential conflicts from differing philosophies minimized.

programs aren't necessary as preschoolers are already receptive to learning and gain knowledge simply through their everyday exposure to new ideas and activities. For parents who live in highly competitive areas or who have certain goals for their child, however, a more formal preschool curriculum is desired.

Preparatory programs are typically more expensive than regular preschools or similar care programs and admission is often limited. Many prep programs require interviews with the family and testing of a child before admittance.

Immersion

- Parents who speak more than one language often place their child in an immersion-based program to provide their preschooler with early learning of a second, and even a third, language.

- Studies show that the younger a child, the more easily a second language is learned.

- Immersion programs are also offered in particular subject areas, such as music, art, or science, to help foster a child's natural talent at the same time that academics are being learned.

Public Versus Private

- Numerous studies support the notion that it is the individual teacher—not the program itself—that contributes most to the overall success and academic readiness of individual children.

- If your child feels an emotional attachment to and strong trust of his teacher, he is more likely to focus and engage in active learning.

- The power of a teacher can mean the difference between your preschooler loving or hating preschool and all that it entails, so make sure the relationship is positive and successful.

PRESCHOOL COSTS

High costs of child care mean many quality programs are out of reach for most families

In many other countries, a free quality preschool education is provided for all children beginning at ages three or four. That's not true in the United States, however. American children are guaranteed a free public education beginning with kindergarten. Free programs like Head Start are available to qualifying families, but for the rest of the population, child

care is expensive. Annual costs and related fees can put a staggering dent in an often already-tight family budget.

According to a 2009 report by the National Association of Child Care Resources and Referral Agencies (NACCRRA), an American family with a four-year-old pays between $4,055 and $11,680 in annual fees. Further, the price of child care

Tuition

- You may be asked to pay administrative fees to have your child's application reviewed and, in select cases, to secure an interview for your child. Many programs charge a one-time enrollment fee, which can range from as little as $25 to up to several hundreds of dollars.

- Ask about discounts for paying by the month or even a whole year at a time. There may be enough of a discount to make it worthwhile.

- Some programs charge a sliding scale depending on a family's total income.

Clothing and Supplies

- Uniforms are sometimes required and may range from simple solid-color, polo-style shirts and khaki pants or skirts to custom purchased items. A particular-style shoe may also be required.

- Some programs require particular backpacks and roll-up nap bedding.

- Expect to pay mandatory supply fees at least once, but often several times, each school year. In addition, parents may be asked to restock classrooms with tissues, pencils, and other materials that children go through rather quickly.

is rising faster than inflation in many areas. In many cases, monthly child care expenses are as high or higher than the average amount that parents spend on food—especially when there is more than one young child in the family.

These costs typically don't include extra fees and enrichment-style activities that many parents consider an important aspect of a preschooler's world. Rates paid in urban areas are higher than in suburban and rural areas of the country. The costs of high-quality care from accredited or specialty programs are typically even higher—up to more than 30 percent higher.

So, what do most families do? Many hunker down and scrimp everywhere else so that they can afford a quality preschool program. Some families may choose to have a partner stay home. Others choose less expensive child care options, such as family child care or using family members to watch their kids while they work.

While many family care centers raise children in a protective, nurturing, and educational environment, in-home caregivers are not always licensed. This means that the home environment and practices are not evaluated or inspected.

The "Extras"

- Make sure you have a clear understanding of any required extras that may be assessed throughout the year.

- Programs may include enrichment electives that are not always considered part of the base tuition. While you may be able to opt-out of these activities, some schools may frown upon a child not receiving the additional instruction.

- Field trips can be exciting for kids but may come at a price for parents. Often, extra charges are assessed.

Dependent Care Deductions

- Don't forget that dependent care expenses can be deducted from your income taxes each year. It's surprising how many families don't deduct these expenses from their tax returns—essentially throwing away money.

- See if your employer offers a flexible spending account, which allows you to set aside a portion of your earnings to pay for qualified expenses. This money is not taxed, resulting in significant savings.

DAYCARE VS. PRESCHOOL

Differences exist between general child care and care that specializes in preparing a preschooler for school

Are there differences between daycare and preschool, and if so, what are they? Knowing what to look for and what you should or shouldn't expect with services varies with what type of program you are considering. The terms can be confusing and even misleading because "preschool" is often used interchangeably for what is essentially daycare (i.e.,

child care) for preschool-age children.

That's a significant difference from a pure preschool program, which typically features a more structured curriculum to prepare students to be successful when they start school. Even more confusing is many daycare programs offer in-house preschool programs, usually for 4-year-olds.

Enrollment Versus Applicant

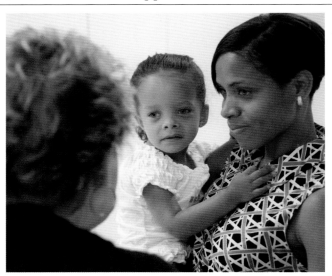

- Most daycare centers accept any normally developing child. Enrollment is accepted year-round.

- Private preschools accept applications and then screen and interview potential students before determining acceptance. Enrollment is usually limited to either once or twice annually.

- A limited number of scholarships are usually offered at private preschools for qualifying families.

- Quality child care services may not always be available for children with special needs.

Screening

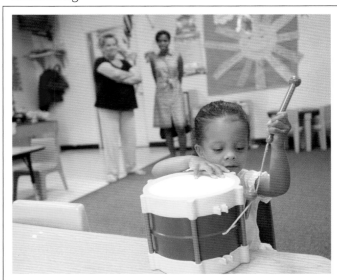

- Screenings are rare for child care and public preschool programs. Placement is determined by age group, and in certain settings, by gender.

- What do administrators look for when screening young children for admission to a private preschool?

Surprisingly, it's not necessarily academic readiness. Interviewers look for kids who demonstrate self-control through sitting still, receptiveness to learning, and ability to focus. Interviewers may also observe the dynamics between parent and child.

Daycare is a generic term that is used to describe child care for infants through school-age primary school kids before and after school. Daycare centers may be individually owned and operated or may be a franchised program with various locations across a particular region or even the country. Workers may or may not have early advanced childhood training, although typical training is more likely to consist of certifications and safety skills.

By comparison, a preschool program typically refers to early academics with an emphasis on learning. That doesn't mean kids don't get ample play time and exposure to enrichment-style activities, because they do. However, preschool programs are just that: They specialize in the preschool-age child. Teachers in structured preschool programs are often educated in early childhood education.

Preschool and daycare aren't the only child care options. Parents can also consider using family home care (where a child is taken to a person's house) where he is cared for along with other children. Using a nanny, au pair, or babysitter can also provide safe care.

Expectations

- Mastery of social and emotional skills along with self-regulatory abilities is emphasized at any child care setting involving preschool-age children. Teachers and caregivers alike agree that this is a primary focus for overall social success and transition to kindergarten.

- Preschool prep programs typically have a greater emphasis on academics. Expectations are often that kids attending preschool prep programs will demonstrate higher skills in reading, writing and math at an earlier age than other peers.

Is Preschool Even Necessary?

- While kids regularly attending preschool have an academic advantage when entering kindergarten, research shows that other kids eventually catch up when placed together in a similar primary school program.

- Preschool helps kids to develop stronger skills concerning appropriate behaviors, making friends, paying attention, and even eating in a group environment. Children who have only limited exposure to peers may struggle with the adjustment to a classroom setting initially, but can still learn and thrive.

INDEPENDENCE

Loosen up and let your child experience the rewards and frustrations of making decisions

Except for occasional twangs of sentimentality about when their child was a wee infant, parents are typically delighted about their preschooler's strides in independence. After all, what's not to like about telling your child to do something and having her actually be able to do it—and willingly!

Independence also involves your being able to have

meaningful exchanges so you can explain the "why, what, how, and when" of things in a way your child can understand. She is now truly able to comprehend how things relate to her world.

Your child may even begin the very normal phase of separation and detachment from you, especially as she edges toward beginning kindergarten. Your child still craves your

Self-Entertainment

- Your preschooler may begin to like "just hanging out" with nothing structured to do. As your child's daily routine becomes busier at the same time maturity increases, just doing nothing is okay at times. Just watch that inactivity doesn't become the rule.

- Your child may enjoy playing independently with toys rather than always requiring someone to interact with her.

- Encourage daydreaming and using her imagination as various forms of self-entertainment. Ask your child to let you know what she's thinking about.

Skills

- Encourage your child to complete as much of his daily routine as possible without reminders. Most kids like the ability to choose their clothes, straighten their room, and perform general hygiene care without a parent hovering over their every move.

- Reward your child's progress in improved independence skills rather than just the result. Avoid the common parenting mistake of either criticizing or redoing a child's efforts. Instead, talk about how well she is doing and show your support.

attention and approval, but is also quite happily able to make decisions for herself and to play independently. You might even be able to relax a bit when supervising your child—although vigilance is still needed.

An older preschooler may actually crave some personal time rather than being in your face or hanging on your leg every waking moment, and may make choices about what to do or even what to eat like never before. Congratulations are in order for a parenting job well done when your child says, "I can do it," and does!

Privacy

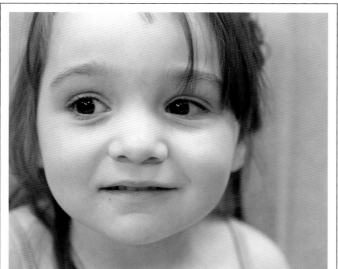

- You may notice your kid begins occasionally craving personal space.

- Many parents get caught off-guard with their child's seemingly sudden need for privacy. Unless safety dictates having direct supervision, begin giving her privacy while getting dressed or undressed or using the bathroom.

- Bath times must still be directly supervised to protect against drowning.

- This is a good time to talk about respecting your body and what personal space means to others.

············· YELLOW ● LIGHT ··············

Be careful that you are not inadvertently undermining your child's growing sense of independence. Parents are so used to "doing for" their child that they may struggle at times to just let go, and let preschoolers experience decision making, challenges, and even small failures on their own. That's the best way to learn. Your child also needs to learn how to handle situations when things don't go the way he anticipated.

Fostering Independence

- Provide the means for your child to demonstrate independence. If your child likes to create pictures, give her an art area stocked with art supplies, for example.

- Consider letting your child awaken to her own alarm clock rather than relying on you for a morning wake-up call.

- Let your kid try her own solutions to problems before you insist on following your own.

SELF-CONTROL

Maintaining focus and sitting still without bothering others are traits needed for school

A certain amount of the wiggles and giggles are absolutely normal. After all, your preschooler is just a young kid! At the same time, one of the signs of kindergarten-readiness is a youngster's ability to control himself. Signs of self-control can be demonstrated by a child sitting in a chair quietly when told and not flailing or running around, and by listening to a teacher's instructions instead of incessantly touching, moving, and examining objects every chance he gets.

Not surprisingly, kindergarten teachers often lament that teaching kids to keep their hands, feet, and "stuff" to themselves is the greatest challenge and most common distraction at school. All kids get restless at times, that's why recess

Touching Others

- Touching other kids in playful ways is a typical behavior for preschoolers, but isn't appropriate for school. A kindergarten teacher's least-popular but most-often cited refrain is, "Keep your hands and feet to yourselves."

- Group desk arrangements

often provide temptations for kids to kick others, to mess with someone's hair, or play with their backpack—all considered no-nos.

- Kids should also learn to respect personal space— no "in your face" actions allowed!

Wiggles and Squirms

- Fidgeting during instructional times or constantly playing with personal supplies is another top concern cited by kindergarten teachers.

- While kindergarteners have bursts of high energy, curriculum is structured to provide appropriate outlets

and high activity levels balanced with classroom "seat time." But if your child simply cannot—or will not—stay still for longer than a few minutes without squirming, or keeps getting up out of her seat, that could be a flag for whether or not she is ready for school.

and free-play times are built into a child's busy daily routine. However, some kids are simply unable to control themselves yet, and countless reminders and strategies such as adapting schedules, routines, or even moving their desks away from distractions don't work.

If parents and caregivers are unable to find ways to help a child remain in control, a more thorough evaluation with the family pediatrician may be advised. If any developmental delays or medical reasons are ruled out as causes, the truth is that your child may simply just not yet be ready for school!

ZOOM

When are overly active kids normal and when are they not? This is a debate that isn't easily answered, and opinions are sharply divided about whether to "let kids be kids" or to assign labels such as having Attention-Deficit Disorder or Attention-Deficit Hyperactivity Disorder to children with focusing or hyperactivity issues. Avoid making comments like, "That kid must have ADHD!"

Focus

- Kindergarten teachers talk of kids who seem to be so "out there" that they are certainly not listening or focusing on anything an educator has to say.

- A child who isn't focused means instructional time is taken away from the class as a whole while the teacher spends time trying to engage and constantly repeating instructions to individual students.

- Teachers report that many kids come to school without enough sleep, and actually frequently fall asleep in class.

Controlling Outbursts

- Kindergarten teachers instruct kids to raise their hands before speaking and not just shout out answers.

- An inability to control outbursts or keep emotions in check can result in behavioral issues and discipline challenges in the classroom.

- Kids need to grasp that all opinions are valued, and that there is a time, place, and way to express them appropriately and with respect.

SEPARATION & DETACHMENT

Begin talking up school and what exciting new opportunities it will mean for your child

Anxiety over separating from a loved one—even just for a few hours—is completely natural. For some kids, giving parents a hug and a kiss and being off on their way is no big deal. For others, however, saying goodbye can be a traumatic experience. By now, you already know whether your child falls into the former or latter category about separation. And

you've likely developed strategies about what to do to calm nerves and ease adjustments—yours and your child's.

Preparing your child emotionally for kindergarten, however, can require some additional preparation. If your child has stayed home with a parent up until now, transitions may be particularly tough. Regardless of your child's care arrangements,

Preparing Your Child

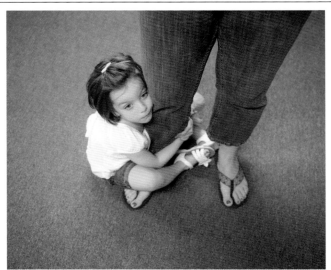

- Learn as much as you can ahead of time about kindergarten, including classroom and school expectations and activities, and talk them up to your child.

- Talk casually about school rules but don't overdo it. You want to alleviate stress, not add to it.

- If your child isn't used to being separated from you, consider utilizing occasional parents' day out programs or other activities where she is under the care of someone else for a period of time.

Factors that Affect Separation

- Changes in a child's life— even those that aren't particularly recent—can have an impact on a child's ability to cope with separation.

- The most common reason is a change in status in the family, including marriage,

- divorce, death, birth of a new baby, or change in custodial arrangements.

- If your child was recently separated from a loved one (such as getting temporarily lost at a store), she may be particularly clingy.

separation anxieties can be worked out successfully through advance planning, understanding the reasons behind your child's fear of separation and working through them, and acknowledging any normal stages of detachment.

If you already know which school your child will be attending (whether it is an academic preschool for four-year-olds or kindergarten), you can start the adjustment and transition process now. Show your child the actual school building while highlighting any features that might be considered attractive. If your child knows friends who will also be going there, be sure to mention them as well. If allowed, let your child check out the playground equipment when school isn't in session. Look on the Web site for more information and show your child any pictures that are posted.

Many schools have open houses or even public festivals and events throughout the year. Look for dates when activities like this might occur, and plan to stop by with your child—even if she won't be starting school for several months or even a year. The key is to begin building anticipation about an imminent change in your child's life.

Exhaustion

- Kids often come to school utterly exhausted from lack of sleep or from too many activities. This greatly affects their attitude and contributes to emotional anxiety.

- Kindergarten teachers report that some kids are simply unable to stay awake and alert throughout the school day, which often contributes to increased frustration and clinginess.

- Parents may opt for a half-day kindergarten program instead of full-day, if available. Attending after-school care or scheduling enrichment programs can be overwhelming.

When Stress Turns to Distress

- It's not unusual for kids to cry the first week of daycare, preschool, or even kindergarten. But, if stress turns to distress and your child exhibits signs of becoming physically ill, you may need to call the pediatrician for help.

- Signs of distress may include diarrhea, vomiting, inability to sleep, and feeling sweaty or clammy. Though rare, some kids simply aren't ready to handle big changes and work themselves into a state of anxiety to the point where intervention is needed.

BEHAVIOR

It's often a case of what your child won't do that determines school readiness

Most behavioral concerns when it comes to determining school readiness don't have to do with what your child can do, but rather, whether or not he will do things *when asked*, especially when he doesn't want to.

Preschool and kindergarten are filled with activities that encourage cooperative learning, getting along with others,

learning tolerance of other children's beliefs and actions, and trying new things. While much of a school day is typically filled with activities that are hands-on, fun, or innovative, there are also lessons that may require a child to really work at something before the skill is learned. That's often when bad behaviors begin to emerge.

Compliance

- Compliance doesn't come at the cost of individuality. Rules are there for a reason, and kids need to learn that following the teacher's instructions is a requirement, not an option.

- Parents sometimes undermine a child's understanding of compliance by always providing options. While this promotes independence, another skill needed for school, kids need to know that not everything will be about personal preference and that they need to listen to their teachers.

Cooperation

- Most preschool and kindergarten programs revolve around cooperative learning. Kids often share common supplies and work in teams to accomplish a project, which promotes team-building and helping one another.

- Your child should be willing to cooperate with other classmates, and to work together in a nice way even though it may not be with a preferred peer.

- Teach your child the concept of being equal, but not always fair (i.e., everyone gets a turn, but only one will be first).

Kids are usually at their best and most charming selves when getting to do what they want to do. Undoubtedly you've already noticed how angelic your tot can be when he thinks there is a reward coming for acting a certain way that pleases you. The test is what your cherub does when the activity involves something he considers boring or requires him to be quiet.

Most teachers already have a way to motivate reluctant learners and to turn even mundane tasks like practicing writing letters into fun. But your child still needs to be willing to try!

Tolerance

- If you express biases or prejudices around your preschooler, it shouldn't be surprising to hear her repeat similar things at school or when out and about.

- Tolerance of others—whether it is based on gender, religion, political beliefs, race, or even favor-ite color—is an expectation that is commonly discussed and taught to young children.

- Help your child learn to value differences and teach her how to act when around someone who is different from what she is used to.

All kids are defiant on occasion, especially when they are stressed, upset, tired, or even hungry. Typical reactions include arguing, talking back, and opposing parents, teachers, and other adults. However, if uncooperative and even hostile behavior becomes so frequent it is a serious concern, further evaluation may be needed. Oppositional Defiant Disorder (ODD) is a possible diagnosis. The good news is that most kids respond well to positive parenting and treatment approaches.

When Your Child Isn't Adjusting

- If your child seems to be struggling with a program—or even saying he "hates" it—start by talking privately with the teacher. Often, what your child says to you isn't at all how he acts when you're gone. He may just miss you!

- Don't allow your child to think simply saying he doesn't like something gets him out of a situation. At the same time, listen to your child and follow up to see if concerns have merit.

199

RULES & STRUCTURE

Even waiting in line to use the bathroom is new behavior many kids must learn

Your child most likely knows how to dash off to the restroom whenever he needs to go at home—often at the very last instant—and to wash his hands himself at the sink. He may also know how to turn on the television when he wants to relax and watch a favorite show, to set up a simple board game and challenge you to a match, and to pour himself a drink of water whenever he's thirsty. So, what's the problem? Absolutely nothing, of course, except that these accomplishments may not be in accordance with a structured day at school or preschool. And that can cause some anxiety and gaffes as children adapt to rules and structure.

Bathroom breaks can be pretty challenging at first for kids.

Lines and Turns

- Waiting in line is a hard concept to master. At school, there seems to be a line for just about everything a kid may want or need to do, from sharpening a pencil, to getting served lunch, to boarding a bus.

- Kids find out quickly that while they may attempt "cutting" in line, their peers will cry foul!

- Your child should be able to take turns successfully—a necessary social skill for playing with others.

Rules

- Most teachers require designated places for backpacks, lunch boxes, jackets, and personal supplies—necessary for keeping order in the classroom. Have your child do the same at home so he'll be prepared for keeping things organized in the classroom.

- Teach your child about saying the Pledge of Allegiance at the start of the day and other school customs. Depending on what type of program your child attends, prayers may also be part of the daily routine.

Teachers set designated times whenever possible so that they don't spend the day taking trips to the restroom instead of focusing on teaching new concepts. Many programs now feature a restroom and sink within the confines of the classroom, so that children can go as needed without causing a disruption to the rest of the class.

Other rules that may require frequent reminders and repetition include asking permission to do something instead of just doing it, waiting in line, and not interrupting others when speaking.

······· GREEN ● LIGHT ··············

Most preschoolers crave a sense of routine and knowing what's next. Post their daily schedule in their bedroom so they can refer to it as desired. Be creative: You can draw pictures to show the activity and then write the times in numbers using the same format as a digital clock. Ask your child whether he wants to include other parts of his day in the schedule as well.

Asking Permission

- Young children often struggle with the concept of asking permission before doing something they consider practical or essential, such as going to the bathroom or retrieving something from a backpack.

- Kids need to learn that not only do they need to get permission, but they need to do it in an unobtrusive way—most likely by quietly raising their hand and waiting for a teacher's acknowledgement.

- Ask how your child's program does it, and practice at home.

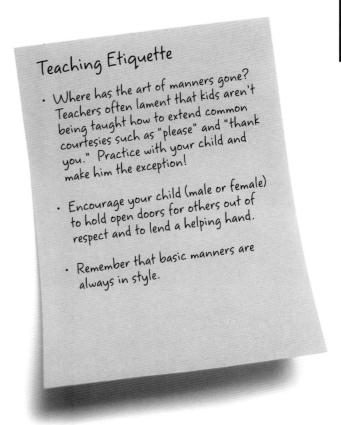

Teaching Etiquette

- Where has the art of manners gone? Teachers often lament that kids aren't being taught how to extend common courtesies such as "please" and "thank you." Practice with your child and make him the exception!

- Encourage your child (male or female) to hold open doors for others out of respect and to lend a helping hand.

- Remember that basic manners are always in style.

201

PUTTING OFF SCHOOL

Turning five years old doesn't mean your child is ready for kindergarten

Just because your child is old enough to attend kindergarten doesn't mean he is emotionally, socially, and even physically ready. There are numerous factors to consider besides your child's birth date, and parents should carefully weigh them all before making a decision about school readiness.

A well thought out decision that leads to either starting school or waiting a year can ultimately shape whether the year is successful or full of challenges, frustrations, and disappointments all around. Your child's overall outlook on school, sense of self and confidence in abilities build the foundation for future school achievement. If your child is miserable in his first year of school, you may find yourself fighting a poor

Advantages of Waiting

- Maturity (or lack thereof) is a commonly cited reason for waiting to start school. Whereas your child may be extremely immature now, a year's wait will most likely mean he begins school being more mature than most of his classmates.

- Another advantage is enhanced developmental readiness. This often equates to knowing more than counterparts and enhances self-confidence.

- Some parents wait when their child's physical size is much smaller than their peers, to allow for an extra year of growth.

Disadvantages of Waiting

- Your child may feel left behind if his peers or similar-age friends begin school and she doesn't.

- Kids who wait to start school may sometimes feel bored and unchallenged by the time they do start the kindergarten curriculum.

- Holding a child back simply because of size may initially allow your child to fit in physically, but growth patterns can change dramatically in future years.

- Some kids do not like being in a classroom filled with younger kids.

attitude, low self-confidence and a fear of failure throughout his academic life. So, how do you know whether your child should start now or wait?

Your child is eligible to begin kindergarten if he is five years old (check cut-off dates) and has acquired basic skills that have to do with self-control, independence, and early academic learning. Your child does not need to be able to read or know math skills when he begins, but it can be advantageous for him to be able to identify alphabet letters, recognize simple sight words, and sort similar objects by color, size, and shape.

If your youngster currently attends any type of child care program, ask the caregiver or teacher her opinion about your child's school readiness. The kindergarten program your child is planning to attend most likely will also have a checklist of readiness skills for you to look over.

If you're leaning toward waiting a year, consider whether your child will most likely feel a sense of pride about being among the oldest in a classroom or feel embarrassed about being placed with younger kids. Remember that you are your child's best advocate regarding whether or not he is ready.

Options to Consider

- A growing number of families who are unsure about whether their child is ready consider a two-year kindergarten program.

- Some kids participate in kindergarten twice—often at different schools or programs—to avoid feelings of being held back.

- Some children attend a half-day kindergarten program at age five and then a full-day program at age six.

- Another option is to add a year at a more academically rigorous preschool before transitioning to kindergarten.

Public or Private?

- Just as there are significant differences between many public and private preschools, there are differences between kindergarten programs as well.

- A child who is "iffy" about being ready for kindergarten is more likely to struggle in an academically focused or highly structured private kindergarten program.

- Expectations about learning, homework, and abilities should be evaluated when deciding whether the program is right for your child.

ACADEMIC PREP

Early reading, math, and writing skills can help boost confidence, provide extra school readiness

Many eager parents want to provide their preschooler with a strong academic foundation prior to kindergarten. Early academic instruction, which typically occurs most through active, hands-on learning, can help build a core of reading, math, and writing abilities. These skills can help boost your child's confidence before ever setting foot in a kindergarten classroom.

Of all core subjects, reading is most emphasized as an early academic achievement. By no means does this indicate your child must know how to read by kindergarten. But parents and caregivers can help with pre-reading skills by fostering a love of reading and reading books to children on a daily basis. If your child does learn to read before kindergarten,

Reading

- Participate in reading hours at local libraries or bookstores, and while there, let your child leisurely explore the shelves and how they are organized.

- Have a kid-designed reading log of sight words. As your child learns sight words such as "stop" or "I,"

have her write the words or glue letters that comprise the word into a spiral.

- Say out loud a sentence that doesn't make sense, and ask your child to explain why not.

- Set up designated reading times.

Math

- Let your child carry your change and count it for you.

- When shopping, ask her to pick out five apples or two peppers, for example. In fact, make it a practice to count everything you do.

- Teach your child the value of money, and have a bank at home.

- Ask your child to solve practical counting problems (We have three glasses out but need five. How many more should I get out?).

there will be numerous age-appropriate books for her to read and explore.

Math skills often come easily to a child, as most kids begin early counting and grouping at a young age. Being able to recognize groups of one, two, three, four, and even five objects is helpful, though not necessary.

If possible, your child should begin kindergarten being able to write her first name and possibly her last one too, though some names are pretty difficult to master yet. She should know her address, the names of her parents, and basic family details.

ZOOM

Should kids ever skip kindergarten? Your child may surpass other classmates in academics, but that doesn't mean he is ready for first grade. Social and behavioral maturity, physical size, and even consideration of how it might affect peer group acceptance at a later age, should also be considered. Rather than having kids skip a grade, ask for more challenging assignments.

Writing

- Kids need more than a lap desk while sitting on the couch in order to properly practice writing. Designate a spot for your child that is ergonomically correct for her height and has proper lighting.

- Let your child trace and copy shapes of interest— not just letters—as a way to practice holding a pencil. Consider toy products that let kids draw and then erase.

- Painting, stenciling, or chalk art are fun ways to encourage writing skills.

Skills Checklist

- Recognizes rhyming sounds and words; can identify some alphabet letters and the beginning sounds of some words

- Pays attention to adult-directed tasks and is able to recognize and respect authority

- Able to use the bathroom independently and get dressed and undressed without help

- Can use scissors, trace shapes, count to ten, and follow rules

- Speaks understandably and talks mostly in complete sentences

- Maintains self-control and keeps emotions in check.

ACADEMIC READINESS

RAISING LEARNERS
Start early to build excitement about acquiring knowledge and trying new things

Your child won't learn to her best potential if you just passively stand by. Rather, most children flourish through being challenged to think, to actively investigate the "why" and "how" of things, and to solve problems instead of just being given the answer. Raising an active learner means you should be engaged with the process, including allowing your child to experience cause and effect, trial and error, and even success and failure.

A key to raising learners and kids who are independently motivated to explore and investigate is to start early. Don't wait until your child is nearly school-age to begin introducing new concepts. Rather, make your home a place of learning

Preparation at Home

- Kids learn best from their parents. Even though most parents are extremely busy, quality time spent together and modeling desired behaviors is still the best way to promote learning.

- How we act, what we say, and what we do around our kids influence them more than education or socioeconomic levels.

- Promote strong communication skills, and encourage questions and follow-ups.

- Engage in active conversations and talk about how skills like math and reading are life essentials.

Support at School

- While you may not be able to personally volunteer or chaperone field trips at your child's preschool, you can help set the stage for active parenting by supporting what skills your child is currently learning.

- Promote the value of hard work and the importance of education.

- Ask your child what he did in school each day and provide your undivided attention when she shows you art projects or demonstrates new skills.

- Support the school's teachers.

from the very start.

Simple ideas on raising learners include creating "centers" in your home as is a common practice in classrooms of pre-schoolers and kindergarten-age children. It need be nothing more than designated areas where "creative" supplies are kept separate from the "science" or "building" supplies. Be imaginative! Another option is to go on regular "fact hunts" and track down solutions or information on whatever it is your child is interested in.

You can also help motivate your child to contribute to the household. Keep pencils and paper on hand and invite your child to help you with a grocery or "to-do" list.

Teach your child to do as much as possible for himself at as young an age as possible. Extra patience may be required when your preschooler is young, but the rewards will quickly pay off as your child matures and he is able to do things for himself. This independence will carry over to the classroom as well.

Homework Help

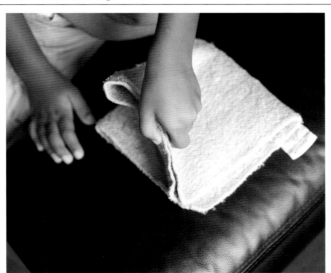

- Teach your child that "homework" isn't a bad thing, and why it is important. Explain that you have homework, too.

- Parents can give their kids so-called homework at an early age. Have them group their money by size or learn how to fold a towel.

- Set up a dedicated study place at home while your child is a preschooler, and encourage quiet time there for coloring, independent play (like looking at pop-up books), or other learning activities.

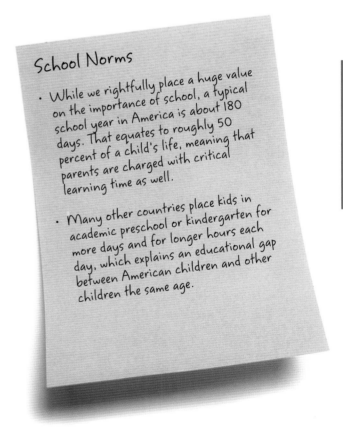

School Norms

- While we rightfully place a huge value on the importance of school, a typical school year in America is about 180 days. That equates to roughly 50 percent of a child's life, meaning that parents are charged with critical learning time as well.

- Many other countries place kids in academic preschool or kindergarten for more days and for longer hours each day, which explains an educational gap between American children and other children the same age.

SOCIAL SKILLS
Doing the right thing can be influenced by leader and follower traits

Playing nicely and fairly, sharing cooperatively, and respecting others are good social skills every preschooler should master. But there are other actions and deeds that will need to be understood as well, as your youngster begins to interact with others in a school setting.

Parents should explain that sometimes the best behaviors aren't what you do—it's what you don't do. That can be a confusing concept for a preschooler, but with a little practice and frequent examples, she'll understand more about judgment.

Why is judgment an important skill to begin learning? The obvious first answers have to do with a child's health and safety needs. Beyond that, kids can easily be led astray and take missteps, typically due to peer pressure, which can

Leaders

- Leadership isn't genetic, but personality traits that define who is seen as a leader are.

- Charisma, self-confidence, and the ability to come up with fun ideas and capture others' attention are common factors in preschool-age leaders.

- Leadership roles can change with time and be environmentally based as well. A child may be a leader in dance class but a follower in the classroom.

- Watch out for leaders who become overly bossy, critical, or even make dictatorial commands.

Followers

- Children who are shy or timid may be viewed as being followers, but that isn't always the case.

- Don't push a follower-style child to lead others. You may be stressing your child by applying pressure and trying to force him into a role he is uncomfortable with.

- Kids who nurture and feel empathy toward others may become leaders in their own right as kids begin to admire and respond to traits like caring over being outgoing.

occur in even simple ways in kindergarten. The most common reason attributed to poor judgment is a desire to be noticed and accepted by others.

Early childhood educators often use the "pack mentality" throughout the day to maintain structure and discipline in the classroom. Kids typically want to please, and if everyone is expected to be seated and quiet or walk in the hallways with their hands behind their backs, most likely they will do so without a second thought.

There are kids that seem born to lead while others feel more comfortable with blending in with a group. All types are needed for successful group dynamics, but sometimes a leader can lead others astray without proper direction. Followers may sometimes feel they have to do something that they aren't comfortable with or is wrong, just to fit in, so parents need to maintain a close eye on social groups and activities.

Adult Roles

- Adults can help with leader/follower dynamics and avert potential issues by voicing expectations clearly in front of all kids and asking whether everyone understands. This helps avoid having a child who "interprets" to others what was meant.

- Empower kids to speak up if they are being bullied.

- Adults shouldn't intervene with normal group dynamics but should step in if a child is either leading bullying or bossy behaviors or is being made to do something against her will.

Accepting Responsibility

- A key trait of leadership is the ability to accept responsibility for errors in judgment or speaking up when things go wrong.

- Preschoolers who are able to be truthful without rationalizing why someone else must be to blame often emerge as a friend peers admire.

- Parents should emphasize the importance of accountability and confessing upfront when appropriate.

ACADEMIC READINESS

EDUCATIONAL GAMES
Learning activities you can play, make, buy, or find online

Some of the most effective educational games are tried-and-true classics such as Go Fish or flash cards. But, if you're looking for something new, there's no shortage of choices out there. Gone are the days when the Internet needed to be feared, as there is an almost endless array of free educational games that can provide hours of safe fun, with many activities being educator approved!

Keep in mind that any activity you can come up with that not only entertains, but also teaches your child something new or reinforces learning in a different and entertaining way can be called an educational game. Most early rhyming games are just exchanges between a parent or caregiver and a child. Something as simple as asking a child to help set the table can become a fun exercise in counting, and stringing

Are Online Games Safe?

There is an assortment of free Web sites that feature safe fun for preschoolers. As with any online play or search, parents should exercise caution. Consider these tips:

- Only click on sites that you are familiar with or trust. Many respected companies feature free preschool games.

- Be aware that advertisements will appear on most of these sites, including the pop-up kind that some people find annoying.

- Always directly supervise your child when on the Internet.

Computer Games

- Many preschool programs feature computers in the classroom with age-appropriate educational games.

- Computer games often promote reading skills through interactive play. They may feature a story being read out loud with accompany-ing graphics (often that come alive and do something when clicked on). To help with a preschooler's word association, words and phrases are highlighted as the story is read out loud.

- Ask your child's preschool if any particular software programs are recommended.

beads, sorting objects, color-coordinating outfits, and playing "I Spy" games while on the road all contribute to your learning.

A simple search on the computer can identify a host of education-oriented games that are free just for the clicking. How is this so? Most sites receive necessary funding through advertising that is either targeted to the young child or to parents of young children. The ads are usually similar to ones seen during child programming on the television, but parents need to be vigilant and should pre-screen all computer games as well as directly supervising their children when they are playing. Well-known kid-focused companies such as Disney and Fisher-Price, for example, feature online preschool games and activities that parents can play with their child.

If you're willing to spend some money, there are numerous kindergarten readiness games and products on the market. Just remember that just because a game claims to be "education-based" doesn't mean that's always the case. In many cases, it is simply a marketing ploy. Ask yourself what your child will learn from it.

Home Educational Fun

- Creative parents can transform their daily routine into one filled with educational games and fun without spending a dime.

- Kids can hunt for letters or look for simple sight words on the back of their favorite cereal box or can cut out letters from a magazine (with your permission, of course!) and create a collage or glue onto paper.

- Create a box of clues that your child looks through to deduce the day's activities or even what you'll be making for dinner!

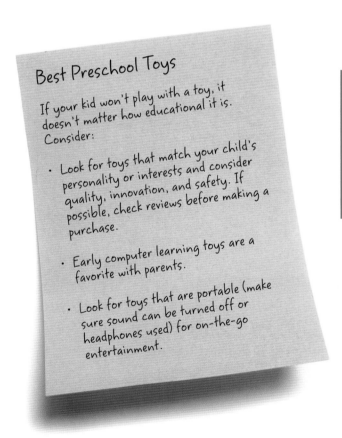

Best Preschool Toys

If your kid won't play with a toy, it doesn't matter how educational it is. Consider:

- Look for toys that match your child's personality or interests and consider quality, innovation, and safety. If possible, check reviews before making a purchase.

- Early computer learning toys are a favorite with parents.

- Look for toys that are portable (make sure sound can be turned off or headphones used) for on-the-go entertainment.

FAMILY SUPPORT

Encouragement, positive communications, and consistent daily routines all impact academic success

Going to school for the first time (whether it is preschool or kindergarten) requires preparation and the support of the entire family to make the transition go smoothly.

Parents play a key role in that success by establishing a consistent family routine with established meals and bedtimes and a healthy lifestyle. Place limits on television, computer, and video game time —even if your child complains that she's spent most of the day at school, there are many other interesting things that can be done instead.

Establish a sense of positive communications, and set the stage for successful learning by sending positive messages about going to school. Keep in mind that children tend to

Gestures of Thanks

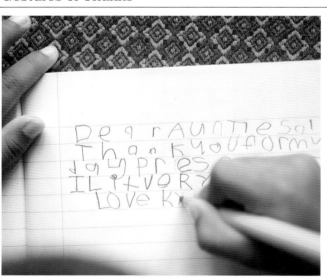

- Have family members find ways to express appreciation for assistance and support. Seek out ways to make each household member feel special and valued.

- Have your child write thank you notes for gifts received or for special efforts. Even young preschoolers can use "fill in the blank" style thank you cards or draw pictures as a sign of appreciation.

- Implement random acts of kindness, a compliment jar, or similar approaches to recognize good deeds.

Chores and Roles

- Help your child to learn the value of chores and family roles.

- Your child most likely will be expected to pick up after himself and help straighten the classroom at school—forms of chores.

- Have your child push in his chair at home and tell him the same is expected with his chair at school.

- Your child should develop an understanding that all students should work together in collaboration with the teacher as a team, much like family members do at home.

follow and adopt our ideals and attitudes. If we say they "must" go to school they'll have a different outlook than if you talk about how they "get to go" to school and learn new skills and become smarter.

Parents should set rules about how they expect their child to contribute, how to act (both at home as well as away from home), and about practicing skills. It's no surprise that kids will continue to push and bend rules or extend limits, but they still actually behave better overall when they know what is expected and that rules will be enforced.

ZOOM

If your child will be riding a school bus, review expectations and safety rules early and often. Your child should memorize the bus driver's name, bus and route numbers and know where to stand while waiting and what to do when getting off the bus at school. Teach your child never to walk between buses or cars or to cross the street without supervision.

Homework Help

- Homework should be considered your child's job, just as other family members have their various jobs to perform as well.

- Tell your child how you appreciate him doing his homework, and to ask for help if he needs it.

- Do not expect your child to complete homework assignments and tasks without adult supervision. You'll need to help, support and encourage!

- Teach your child to learn to respect the need for quiet time and concentration.

Key Family Messages

- Promote common bonds of school memories, like showing your child photos of yourself when you started school and talking about how you felt.

- Discuss the future with your child, and how learning opens up the world to a whole new realm of possibilities. If they want to be an astronaut, for example, talk about necessary science and math skills.

- Encourage family members to support and encourage everyone else.

ACADEMIC READINESS

SCHOOL GEAR

Check program requirements and restrictions before heading out to shop for supplies

If your child will be attending a preschool or kindergarten program where school supplies and backpack styles are pre-selected and uniforms are required, then school gear is one less thing to worry about. For everyone else, knowing what to purchase and what your child should wear requires some effort. After all, for many youngsters who will be venturing to a school setting for the first time, having the perfect backpack and school outfit is all that it is about—at least initially, anyway!

Purchasing a school backpack is considered a rite of passage for many children heading to school. There are a wide variety of options available, ranging from wheeled backpack

Backpacks

- Overall comfort, quality, and safety should be key considerations above design or color.

- Kids should carry no more than 10 to 20 percent of their body weight in a backpack. For a young preschooler, carrying a lunch, water bottle, jacket and any school supplies can add up to that maximum amount quickly.

- Backpacks that are too heavy or that require a child to shift body weight or lean forward can result in back pain and injuries.

Clothing Rules

- Many programs have dress codes about what kids can—and cannot—wear to school.

- Length of skirts and shorts, and whether shorts are required under dresses, may be specified. Many schools don't allow sleeveless shirts for boys or spaghetti straps or tank tops for girls. Some schools require shirts to be message-free or of a certain color. Hats are often not allowed.

- Consider comfort first and styles that are easy to unfasten for urgent trips to the bathroom.

varieties that can be pulled instead of carried, messenger-style bags, sling-style bags that are carried cross-ways over the shoulder, and traditional styles carried on the back.

Before even so much as browsing over selections, however, find out what types of backpacks are even allowed at your child's school. Space limitations and narrow lockers (for schools that have lockers) may impact the type of design that is recommended. Many early educators say they simply don't have space in classrooms to accommodate the wider, larger styles with wheels and ask for small bags that can be hung on pegs. Consider also the ease of opening and closing the backpack. While most feature simple zip styles, some trendier backpacks feature snap-in or drawstring styles that work well with older kids but not so well with young kids.

Ask about the program's dress-code policy and any other requirements and restrictions before back-to-school shopping. Many programs have certain rules about skirt or dress lengths for modesty reasons and may require shorts under dresses or a certain style of shirt for both boys and girls.

Foot Apparel

- Kids often come to school in trendy but impractical shoes for the day's activities. Shoes should be in styles that can be worn to recess or in physical education class.

- Some schools allow kids to change shoes for gym, but require children to do so independently and within a very brief amount of time.

- Kids' feet often get hot and sweaty when stylish boots are worn in the classroom.

- Provide appropriate socks to minimize blisters or foot odor.

Car Booster Seats

- Once children outgrow their forward-facing car seats (usually around age four and 40 pounds), they should ride in booster seats in the back seat.

- Booster seats should be used until a vehicle seat belt fits properly, which is usually when a child is 4' 9" and at least eight years old.

- Children younger than thirteen should ride in the back seat.

- Some states have enacted specific laws requiring child booster seats. Be sure to check what your state requires.

ENVIRONMENT

Work together to identify environmental health and safety issues and eliminate or mitigate problems

Not a day goes by when there isn't some type of health warning about something that could affect our child's overall wellness or safety. While our environment provides for some joyous times outdoors, it can also create some risks when it comes to air quality, the sun's rays, and even exposure to indoor toxicants and combustion gases. Risks also are ever-

present when it comes to asbestos and lead poisoning.

On top of that, some kids have severe seasonal allergies or asthmatic health conditions that are triggered by both indoor and outdoor pollutants and environmental factors. So, what's a conscientious parent to do?

Luckily, exposure to most potentially hazardous conditions

Lead Levels

- All houses built before 1978 are likely to contain some lead-based paint. However, it is the deterioration of this paint that causes a health problem.

- The U.S. Consumer Product Safety Council announces all recalls on its Web site at www.cpsc.gov, along with a full description of the product and the hazard noted.

- Toys that are recalled often contain excessive levels of lead in the paint, which is toxic if ingested and may cause adverse health effects.

Air Quality

- Poor air quality can aggravate asthma and affect children with any type of respiratory weakness. The culprits are typically ground-level ozone and airborne particles, two pollutants that pose the greatest threat to humans.

- The seemingly prettiest days—when it's sunny, warm, mostly wind-free, and clear—is when ozone is at its worst.

- Understand the Air Quality Index (AQI), and its associated colors, which is broadcast to viewers in a majority of communities.

can be minimized, if not eliminated, with proper safeguards. A key nationwide campaign involves the elimination of children's exposure to lead. The Centers for Disease Control and Prevention (CDC) indicates that approximately 250,000 U.S. children ages one through five have elevated blood lead levels. Because lead poisoning can affect nearly every system in the body and often occurs with no obvious symptoms, it frequently goes unrecognized.

Children under the age of six are at greatest risk for lead poisoning because they are rapidly growing and because they tend to put their hands and other objects, such as toys—which can be contaminated with lead-based paint—into their mouths. Lead-based paint and lead-contaminated dust are the main sources of exposure for lead in the United States. Ongoing efforts have also resulted in product recalls of items that have been found to contain lead.

The CDC has implemented a Healthy Homes initiative concerning housing conditions that can adversely affect public health. The focus of the initiative is to identify health, safety, and quality-of-life issues in the home environment.

UV Rays

- Don't forget to protect your child's eyes from bright sunlight, which can increase the risk of eye-related ailments.

- UV radiation from the sun's rays can damage eyes' surface tissues as well as the cornea and lens.

- Eyes are at risk from getting injured year-round and not just in the summer months.

- Protect your kid's eyes with hats and sunglasses. It's especially important to wear glasses during peak sun times and at higher altitudes, where UV light is more intense.

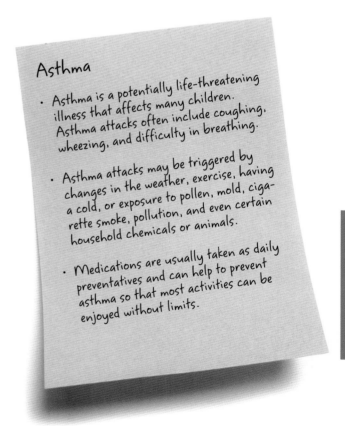

Asthma

- Asthma is a potentially life-threatening illness that affects many children. Asthma attacks often include coughing, wheezing, and difficulty in breathing.

- Asthma attacks may be triggered by changes in the weather, exercise, having a cold, or exposure to pollen, mold, cigarette smoke, pollution, and even certain household chemicals or animals.

- Medications are usually taken as daily preventatives and can help to prevent asthma so that most activities can be enjoyed without limits.

CONTAGIOUS AILMENTS

Frequent hand washing helps but doesn't always prevent exposure to common childhood illnesses

Catching and spreading contagious illnesses are a common part of childhood. Despite adults' best efforts, preschoolers and hygiene don't always go hand in hand. Kids frequently wipe runny noses with their hands and then touch objects, pick their nose, put their fingers in their mouth, and openly sneeze and cough in a room.

As such, it should come as no surprise that child care facilities, classrooms, playgroups, and about anywhere where kids play are potential breeding grounds for the ickies.

Chances are good that your child—or another sibling—will at some time get conjunctivitis (a.k.a. pinkeye), impetigo (skin rash), or head lice (that's not dandruff you're seeing). Luckily,

Conjunctivitis (Pinkeye)

- Unless eye irritation is caused by an allergy or other irritant, most causes of pinkeye are contagious.

- Bacterial pinkeye causes a green or yellow discharge from the eye. The white parts of the eye will be red. Pinkeye may be in only one eye, or both.

- Pinkeye will cause a child's eyelids and lashes to become matted and frequent wiping of the drainage will be necessary.

- Topical antibiotic drops are usually prescribed for preschoolers with pinkeye.

Skin Diseases

- Impetigo is a bacterial skin condition. Kids may develop honey-colored crusted lesions. Nostrils are commonly affected. Topical antibiotics are usually required.

- Hand, Foot, and Mouth disease is a common viral infection. Typical symptoms include ulcers in the mouth, blisters on hands and feet, and possible rash. There is no specific treatment, and symptoms typically last three to six days.

- Fifth disease is also a common viral infection. Symptoms include red cheeks and then a lacelike rash on the child's arms.

while not pleasant, they are easily treated.

Your child will also likely catch the common cold and perhaps even strep throat. Teachers report that these communicable sicknesses can temporarily transform a very busy and active classroom into a ghost town.

The flu—including the worrisome H1N1 virus—can be more serious for youngsters, especially ones with respiratory conditions. Flu shots can help protect against this very serious contagious ailment, and pediatricians recommend that children receive a flu shot every year as a preventative measure.

Head Lice

- Head lice are a common problem that affects up to 12 million kids each year across all socio-economical groups. It is not caused by poor hygiene.

- Lice are about the size of a sesame seed. The main symptom is an itchy scalp from the bites of the lice, which then can become infected and may appear red or crusty.

- Treatment involves a head lice shampoo and removal of lice and nits, which hatch in seven to ten days.

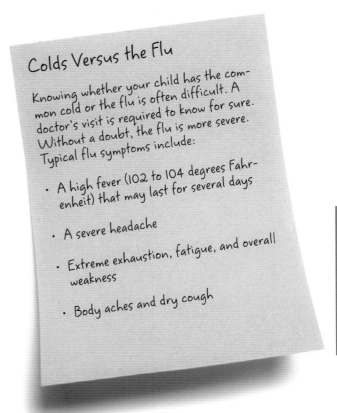

Colds Versus the Flu

Knowing whether your child has the common cold or the flu is often difficult. A doctor's visit is required to know for sure. Without a doubt, the flu is more severe. Typical flu symptoms include:

- A high fever (102 to 104 degrees Fahrenheit) that may last for several days

- A severe headache

- Extreme exhaustion, fatigue, and overall weakness

- Body aches and dry cough

POSSIBLE CONCERNS

219

COMMON INJURIES

Cuts, scrapes, bruises, and even fractures come with physical play and energetic actions

By now, you're probably pretty comfortable in treating a host of common boo-boos that result from your exuberant preschooler's active play. Typically, a quick treatment of cleaning up the wound, applying antiseptic, and then giving a kiss or hug is all that is needed for minor injuries. Because scratches and scrapes, bruises and minor ouchies like stubbing a toe are

quite commonplace, it doesn't take much to return a howling preschooler back to play—perhaps even with a badge of honor in the form of a trendy bandage for everyone to see.

Occasionally, however, injuries are more severe and require a visit to the pediatrician or even to the emergency room. Because preschoolers are typically physically active and

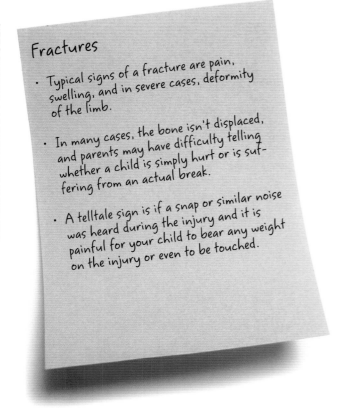

Fractures

- Typical signs of a fracture are pain, swelling, and in severe cases, deformity of the limb.

- In many cases, the bone isn't displaced, and parents may have difficulty telling whether a child is simply hurt or is suffering from an actual break.

- A telltale sign is if a snap or similar noise was heard during the injury and it is painful for your child to bear any weight on the injury or even to be touched.

Cuts and Scrapes

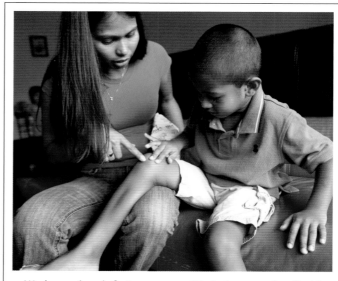

- Wash your hands first before treating your child's injury. If the wound is bleeding, apply direct pressure with a clean towel or bandage until bleeding stops.

- Check for and remove any foreign objects or debris in the wound.

- Wash the wound well with soap and water and use a non-sting antiseptic.

- Skip the bandage if the cut or scrape is minor or is in an area that won't get rubbed; wounds heal best left open to air.

220

sometimes don't have a true understanding that their careless actions can result in getting hurt, lots of accidents still occur at this stage.

Broken bones or fractures occur often—either from a daredevil stunt gone awry, from participating in sports, or just from active play. Most fractures occur in the wrist, the forearm, and above the elbow because kids instinctively will throw out their hands in an attempt to stop or break a fall.

If you suspect a broken bone, seek medical care immediately so an x-ray can be performed.

Head Injuries

ZOOM

Broken bones typically heal best when put into a cast that restricts movement. Casts are usually made from either plaster or synthetic (fiberglass) material. The cast has two layers: soft cotton wrap that rests against the skin and a hard layer that protects the bone. Some waterproof cast options exist, but not all doctors recommend them because of an increased risk of skin infections.

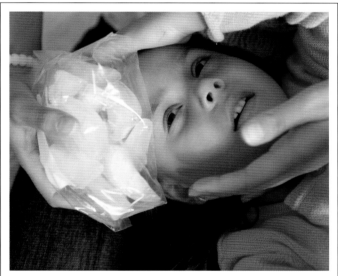

- Kids often suffer from minor bumps to the head without any penetration of an object or bleeding. Closed-head injuries are called concussions.

- Parents must be particularly vigilant in observing their child after a fall.

- If your child is breathing irregularly, loses consciousness, has convulsions, or vomits, seek immediate medical care.

- Also watch for signs of dizziness, nausea, disorientation, and headaches.

Family First-aid Kit

- Keep a well-stocked first-aid kit at home and another one in the car.

- Convenience kits can be purchased at almost any store, or assemble your own.

- Include essentials like gauze, adhesive bandages and tape, elastic bandage and fasteners, antiseptic wipes, and common Band-Aids.

- Add scissors, tweezers, thermometer, alcohol wipes, acetaminophen and ibuprofen, flashlight, and extra batteries.

- Include a first-aid manual.

POSSIBLE CONCERNS

CONDITIONS
Check with your doctor when unsure about your child's activity levels, ability to focus, and headaches

Kids are kids, and their development, behaviors, and overall temperament are different. It would be quite boring if all kids acted the same; however, what parent hasn't wondered at times whether their child is typical?

A common behavioral issue that parents ask their child's pediatrician about is whether a particularly energetic and always-on-the-go behavior and personality is normal, or whether their child's inability to focus and concentrate might signify a condition such as attention deficit hyperactivity disorder (ADHD) or attention deficit disorder (ADD).

A first step is determining whether your child is normally active as compared with peers or too active to the point

Hyperactivity

- Signs of hyperactive behaviors may include running or climbing inappropriately, talking too much and playing too loudly, and constant fidgeting and a sense of restlessness.

- Kids who are hyperactive often interrupt others—even when told to wait—cut in line, are unable to wait for a turn, and seem unable to sit still for quiet games.

- Kids may not sleep well and don't like to have unstructured, down time, and may "find trouble" when not given an outlet.

Medication for ADHD?

- There is much debate concerning whether hyperactive kids should be labeled as ADHD and whether medication is needed.

- Medications can help calm out-of-control behavior and increase focus; parents sometimes say they can restrict a child's natural personality.

- Medication is not a miracle cure for everyone; treatment plans and results vary.

- Kids who take medication may not always stay on it; some are able to self-manage their condition as they mature.

where it could be a problem at school. Determine for how long a child seems too active, whether the impulsiveness and restless behaviors occur in various settings, and whether a child can stick to a routine or finish tasks that are assigned.

A starting place is with the family pediatrician, who may want to discuss your child's actions further, offer suggestions, or refer your child to a specialist.

Other conditions may impact your child's overall health and how he feels over the course of a day. High cholesterol, migraines or frequent headaches, and allergies are examples.

Headaches

················· YELLOW ● LIGHT ·················

Seasonal allergies can take their toll on young children and result in headaches, lethargy, and overall just feeling poorly. Kids can also develop painful sinus infections or ear infections that may have started with severe allergic symptoms or a common cold. How a child feels has an obvious correlation to activity level and overall focus and behavior. Control what you can in your child's environment and consider allergy medications, if needed.

Cholesterol and Kids

- High cholesterol is a huge health concern with kids, yet most parents overlook it as a potential issue with their child. The liver produces this waxy substance for healthy body function, but high levels contribute to cardiovascular disease and stroke.

- Food choices matter. Vegetables, fruits, and grains don't have cholesterol but meat, poultry, seafood, dairy, and egg yolks do.

- Diet, heredity, body weight, and activity levels all contribute to high cholesterol.

- Headaches are very common in school-age children. Reports indicate 30 to 50 percent of kids suffer from them occasionally.

- Migraine headaches are also common and occur in up to 3 percent of pre-schoolers and 11 percent of primary school students.

- Migraines are thought to run in the family.

- Kids can take an age-appropriate dose of pain reliever and often avoid common triggers like skipping meals, poor sleep habits, lack of exercise, or listening to loud music with headphones.

POSSIBLE CONCERNS

223

FLAGS & DELAYS

Concerns about speech and motor skills should be discussed and reviewed with your pediatrician

Since children develop at different paces, true developmental delays are sometimes initially overlooked. By the time a child is of preschool-age, however, most development delays are easier to spot. As with any concern, early intervention is the key to long-term success.

Common flags with preschoolers include possible speech and language delays as well as delays in gross and fine motor skills. Youngsters who don't demonstrate an increasingly fluent vocabulary, speak only in phrases or brief answers rather than complete sentences, or have difficulty in being understood should be screened for speech delays or language disorders.

Common Flags

- Learning flags include a slow response to learning new things and not remembering skills that have just been taught.

- Motor skills flags include poor balance, a peculiar walk or gait (including only walking on toes or always twirling), excessive clumsiness, or falling.

- Behavior or social flags include aggressive or aggravating behaviors, extreme stubbornness, and an inability to sit still or stay calm.

- Speech flags include saying only a few word responses and not being understood.

Speech Tips

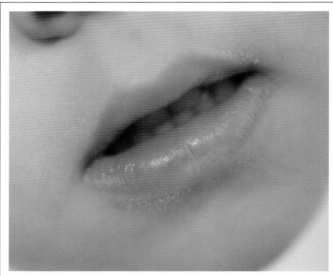

- It is common for preschoolers to pronounce words incorrectly. Your child may have a speech disorder, or may simply be struggling with correct pronunciations.

- Model correct pronunciations and encourage your child to repeat mispronounced words correctly by calling attention to it without being critical or making your youngster feel self-conscious.

- Read books that are written in rhyme or have repetitive lines.

- Avoid teasing your child about mispronunciations.

Flags for fine motor skill delays include preschoolers who can't use silverware or hold a pencil correctly, draw shapes, color within the lines, or get dressed or undressed independently. Flags for gross motor skills include preschoolers who don't walk using a proper gait, are excessively clumsy, and are unable to ride a tricycle or similar riding toy.

Your child's pediatrician may perform a more comprehensive screening. Sometimes, possible delays are simply noted and a follow-up visit scheduled in a few months to see if additional achievements have been made.

Not Like Others

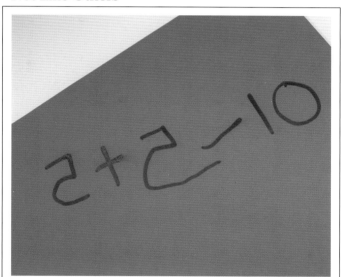

- Being different than other children by no means indicates that your child has any type of developmental disorder. At the same time, achieving typical milestones is one way to identify potential issues.

- Parents should keep track of their concerns by not-ing specific instances or examples of how they feel their child is different.

- If multiple exceptions are observed and a child seems unable to interact successfully with others, a consultation with the pediatrician should be scheduled so concerns can be discussed.

Dyslexia is a reading disability caused by subtle problems with how the brain processes information, especially in the so-called language regions. Preschoolers are typically too young to be tested and diagnosed with dyslexia. However, they may exhibit signs if they have difficulty with learning to talk, rhyming, learning sequences such as the alphabet and days of the week, sounding out simple words, and even learning to read and write their own names.

Can Preschoolers Become Depressed?

Even preschoolers can get depressed. A recent change in the home such as divorce or a move or low self-esteem can cause depression. Common symptoms include:

- Persistent sadness or irritability
- Loss of interest in activities and friends
- Feelings of worthlessness
- Difficulty in sleeping or wanting to sleep all the time
- Loss of energy and change in appetite

Parents should provide constant reinforcement of their love and support, and if symptoms continue, seek intervention.

POSSIBLE CONCERNS

225

SPECIAL NEEDS
An array of free services and programs are available for children with disabilities

While many developmental delays can be successfully treated with therapy, some kids are diagnosed with lifelong disorders or conditions. Children who have medical, developmental, behavioral, learning, and mental health issues that may range from mild to severe are guaranteed special services in order to thrive and meet their maximum potential.

The Individuals with Disabilities Act (IDEA) is a federal law that ensures services to children with disabilities. IDEA governs how individual states and public agencies provide intervention, special education, and related services. More than 6.5 million infants, toddlers, children and youth with disabilities are eligible for services, according to the U.S. Department of Education.

Evaluation & Qualification

- Children must be evaluated by trained school personnel to determine whether they qualify for special education services.

- Parents have the option of having an Independent Educational Evaluation

(IEE) if they feel the school's evaluation is incomplete or if you disagree with the conclusions of the district's evaluation. Some parents like having an independent evaluation for additional insight on their child's needs.

ARD

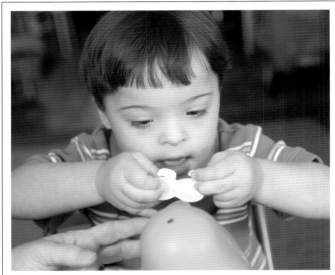

- The Admission, Review and Dismissal (ARD) Process helps families of students who qualify for special education services take an active role in planning their child's educational program.

- An ARD committee includes the child's parents along

with educators and special education specialists.

- An ARD meeting is needed for initial placement or any time school staff or parents feel a change is needed in a student's special education program or to review additional assessments.

Parents of a child with special needs should become familiar with services that are provided and the array of programs offered. It is also important to understand other laws that relate to children with disabilities, including No Child Left Behind Act, the Family Education Rights and Privacy Act, and Americans with Disabilities Act.

Special education laws guarantee children ages three to twenty-one a free appropriate education. Parents will need to advocate for their child and will work in partnership with the assembled team of special education professionals.

ZOOM

"Early intervention" services are typically offered for children with special needs (up to age three) to get the services and therapies they need. Sometimes it is offered in groups, other times individually. At age three, a child is referred to a school district for special-education preschool. Ask a school official about what you need to know to see if your child qualifies for the PPCD.

IEP

- An Individualized Education Plan (IEP) spells out exactly what special education services your child will receive and why.

- The plan will include your child's classification, services such as an aide and therapy, academic and behavioral goals, and placement. The IEP will be tailored to your child's needs.

- It will also include time to be spent in regular education with typically developing peers and progress reports.

- The IEP must be reviewed at least once a year.

Starting PPCD

- The public school program for young children, ages three to five, is called the Preschool Program for Children with Disabilities (PPCD). Parents who believe their preschooler may be in need of special education services should request a referral to the local school district's special education office.

- Eligible preschoolers are provided a language-rich environment that promotes speech and early literacy and teaches developmental skills through active play. Children may need accommodations or modifications to the curriculum guidelines.

POSSIBLE CONCERNS

227

RESOURCES

Parents have lots of questions about raising preschoolers, especially concerning development, behaviors, nutrition, child care, and preparing for kindergarten. A wealth of information about general parenting or school preparation can be found on the Internet, and some favorite resources are listed below. This is by no means an exhaustive list, but it can help you get started in your search. Keep in mind that parenting approaches and guidance about health and safety, general care, early childhood learning, and kindergarten readiness may vary. Ultimately, it is up to you—as parents—to advocate for your child and determine what is in your preschooler's best interests overall.

Ages & Stages
Adoption www.adoption.com
Child Care http://childcare.about.com
Child Care Aware www.ccaparentnetwork.org
ChildCare.gov www.childcare.gov
International Nanny Association www.nanny.org
Moms of Multiples www.momsofmultiples.com
Nanny.com www.nanny.com
National Association for the Education of Young Children www.naeyc.org
National Association of Family Child Care www.nafcc.org/include/parents.asp
National Head Start Association www.nhsa.org
Stay-at-Home Dads http://stayathomedads.about.com
Twins and Multiples http://multiples.about.com

Age 3: Milestones
Child Development Institute www.childdevelopmentinfo.com
Childproofing www.childproofing.com
Family Education www.familyeducation.com
Kids Health http://kidshealth.org/parent
National Network for Child Care www.nncc.org
Parents www.parents.com

Pediatrics http://pediatrics.about.com
Preschoolers News www.topix.com/family/preschoolers

Age 3: Care
American Academy of Pediatrics www.aap.org
American Dental Association www.ada.org
American Dental Hygienists' Association www.adha.org
Keep Kids Healthy www.keepkidshealthy.com/
Kids' Fashion http://kidsfashion.about.com
National Highway Traffic Safety Administration www.nhtsa.dot.gov
Safe Kids Worldwide www.safekids.org
Seat Check www.seatcheck.org
Single Parents http://singleparents.about.com

Age 3: Play & Learning
Child Fun www.childfun.com
Children's Books http://childrensbooks.about.com
Children's Music http://kidsmusic.about.com
Discovery Health http://health.discovery.com
Education.com www.education.com
National Institute of Child Health and Human Development www.nichd.nih.gov
Preschoolers http://preschoolers.about.com
Science for Preschoolers http://scienceforpreschoolers.com
Single Parents http://singleparents.about.com
Toys http://toys.about.com
Wonder Time www.wondertime.go.com

Age 3: My World
Dr. Greene www.drgreene.com
Fatherhood http://fatherhood.about.com
Family Doctor http://familydoctor.org/online/famdocen/home children.html

Focus on the Family www.focusonthefamily.com/parenting.aspx
Healthy Kids, Healthy Care www.healthykids.us
It's a Mom's World www.itsamomsworld.com
iVillage www.parenting.ivillage.com
Kidsource www.kidsource.com

Age 4: Milestones

American Dental Association www.ada.org
American Dental Hygienists' Association www.adha.org
Childproofing www.childproofing.com
Family Education www.familyeducation.com
Kids Health http://kidshealth.org/parent
Kids' Movies and TV http://kidstvmovies.about.com
Pediatrics http://pediatrics.about.com
Parents www.parents.com

Age 4: Care

American Academy of Pediatrics www.aap.org
Bisphenol-A www.bisphenol-a.org
BMI Calculator http://pediatrics.about.com/cs/usefultools/l/bl_bmi_calc.htm
Centers for Disease Control and Prevention www.cdc.gov
Child Care http://childcare.about.com
FirstAidWeb www.firstaidweb.com
Keep Kids Healthy www.keepkidshealthy.com
Safe Kids Worldwide www.safekids.org
Single Parents http://singleparents.about.com
The U.S. Consumer Product Safety Commission www.cpsc.gov

Age 4: Learning & Play

Children's Books http://childrensbooks.about.com
Discovery Health http://health.discovery.com
Education.com www.education.com

Kids' Clubs http://kidsclubs.about.com
National Institute of Child Health and Human Development www.nichd.nih.gov
Preschoolers http://preschoolers.about.com
Toys http://toys.about.com
Wonder Time www.wondertime.go.com

Age 4: My World

Dr. Greene www.drgreene.com
Family Doctor http://familydoctor.org/online/famdocen/home/children.html
Fatherhood http://fatherhood.about.com
It's a Mom's World www.itsamomsworld.com
iVillage www.parenting.ivillage.com
WebMD www.webmd.com
ZOOM http://pbskids.org/zoom/activities/preschool

Age 5: Milestones

American Dental Association www.ada.org
American Dental Hygienists' Association www.adha.org
Childproofing www.childproofing.com
Family Education www.familyeducation.com
Kids Health http://kidshealth.org/parent
Parents www.parents.com
Pediatrics http://pediatrics.about.com

Age 5: Care

American Academy of Pediatrics www.aap.org
How Kids Develop www.howkidsdevelop.com
Keep Kids Healthy www.keepkidshealthy.com
Love to Know http://kids.lovetoknow.com
Single Parents http://singleparents.about.com
WebMD www.webmd.com

Age 5: Early Learning

Child Development Institute www.childdevelopmentinfo.com
Children's Books http://childrensbooks.about.com
Education.com www.education.com
National Institute of Child Health and Human Development www.nichd.nih.gov
Preschoolers http://preschoolers.about.com
Preschoolers Today www.preschoolerstoday.com
Toys http://toys.about.com

Age 5: My World

Dr. Greene www.drgreene.com
Fatherhood http://fatherhood.about.com
Family Doctor http://familydoctor.org/online/famdocen/home/children.html
It's a Mom's World www.itsamomsworld.com
iVillage www.parenting.ivillage.com
KidsCom Jr www.kidscomjr.com

Nutrition

About Nutrition http://nutrition.about.com
Act Against Allergy www.actagainstallergy.com
Centers for Disease Control and Prevention www.cdc.gov
Food Allergy Help www.actagainstallergy.com
Keep Kids Healthy www.keepkidshealthy.com/
U.S. Department of Agriculture www.mypyramid.gov/preschoolers/index.html
U.S. Food and Drug Administration www.fda.gov

Behavior & Discipline

Discovery Health http://health.discovery.com
Keep Kids Healthy www.keepkidshealthy.com
Pediatrics http://pediatrics.about.com
Preschoolers http://preschoolers.about.com

WebMD www.webmd.com
Wonder Time www.wondertime.go.com

Preschool Options

Bank Street College www.bankstreet.edu
Child Care http://childcare.about.com
Early Childhood Learning & Knowledge Center http://eclkc.oh.acf.hhs.gov/hslc/HeadStartOffices
HighScope www.highscope.org
Homeschooling http://homeschooling.about.com
Montessori www.montessori.edu
Montessori Foundation www.montessori.org
National Association of Child Care Resources and Referral Agencies www.naccrra.org
National Association for the Education of Young Children www.naeyc.org
National Head Start Association www.nhsa.org
North American Reggio Emilia Alliance www.reggioalliance.o
The National Association for the Education of Young Childr www.naeyc.org
Waldorf Answers www.waldorfanswers.org

Emotional/Behavioral Readiness

ADD/ADHD http://add.about.com
Healthy Kids, Healthy Care www.healthykids.us
Kids Psych www.kidspsych.org
National Network for Child Care www.nncc.org
Preschoolers Today www.preschoolerstoday.com
WebMD www.webmd.com
Whole Family www.wholefamily.com/

Academic Readiness

Child Fun www.childfun.com
Funbrain www.funbrain.com

Gifted Children http://giftedkids.about.com
Kaboose http://funschool.kaboose.com/
Kids' Fashion http://kidsfashion.about.com
National Highway Traffic Safety Administration www.nhtsa.dot.gov
Preschool Express www.preschoolexpress.com
Seat Check www.seatcheck.org

Concerns & Considerations

Afterschool.gov www.afterschool.gov
Attention Deficit Disorder Association www.add.org

Centers for Disease Control and Prevention www.cdc.gov
FirstAidWeb www.firstaidweb.com
IDEA 2004 http://idea.ed.gov
LDonline www.ldonline.org
Learning Disabilities http://learningdisabilities.about.com
Mayo Clinic www.mayoclinic.com
National Center for Learning Disabilities www.ncld.org
Special Needs Children http://specialchildren.about.com
The U.S. Consumer Product Safety Commission www.cpsc.gov

GLOSSARY

ADD/ADHD: Attention Deficit Hyperactivity Disorder (ADHD) and Attention Deficit Disorder (ADD) are often used interchangeably. ADD is essentially ADHD without the hyperactivity component. Symptoms may include impulsivity and inattention. Medication is sometimes used to decrease restlessness and enhance focus.

ARD: The Admission, Review and Dismissal (ARD) Process helps families of students who qualify for special education services take an active role in planning their child's educational program.

Au pair: "Au pair" is a French term which means "on par" or "equal to" and the term describes a young person between the ages of eighteen and twenty-six who enters the United States through the U.S. Department of State, Bureau of Educational and Cultural Affairs Au Pair Exchange Program to experience American life for up to two years. Au Pairs are paid a salary by the host family to provide child care services.

Babysitter: A babysitter is a teenager or adult who occasionally comes to a family's home and watches young children for pay. No experience is required, although many sitters have basic first aid training.

Bilingual/Multilingual: A person is bilingual if he speaks and understands two languages, and is considered multilingual if he speaks and understands more than two languages. Some children become fluent in two languages at a very young age through having parents speak different languages at home.

Birth order: A child's placement in the order of births among siblings is believed to impact overall psychological development, including sense of self.

Bisphenol A: The chemical bisphenol A is commonly used in the making of plastic water bottles as well as food and beverage can linings. Its hazard is debated, but many infant and food storage products are now being made without the chemical and have a label that says BPA-free.

Bodily-kinesthetic intelligence: This learning style refers to a child's ability to process information through hand and body movement, control, and expression.

Body Mass Index: BMI is a measure of normal to obese weight ranges and is based on a child's height and weight, although it doesn't directly measure body fat. BMI is considered a reliable indicator of overall body fat for children and adults. If you are using pounds and inches for a child's weight and height, the formula to calculate BMI is: BMI = [weight / (height x height)] x 703. Simple charts are also available on the Internet or from your child's pediatrician.

Childhood obesity: This is a serious health condition in which excess body fat affects a child's overall well-being. Obesity is often detected based on body mass index, which compares a child's height and weight.

Childproofing: This refers to the practice of locking up, gating off, or otherwise protecting medications, hot tubs, swimming pools, doors, and other potentially hazardous household areas and objects to protect children from harm.

Cholesterol: Cholesterol is a waxy, fatty substance made in the liver and also found in many foods (typically animal products, like meat, eggs, and dairy). Our body needs cholesterol but too high levels pose a health risk. The American Academy of Pediatrics recommends that children at risk of cardiovascular disease have a fasting lipid profile at their well-child visit between the ages of two and ten. Risks include having family members with high cholesterol or premature cardiovascular disease or having family members who are overweight or obese or who have high blood pressure or diabetes, or who smoke. Check with your pediatrician for an individualized recommendation.

Cognitive development: Cognitive development relates to thinking or thought processes and how a preschooler learns and solves problems.

Concept of conservation: This refers to a child's understanding of whether they truly know what they think they know. It applies to certain features of things remaining the same (conserved) despite other changes. Preschoolers typically don't yet understand this concept. An example is two equal amounts of juice being poured into two different-sized cups, one big and one small. A young child will think the big cup has more juice than the small cup.

Concussion: Closed-head injuries from falls or bumps are called concussions. Mild head injuries may be nothing to worry about, but others can lead to more serious concussions. Parents must be particularly vigilant in observing their child after a fall, however. If your child is breathing irregularly, loses consciousness, has convulsions, or vomits, seek immediate medical care.

Conjunctivitis: Conjunctivitis, commonly called pinkeye, is a common eye infection. It can either be bacterial or viral in nature and is highly contagious. An antibiotic ointment or drops may be required.

Co-op preschool: This is an organization that is owned or managed by members of a group. Parents work together to determine appropriate learning. Parents have an active, hands-on role with their child's early education experiences.

Cryptosporidium: Cryptosporidium is a waterborne illness carried by a chlorine-resistant parasite found in the fecal matter of infected humans and animals. It is sometimes found in public swimming pools, although usually not unless there is an outbreak, which is uncommon. It spreads when liquids or items that have been contaminated by an infected person are swallowed. It can cause diarrhea and dehydration.

Daycare: Daycare typically refers to a child care facility that parents take their children to during the daytime for care, supervision, and learning. Daycare centers specialize in care of infants through preschoolers, although some daycare facilities also offer before- and after-school care for school-age children as well. Centers can either be national or regional chains or independently owned. Be sure to check with your state to determine regulations, licensing, or accreditation requirements.

DEET: This is the most widely used active ingredient in keeping mosquitoes, ticks, and other bugs away. Bug sprays with DEET are considered safe for use on children over the age of two months, according to the American Academy of Pediatrics. DEET-based sprays or products are recommended to help minimize a child's risk of getting potentially serious diseases carried by mosquitoes and ticks.

Drop-and-run child care: This refers to parents masking the symptoms of a sick child with over-the-counter medication and then dropping the child off to child care before the symptoms reappear. In the meantime, other children in the program are exposed to the illness. This frequently occurs because working parents do not have a back-up child care plan.

Drop-in care: This style of care doesn't require parents to have advanced reservations for child care, and lets them bring their child by for a few hours, as long as space is available. Drop-in care centers often feature evening and weekend hours and cater to parents who have evening functions or just want to enjoy a child-free evening.

Dyslexia: Dyslexia is a learning disability that has to do with the brain's ability to translate written images received from the eyes into a meaningful language. It most commonly is observed through a child's difficulties in reading and spelling.

Early childhood education: This term refers to the years before children enter kindergarten, which is considered the most critical time to influence learning and prepare for success in school.

Early intervention: Early intervention services are typically offered for children with special needs up to age three to get services and therapies they need. At age three, a child is referred to a school district for special-education preschool.

Emotional skills: This child development skill relates to a preschooler's ability to express and control feelings. Most preschoolers are beginning to learn to control tantrums and show consideration and respect of others.

English as a Second Language: ESL refers to the study of English by children or adults with a different native language. Programs provide instruction in speaking, listening, reading, and writing for non-native speakers of English.

Enrichment: Enrichment activities refer to any extracurricular activities that may foster a new skill or expose a child to a new interest, such as dance, music, or art lessons.

Escapism: Escapism is what some kids do with daydreaming, pretend, and fantasy. Preschoolers often immerse themselves in a make-believe world rather than engaging in the day's routine or events. Usually, they do this simply because it is more fun, although some may do this to escape from an unpleasant situation.

Family child care: This type of child care takes place in the home of an individual child care provider. Often, the provider takes care of a span of different-age children and provides similar activities and structure to what a child experiences at home. Parents should check with their state to determine regulations, licensing, and accreditation requirements.

Fifth disease: Fifth disease is also a common viral infection. Symptoms include a lacelike rash after pink cheeks that can last for several weeks. Typically no treatment is needed.

Fine motor skills: Fine motor skills use small muscles for grasping and basic hand-eye coordination such as reaching for and holding an object.

Flu: Parents need to be informed and protect their children against both the seasonal flu as well as the H1N1 swine flu. Symptoms are similar and may include fever, cough, body aches, sore throat, chills, fatigue, and either a runny or stuffy nose. The H1N1 flu is more likely to cause diarrhea and vomiting than the seasonal flu.

235

Food intolerance: Food intolerance is a reaction to foods that don't involve the immune system. Food such as milk containing lactose, chocolate, or monosodium glutamate (MSG) are examples.

Fractures: Broken bones, or fractures, usually occur in the wrist, the forearm, and above the elbow because kids instinctively will throw out their hands in an attempt to stop or break a fall.

Green products: This term applies to products that are considered environmentally friendly. An increasing number of child care programs are touting the use of green cleaning products to help minimize a child's exposure to chemicals.

Gross motor skills: Gross motor skills involve the large muscles that preschoolers will develop in order to ride a tricycle, jump rope, or kick a ball.

Growing pains: The preschool years are when about 30 percent of children experience growing pains in their legs, usually the front of the thigh, the calf muscles, and muscles in the back of the knee. Pain usually flares up either late in the day or during the middle of the night. Occasional use of ibuprofen can help.

Halitosis: This health condition is better known simply as bad breath.

Hand-eye coordination: This fine motor skill refers to the coordination between eye movement and hand movement that is required for activities like catching a ball.

Hand, Foot, and Mouth: Hand, Foot, and Mouth disease is a common viral infection. Typical symptoms include ulcers in the mouth, blisters on hands and feet, and possible rash. There is no specific treatment, and symptoms typically last three to six days.

Head Start: This federally funded child development program of the U.S. Department of Health and Human Services provides free comprehensive education, health, nutrition, and parent involvement services to low-income and other qualifying children and their families.

Helicopter parents: This term refers to parents who constantly hover over their child and micromanage their every decision and action.

HighScope: The HighScope educational approach was founded in 1970 and is perhaps best known for its research on the lasting effects of preschool education and its preschool curriculum approach.

Home schooling: Some parents opt to provide preschool and school-age instruction themselves, typically within their own home.

IDEA: The Individuals with Disabilities Act (IDEA) is a federal law that ensures services to children with disabilities. IDEA governs how individual states and public agencies provide intervention, special education, and related services. More than 6.5 million infants, toddlers, children and youth with disabilities are eligible for services, according to the U.S. Department of Education.

IEE: Parents may choose an Independent Educational Evaluation (IEE) for their child rather than using a school district's evaluation.

IEP: An Individualized Education Plan (IEP) spells out exactly what special education services your child will receive and why.

Impetigo: Impetigo is a bacterial skin condition. Kids may develop honey-colored crusted lesions. Nostrils are commonly affected. Topical antibiotics are usually required.

IQ: Intelligence Quotient is a score from a series of tests used to measure intelligence.

Interactive learning: This type of learning involves the child rather than just speaking to a child. Interactive learning can take the form of doing experiments, reading pop-up books, or doing motions while singing to a rhyming song.

Interpersonal intelligence: This learning style refers to a child's ability to interact with and understand other kids and adults and social situations.

Intrapersonal intelligence: This learning style refers to a child's ability to analyze and think through solutions.

Lactose intolerance: A child with lactose intolerance lacks the enzyme necessary to digest milk sugar, and as a result may experience abdominal pain, gas, or bloating after consuming milk and other products.

Language disorder: A preschooler who has difficulties in comprehending and or speaking language may have this disorder. It is typically the result of a physical, neurological, or psychological factor.

Learning centers: These are areas set up around a classroom for a particular activity. Often, preschoolers rotate among centers throughout the day.

Learning disability: A child is said to have a learning disability when his ability to learn a particular academic subject is much lower than expected given his estimated aptitude. An aptitude achievement discrepancy is usually diagnosed through various assessments. Learning disabilities are supported with specially designed instruction that is delivered in accordance with a child's style of learning.

Lice: About 12 million children are affected by head lice each year. The main symptom is an itchy scalp from the bites of the lice, which then can become infected and may appear red or crusty. Treatment involves a head lice shampoo and removal of lice and then the nits, which hatch in seven to ten days.

Linguistic intelligence: This learning style refers to a child's ability to solve problems, reason, and learn using language.

Logical-mathematical intelligence: This learning style refers to a child's ability to understand and use numbers and the ability to reason well.

Manipulatives: Manipulatives are physical objects that are used as teaching tools to engage students in hands-on learning.

Migraines: Migraines are chronic headaches that can cause considerable pain or discomfort and are fairly common in children. Migraine headaches can affect a child's daily routine. Consult with your pediatrician if your preschooler frequently complains of headaches.

Milk teeth: These deciduous teeth are also known as baby teeth or temporary teeth. Most children have a total of 20, but will typically lose them all by age twelve.

Montessori: This learning philosophy emphasizes individuality combined with self initiative and independence, regardless of level of ability, learning style, or maturity level.

Musical intelligence: This learning style refers to a child's ability to relate to music in different ways, either as a performer, a music critic, or as a composer.

Nanny: A nanny is employed by a family on either a live-in or live-out basis. A nanny is responsible for all care of the children in the home in a largely unsupervised setting. Nannies may or may not have formal training, though most have training in early childhood education and basic first aid. A male nanny is sometimes referred to as a "manny."

Nanny-cam: This is the commonly-used term for an in-home surveillance device that some parents use to monitor a child care provider who is watching kids while they are away.

Naturalist intelligence: This learning style refers to a child's ability to connect to and appreciate nature.

Night terrors: About 15 percent of children, most commonly between the ages of two and six, have night terrors. Symptoms may include a child suddenly sitting upright with eyes open and a look of panic and fear, and perhaps screaming. They typically last between 5 and 30 minutes. Unlike a nightmare, children usually don't remember them. Most kids outgrow night terrors as they get older.

No Child Left Behind Act: Enacted on Jan. 8, 2002, this federal legislation is based on the belief that setting high standards and establishing measurable goals can improve individual out-comes in education. It requires states to develop assessments in basic skills to be given to all students in certain grades, and has increased federal funding of education.

Pesticides: A pesticide is a substance or mixture of differing substances used as a means for pest control. The Environmental Protection Agency has a program with a mission to protect public health (especially kids and individuals with respiratory illnesses) and the environment from risks of pesticides and to promote safer means of preventing, repelling, and killing pests.

Phonemic awareness: This has to do with structure of sounds and words and is an important pre-reading skill. Before children learn to read, they understand that words are made up of sounds that can be assembled in different ways to comprise different words.

Potty readiness: This refers to physical, cognitive, and behavioral signs that your child is showing trends toward independence and is ready to use the toilet. Not all children are potty trained by the time they become preschoolers.

PPCD: A Preschool Program for Children with Disabilities (PPCD) provides free services to children who have been identified as in need of special education services beginning on their third birth-day. Services may include instruction; speech, physical, and occu-pational therapy; and any specialized services for students with vision and hearing deficits. Parents who believe their preschooler may be in need of special education services should make a refer-ral to the local school district's special education office.

RAST: A radioallergosorbent test, better known as RAST, checks for antibodies against certain foods your child may be allergic to.

Reggio Emilia: This whole-child philosophy of early childhood education encourages the building of thinking skills and collaborative problem solving while retaining each individual's "voice."

Separation anxiety: This is a strong feeling of anxiety over being apart from loved ones and having a fear they won't return. This anxiety sometimes occurs when a child begins a new preschool or child care setting.

Sight words: A sight word is simply any word a young reader knows automatically. First sight words may be I, a, the, an, and the child's name. These are also commonly referred to as high-frequency words.

Sleep routines: This refers to how much uninterrupted sleep, including naps if age-appropriate, a preschooler should have each day for optimal growth and development.

Social development: This child development skill relates to a preschooler's ability to interact with others, such as making and keeping new friends.

Spatial intelligence: This learning style refers to a child's ability to represent his world in his mind. Spatial intelligence is noted in a strong sense of direction, understanding maps, remembering in pictures, and demonstration of strong traits in the arts and sciences.

Speech disorder: This pertains to a preschooler who has articulation difficulties or impairments with verbal language, and may be physical, neurological, or psychological in nature.

Temperament: This refers to innate traits that most accurately describe a child's natural personality, such as being easy-going, extroverted, or even shy.

Tooth decay: Tooth decay, commonly referred to as cavities, is a destruction of the tooth enamel. It occurs when foods high in sugars and starches are frequently left on the teeth. Over a period of time, acids from the bacteria in the mouth destroy tooth enamel, resulting in tooth decay.

Typically developing child: This term refers to what a child of a particular age may typically do or feel, and how they will typically act and respond to situations.

Waldorf: This early childhood learning philosophy emphasizes a child's intellectual powers in harmony with emotions and physical aspects of his nature.

Word bank: This term commonly refers to the number of words a preschooler can either say, understand the meaning of, or both.

INDEX